Daniel

Unlocked for the Final Generation

Scriptural references are based on the New International Version and the King James Version.

Scripture taken from the HOLY BIBLE, NEW INTERNATIONAL VERSION®. Copyright © 1973, 1978, 1984 International Bible Society. Used by permission of Zondervan. All rights reserved.

The "NIV" and "New International Version" trademarks are registered in the United States Patent and Trademark Office by International Bible Society. Use of either trademark requires the permission of International Bible Society. Italics and brackets used in quotations from Scripture have been inserted by the author.

Larry W. Wilson

ISBN 0-9668099-4-7

Wake Up America Seminars, Inc.
P.O. Box 273
Bellbrook, Ohio 45305
(937) 848-3322
http://www.wake-up.org

Cover: Comstock.com

Second Printing (December 2009)

Daniel

Unlocked for the Final Generation

Table of Contents

Forward

The Time of the End

"But thou, O Daniel, shut up the words, and seal the book, even to the time of the end: many shall run to and fro, and knowledge shall be increased." (Daniel 12:4, KJV) If a chart were drawn showing the increase of knowledge on Earth during the past twenty-six centuries, the line would slowly rise until it reached the nineteenth century. Then, the line would suddenly curve upwards because knowledge has dramatically increased during the past two hundred years. In fact, I have heard it said that the half-life of knowledge today is about five years. If this statement is true, this means there will be twice as much knowledge in five years! How can the doubling of knowledge continue at such a rapid pace, and furthermore, who can absorb all of the knowledge that is current? There is so much to learn and life is so short!

School, by definition, is a series of progressive classes. For example, basic arithmetic is a prerequisite for Algebra I, and Algebra I is a prerequisite for Algebra II, and Algebra II is a prerequisite for Calculus and so on. This progression in learning is necessary because knowledge in mathematics is additive in nature. A student must have a working knowledge of basic arithmetic and algebra *before* he* can understand calculus. Bible prophecy is similar to mathematics. The Bible student must understand certain fundamental concepts *before* he can appreciate the larger issues presented in Bible prophecy.

Many people think Bible prophecy is merely future telling. This definition is terribly inadequate. Bible prophecy encompasses the study of an infinite God and His mysterious ways. Bible prophecy has been unfolding for the past 6,000 years and it reveals the actions and plans of God as nothing else can. Bible prophecy proves that God is deliberate and purposeful in everything He does. Bible prophecy not only reveals the foreknowledge of God, it also reveals the plans of God. Bible prophecy has much to say about the future, but there is very little in the future that has not been witnessed in

---

* In this book, for the sake of brevity, the pronoun *he* is used in certain situations to identify both genders, male and female.

times past. This is the beauty of Bible prophecy. Almost everything that God plans to do in the future, He has done at various times in the past. This is why Bible prophecy is an encompassing study of an infinite God and His mysterious ways.

Why Now?

Daniel was told that knowledge would be increased at the time of the end. (Daniel 12:4) True to His word, God has granted mankind more knowledge during the past two hundred years than during the past two thousand years! Why has He done this? Perhaps God planned from the beginning to populate the world with as many people as possible at the time of the end. If so, one could say that God has controlled the population of Earth through knowledge. We know that the resources necessary to sustain life on this planet are limited, and access to these resources was impossible until the nineteenth century. Now that knowledge has been given to mankind, access to these resources has brought about a population explosion. For example, the industrial revolution of the nineteenth century produced mechanical machinery of various types. As a result, farming equipment and agricultural techniques were developed which allow a small number of people to feed an ever expanding global population. Transportation and commerce moves food and supplies to distant places and this translates into larger numbers of surviving people. Advances in medicine also contribute to a longer life span; thus the population of Earth increased because people lived longer and their offspring survived longer. Railroads, freeways, ocean-going super tankers, telephones, banking, energy and computers enable businesses to flourish so that the physical needs of billions of people can be met. Think about this: The expansive infrastructures of our world are built upon knowledge and technology that did not exist a mere two hundred years ago. Consequently, the population of Earth has now passed the *six billion* mark and experts say it will exceed nine billion by 2050. Evidently, this is what God planned. He appears to be crowding this planet with people at the time of the end so that He might populate Heaven with the largest number of people possible!

Knowledge of Bible Prophecy Necessary for Salvation?

When people say, "I don't need to understand Bible prophecy because it has nothing to do with salvation," they are right in a limited sense. Many generations of people have died without understanding apocalyptic prophecy. However, there is a profound difference between past generations and the last generation. A time is coming when prophetic understanding will have everything to do with salvation! (As it did in Noah's day.) The final generation will experience a series of tests that no other generation has faced. This is why God warns us in the book of Revelation about the mark of the beast and the importance of receiving the seal of God.

By increasing our knowledge of His Word and His ways, God has made the plan of salvation so simple that any searching person can understand it. But, God offers more in the Bible than the basics of salvation. (Hebrews 5:11-6:1) *God offers to explain Himself.* People who truly love God and deeply appreciate His generous offer of salvation want to know everything they can about the One who first loved us! A life of discovering a loving God never ends. He is the most interesting subject in all the universe. If the plan of salvation is interesting to study, Bible prophecy is even more interesting because the fulfillment of salvation involves a series of prophetic events!

Five Prerequisites

The study of Bible prophecy forces the student into a theological corner. This occurs because the student has to reconcile his conclusions on prophecy with everything he knows about God into one harmonious theology. Notice how this process evolves: Some people support the doctrine of a pre-tribulation rapture with the idea that God will not allow Christians to suffer wrath during the Great Tribulation. (1 Thessalonians 5:9) These people claim a pre-tribulation rapture *is consistent* with the experiences of Noah, Lot, Rahab, etc. What do Noah, Lot and Rahab have to do with the Great Tribulation? Actually, nothing. "But," they say, "if Noah, Lot and Rahab were saved from God's wrath, God will save Christians from His coming wrath." (Luke 21:36) This use of logic and a few "proof texts" demonstrates how certain prophetic conclusions are reconciled within a theological framework. Even though I do not believe the Bible teaches a pre-tribulation rapture, this example demonstrates why prophetic conclusions and theological beliefs are inseparable.

It is almost impossible for two people to discuss the prophecies of Daniel and Revelation if they are not in agreement on essential Bible doctrines. I find there are five essential doctrines in the Bible, and they are easy to remember because they can be associated with the letter "S." The essential doctrines are: Salvation by faith in Jesus Christ, the Second Coming of Jesus, the Sabbath rest of Jesus, the State of man in death, and God's use of parallel Sanctuaries. These five doctrines are prerequisites for a study of Bible prophecy. Two examples demonstrate the reasons for this conclusion. First, if a person does not understand the state of man in death, then portions of Daniel 7 and 12, Revelation 6 and 20 will make no sense. If a person is judged at the time of death and he immediately goes to Heaven or hell, why is there a resurrection and a white throne judgment at the end of the 1,000 years in Revelation 20 for those who were previously burning in hell? Second, if a person does not understand God's use of parallel sanctuaries, he cannot understand the casting down of the censer at Heaven's Altar of Incense. (Revelation 8:5) One has to understand the services at the *earthly* Altar of Incense before he can understand the services at the *heavenly* Altar of Incense. Again, certain prerequisites are necessary to understand Bible prophecy. This relationship will be identified at various places in this book and you will be referred to my companion volume, *Jesus, The Alpha and The Omega,* for further study on the five essential doctrines.

Four Rules: Trash or Treasure?

There are hundreds, maybe thousands of books on Bible prophecy and most of these books do not agree on the meaning of Bible prophecy. This diversity of opinion leads many people to conclude that no one actually understands what Bible prophecy says. If Bible scholars cannot agree, how are lay people supposed to decipher the meaning of prophecy? This is a good question. Perhaps you should be warned that this book perpetuates the tradition, because it does not agree with thousands of books already written on this subject. Why, then, should another book on Bible prophecy be written? This book was written because I have stumbled, through God's generous grace, into a discovery of four rules of interpretation that allows Bible prophecy to be understood just as it reads. In days to come, this discovery could prove to be more profound than a cure for cancer or AIDS! Of course, time will tell whether my discovery is trash or treasure, but nevertheless, I am excited about the new end-time story that springs from Bible prophecy, because a significant part of the story is about to take place!

Apocalyptic Prophecy Points to the End of Sin

Because Bible prophecy is much more than future telling, the books of Daniel and Revelation offer a lot more than an explanation of how the world will end. These two prophetic books reveal the *ways* of God. Furthermore, Bible prophecy serves many purposes, and its ultimate purpose is a revelation of God's love for man. The five essential doctrines explain *why* our world is in a fallen condition and Bible prophecy explains *how* and *when* God will rescue mankind from the curse of sin.

Many people are surprised to learn that Revelation's story does not end with the Second Coming. Actually, the story continues for 1,000 years *after* the Second Coming because Revelation's story is ultimately concerned with something larger than the end of the world as we know it. This "something" is the elimination of the sin problem. If a person looks into Revelation to merely foretell how the world will end, he will miss the best part of the story because God's greatest problem is the presence of sin within *His* universe. God's solution to the sin problem has cost the Father and the Son everything They could give. Consequently, a correct understanding of the sin problem is a prerequisite for understanding Bible prophecy. Bible prophecy indicates God will ultimately eliminate sin and annihilate a large number of people whom He deeply loves. Even more, Bible prophecy reveals that God will be fully justified in the eyes of His subjects when He does this! This is an incredible story that has many dimensions and it takes some effort to understand it.

An Omnipotent Jesus

The books of Daniel and Revelation declare an omnipotent Jesus. Jesus is the centerpiece of apocalyptic prophecy. He is Sovereign God and He oversees the final events of Earth from His throne during the time of the end. (Daniel 7:13,14; John 1:1-14; Matthew 26:64; John 5:23; Revelation 1:8; 4, 5) A great war is about to begin. At this very moment, two kings are preparing for a war that will determine the fate of everyone living on Earth. Jesus and Lucifer are extremely powerful and they have legions of angels at their command. A declaration of war has existed between them for thousands of years. For the past 6,000 years, human beings have been trapped in a cosmic drama between Christ, the king of righteousness, and Lucifer, the king of evil. To Jesus, we are objects of greatest affection. To Lucifer, we are targets for destruction. Like it or not – believe it or not, the last generation to live on Earth will be caught in the middle of a no-holds-barred *spiritual* and *physical* war that will take place between these two great rulers. The Great Tribulation will become The Great Divide of the human race. God will test the people of Earth to see who will stand on the side of righteousness and who will capitulate and unite with the forces of evil. Because the coming war is both spiritual and literal, the Bible predicts the inhabitants of Earth will see the physical appearing of both kings. Lucifer, the prince of this world (John 16:11; Revelation 17:8), will gloriously appear first. Later, Jesus, the prince of Heaven's host (Revelation 19:11-21), will majestically appear in clouds of glory and Jesus will destroy Lucifer (the Antichrist), and his followers with a single command that comes out of His mouth! (This command is represented as a sharp sword in Revelation 19:15,21.)

The books of Daniel and Revelation tell a drama that involves truth and lies, death and resurrection. The presence of sin has caused God to do things that He would have not done otherwise. If sin had not occurred, Jesus would not have died for sinners. If Jesus had not died at Calvary, the universe would know less about the depths of God's love, because the death of Jesus on Calvary demonstrates what Jesus was willing to do for man *before* He created Adam and Eve. Jesus knew our parents would sin *before* He created them, but His foreknowledge did not keep Him from creating them nor did He predispose Adam and Eve to sin. They were created with a powerful tendency to live in perfect harmony with their Creator. But, they chose to sin of their own free will, and God chose of His own free will to deal with the lemon of sin by converting this tragic event into lemonade. Because of His love for man, Jesus went to His death in order that we might have life. It is incomprehensible that Jesus was willing to perish forever so that Adam and Eve and their offspring might have the opportunity to spend eternity with His Father. What love! What amazing grace! Because God is love, the rise of sin produced an opportunity for the Godhead to reveal their true character of love. Of course, the Godhead did not need sin's presence to reveal their infinite love for their creation. However, sin happened because God's children have the power of choice. The Godhead used this misfortune to expose their souls before a whole universe so that every thoughtful observer might understand the righteousness and fairness of God's government and God's ways. Because we live in the darkness of degeneracy and sin, we need spiritual eyesight to understand a host of things that we cannot physically see. (1 Corinthians 2:12) For this reason Jesus has sent the Spirit, the Spirit of *prophecy*, to guide us into an understanding of prophetic truth. (Revelation 1:9; 19:10; John 16:13) When Bible prophecy is properly understood, the entire Bible harmoniously declares a loving God, an unbelievably generous offer of salvation, the promise of victory over sin, a resurrection to eternal life, and the final annihilation of sin with all its harmful consequences. This is wonderful news that everyone should understand! This is why this book was written. The books of Daniel and Revelation tell us the present world order – which groans under the curse of sin – is soon to end and a new-world order is about to begin. The book of Daniel closes with these encouraging words: **"Blessed is the one who waits for and reaches the end of the 1,335 days** [for he shall behold the Lamb of God without experiencing death]." (Daniel 12:12, insertion mine)

In closing, I would like to express deepest appreciation to those who helped to make this book a reality. Suzy, Gail and Evonne worked very hard to find and correct my typographical errors. Suzy also did the painstaking research necessary to create the index of Bible texts. Marty spent many tedious hours putting the book in its final format and Shelley searched through piles of photos for the best possible picture for the cover. The product of our hands is in your hands. May the Lord use this little book to His glory is my prayer.

Larry Wilson

June, 2003

Chapter 1

Daniel 2 – The Rock of Ages

"Trust in the Lord forever, for the Lord, the Lord, is the Rock
eternal."
— Isaiah 26:4

Because of God's love for Abraham, God chose the descendants of
Abraham to be His representatives on Earth. Beginning with the
Exodus from Egypt, God did everything possible to get the nation of
Israel to love Him and obey His commands. Israel was to be a
nation of priests; they were to be representatives of the Most High
God throughout the earth. They were to be a light unto the world
demonstrating the wisdom of God's laws and reflecting the kindness
and generosity of His love. **"I, the Lord, have called you in
righteousness; I will take hold of your hand. I will keep you
and will make you to be a covenant for the people and a light
for the Gentiles, to open eyes that are blind, to free captives
from prison and to release from the dungeon those who sit in
darkness."** (Isaiah 42:6,7) For more than 800 years, God gave Israel
every blessing and opportunity, and they gave Him rebellion and
rejection in return. Finally, God could not endure Israel's insolence
any longer. Around 620 B.C., God spoke through the prophet
Jeremiah saying, **"O house of Israel . . . . I am bringing a
distant nation against you – an ancient and enduring nation,
a people whose language you do not know, whose speech you
do not understand. Their quivers are like an open grave; all
of them are mighty warriors. They will devour your harvests
and food, devour your sons and daughters; they will devour
your flocks and herds, devour your vines and fig trees. With
the sword they will destroy the fortified cities in which you
trust. Yet even in those days . . . I will not destroy you
completely. And when the people ask 'Why has the Lord our
God done all this to us?' you will tell them, 'As you have
forsaken me and served foreign gods in your own land, so**

now you will serve foreigners in a land not your own. . . .'
This is what the Lord Almighty, the God of Israel, says:
'Listen! I am going to bring on this city and the villages
around it every disaster I pronounced against them, because
they were stiff-necked and would not listen to my words. . . .
I will hand all Judah over to the king of Babylon, who will
carry them away to Babylon or put them to the sword.' "
(Jeremiah 5:15-19, 19:15, 20:4)

These verses reveal three interesting points about God. First, from
these and many other Bible texts, it is clear that God's patience with
sin and rebellion has a limit. God's comments to Jeremiah and His
subsequent actions leave no room for doubt about this. Second, when
the time came to punish Israel, God fully warned Israel about His
forthcoming actions. Even though they did not believe Him, God
told Israel what He was going to do before He did it! He made it
clear that He was going to use the sword of King Nebuchadnezzar
against His people. Third, God's treatment of Israel is a mirror
reflecting how He treats all nations! "**. . .God is no respecter of
persons.**" (Acts 10:34, KJV) In other words, if God destroyed
Jerusalem and His chosen people because of sin and degeneracy, we
can be sure that He has followed the *same* policy with all nations.
Indeed, the Bible confirms this to be the case. (Genesis 6:7, 15:16;
Leviticus 24:18-24; Isaiah 16:6-14; Isaiah 19:1-12; Ezekiel 14:12-21)

Like Pharaoh, who would not let Israel leave Egypt, Nebuchadnezzar
did not know the God of Israel. Yet, God knew the Babylonian king
very well and God empowered Nebuchadnezzar to be a "servant-
destroyer." (Jeremiah 25:9) God moved the heart of Nebuchadnezzar
to put Jerusalem to the sword just as surely as He moved the heart
of King Cyrus to set His people free seventy years later. Notice
these two texts:

" 'I will summon all the peoples of the north and my *servant*
Nebuchadnezzar king of Babylon,' declares the Lord, 'and I
will bring them against this land and its inhabitants and
against all the surrounding nations. I will completely destroy
them and make them an object of horror and scorn, and an
everlasting ruin.' " (Jeremiah 25:9, emphasis mine)

"In the first year of Cyrus king of Persia, in order to fulfill the word of the Lord spoken by Jeremiah, the Lord *moved* the heart of Cyrus king of Persia to make a proclamation throughout his realm and to put it in writing: 'This is what Cyrus king of Persia says: "The Lord, the God of heaven, has given me all the kingdoms of the earth and he has appointed me to build a temple for him at Jerusalem in Judah." ' " (Ezra 1:1,2, emphasis mine)

The Bible indicates that God affects the hearts of men to do His bidding. God used Nebuchadnezzar to tear down Jerusalem and God used Cyrus to rebuild it! Since the Bible declares that God is proactive in managing the nations and kings of Earth, let us consider a vision which God gave to King Nebuchadnezzar about 600 B.C.

The Foundational Prophecy: Daniel 2

Daniel 2 contains the first prophecy in the book of Daniel. In this respect, Daniel 2 is a *foundational prophecy* and all subsequent prophecies in Daniel and Revelation are built on it. The prophecy in Daniel 2 reveals three interesting facts. First, God not only knows the future, but He has also predetermined that certain events will occur in the future. Second, God chooses the kings of Earth and He sets them up and takes them down according to His higher purposes. Third, beginning with the kingdom of Babylon, God has predestined the appearing of seven global empires. Think of the number *seven* as God's signature. He has put His signature on many things to remind us that He is our Creator and our Creator has a plan! The number seven suggests fullness or completion. For example, in Daniel and Revelation there are *seven* kingdoms, *seven* heads, *seven* eyes, *seven* horns, *seven* thunders, *seven* seals, *seven* trumpets, *seven* churches, *seven* bowls and *seven* angels who stand before God. Consider our physical world, there are *seven* continents, *seven* colors in the rainbow, *seven* notes in our musical scale, *seven* days in a week, and Jesus spoke *seven* times when He was on the cross. God's signature is everywhere! Even our seven-day week is terminated with God's seventh-day rest. The use of *seven* in Daniel and Revelation is deliberate and important to God. The seven kingdoms presented in Daniel 2 declare a finished plan. The seven kingdoms presented in Daniel 2 consist of six kingdoms governed by men and an eternal kingdom governed by God. The interesting climax in this vision is that God destroys the kingdoms of men *before* He establishes His kingdom on Earth!

Parts of the Daniel 2 Image

1. **Head - Gold**
2. **Chest - Silver**
3. **Thighs - Bronze**
4. **Legs - Iron**
5. **Feet - Iron & Clay**
6. **Toes - Iron & Clay**
7. **Rock - Indestructible & Eternal**

Note: Even though the toes are made of the same materials as the feet, the "toes" are a *distinct* kingdom separate from the kingdom of the feet. The toes are identified as "a kingdom" in verse 42, just like the "chest" is identified as a kingdom in verse 39. Even though the composition of the feet and toes is identical, they represent two different world orders. Currently, we are living in the kingdom of the feet. During the Great Tribulation, the present order of this world will drastically change and we will enter the final phase of world order represented by the toes. Even though this vision does not explicitly say there are "ten" toes on the metal man, we can safely assume this anatomical feature is implied in Daniel 2 because the book of Revelation predicts that ten kings (ten horns) will rule over the whole world for a very short period of time during the very last moments of Earth's history. (Revelation 17:12-14) Obviously, the kingdom of the toes has not arrived, but it is coming. When it does arrive, Daniel 2:44 says, **"In the time of those kings** [represented by the ten toes], **the God of heaven will set up a kingdom that will never be destroyed, nor will it be left to another people. It will crush all those kingdoms and bring them to an end, but it will itself endure forever."** (Insertion mine)

The Timeline of Daniel 2

605 B.C.	538 B.C.	331 B.C.	168 B.C.	A.D. 476	?	?
Babylon	Medo-Persia	Grecia	Rome	Many Kings	10 Kings	Jesus
1	2	3	4	5	6	7
Gold	Silver	Bronze	Iron	Iron/Clay	Iron/Clay	Rock
Head	Chest	Thighs	Legs	Feet	Toes	Eternal

Chart 1.1

The Vision

"...Thy dream, and the visions of thy head upon thy bed, are these; As for thee, O king, thy thoughts came into thy mind upon thy bed, what should come to pass hereafter: and he that revealeth secrets maketh known to thee what shall come to pass. But as for me, this secret is not revealed to me for any wisdom that I have more than any living, but for their sakes that shall make known the interpretation to the king, and that thou mightest know the thoughts of thy heart.

"Thou, O king, sawest, and behold a great image. This great image, whose brightness was excellent, stood before thee; and the form thereof was terrible. This image's head was of fine gold, his breast and his arms of silver, his belly and his thighs of brass, His legs of iron, his feet part of iron and part of clay. Thou sawest till that a stone was cut out without hands, which smote the image upon his feet that were of iron and clay, and brake them to pieces. Then was the iron, the clay, the brass, the silver, and the gold, broken to pieces together, and became like the chaff of the summer threshingfloors; and the wind carried them away, that no place was found for them: and the stone that smote the image became a great mountain, and filled the whole earth." (Daniel 2:28-35, KJV)

The Meaning of the Vision

"This is the dream; and we will tell the interpretation thereof
before the king. Thou, O king, art a king of kings: for the God
of heaven hath given thee a kingdom, power, and strength,
and glory. And wheresoever the children of men dwell, the
beasts of the field and the fowls of the heaven hath he given
into thine hand, and hath made thee ruler over them all.
Thou art this head of gold. And after thee shall arise another
kingdom inferior to thee, and another third kingdom of
brass, which shall bear rule over all the earth. And the
fourth kingdom shall be strong as iron: forasmuch as iron
breaketh in pieces and subdueth all things: and as iron that
breaketh all these, shall it break in pieces and bruise. And
whereas thou sawest the feet and toes, part of potters' clay,
and part of iron, the kingdom shall be divided; but there
shall be in it of the strength of the iron, forasmuch as thou
sawest the iron mixed with miry clay. And as the toes of the
feet were part of iron, and part of clay, so the kingdom shall
be partly strong, and partly broken. And whereas thou
sawest iron mixed with miry clay, they shall mingle
themselves with the seed of men: but they shall not cleave
one to another, even as iron is not mixed with clay. And in
the days of these kings shall the God of heaven set up a
kingdom, which shall never be destroyed: and the kingdom
shall not be left to other people, but it shall break in pieces
and consume all these kingdoms, and it shall stand for ever.
Forasmuch as thou sawest that the stone was cut out of the
mountain without hands, and that it brake in pieces the iron,
the brass, the clay, the silver, and the gold; the great God
hath made known to the king what shall come to pass
hereafter: and the dream is certain, and the interpretation
thereof sure. Then the king Nebuchadnezzar fell upon his
face, and worshiped Daniel, and commanded that they
should offer an oblation and sweet odours unto him. The
king answered unto Daniel, and said, Of a truth it is, that
your God is a God of gods, and a Lord of kings, and a
revealer of secrets, seeing thou couldest reveal this secret."
(Daniel 2:36-47, KJV)

Comments

Two men saw the vision of the image. King Nebuchadnezzar saw the vision first and later, God gave a copy of this vision to Daniel so that he could explain the vision to the king. The vision occurred around 600 B.C., but it spans a time period of more than 2,600 years so far. This vision has not been fulfilled. We are still waiting for the kingdom of the ten toes and the eternal kingdom that is established when Jesus (the Rock) destroys the kingdoms of men. By right of sovereign authority, God predetermined a chronological progression of seven world empires, and He revealed this information to Nebuchadnezzar *for our benefit.* The real impact of this vision (pun intended) belongs to the final generation. Many people in the final generation on Earth will thoughtfully consider the merits of this vision during the Great Tribulation, and they will discover that God has a predetermined plan that has been unfolding for more than twenty-six centuries. Because this vision and world history are in perfect harmony, the final generation will have a bundle of evidence upon which to base its faith in God's Word. **"Have you not heard? Long ago I ordained it. In days of old I planned it; now I have brought it to pass. . . ."** (2 Kings 19:25)

If we consider the architecture of this vision (see Chart 1.1), we discover three interesting points. First, this vision has a beginning and an ending point in time. The vision begins with the kingdom of Babylon as the head of gold and the vision ends when Jesus, The Rock of Ages, King of kings and Lord of lords, destroys the ten kings who will be ruling over the world at the time of the Second Coming. (See Revelation 17:12,13; 19:11-21.) Second, there is chronological order within the vision. The elements within the vision occur in the order they are given. For example, the kingdom represented by the thighs of brass fell to the kingdom represented by the legs of iron, etc. The third point concerns the use of language. God used the *symbol of a man* to represent a succession of kingdoms that would occur on Earth. Within the context of this vision, the use and the meaning of the symbol is explained by the Bible. These three points are highlighted so you can observe a distinct pattern that emerges from Daniel, and this pattern will prove to be very important later in this book.

The Succession of World Empires

The kingdoms that follow Babylon are represented by metals of lesser value. This decline suggests that fallen man degenerates with the passage of time. According to Daniel 2, the chest and arms of silver represented a kingdom that would succeed Babylon. It is interesting to note that the silver kingdom had two arms (as in two *armies*). This feature accurately reflected the Medo-Persian empire which overran Babylon in 538 B.C. The Medo-Persian kingdom consisted of two kings and two armies. Eventually, the Persian side of this kingdom became dominant.

The third kingdom, represented by thighs of brass, rose to power with the fall of the Medo-Persians. The Grecian empire was noted for its extensive use of bronze. In fact, the Grecian period is sometimes called "The Bronze Age." The fourth empire was represented by legs of iron and this feature accurately represented the Roman empire. The Romans were noted for their ferocious conquests and their weapons of unbreakable iron. The Roman empire also included a larger geographical territory than any of the previous empires. Perhaps this expansion is reflected in the *two* legs of iron. The Romans dominated a large portion of the East, as well as the West.

The fifth kingdom, represented by the feet of iron and clay, represents the breakup of the Roman empire into many kingdoms; some became strong and others weak. When Rome fell in A.D. 476, a distinctive change occurred. After this date, the empires of the world were no longer universal. Instead, the world was permanently fractured into small empires. Through the ages, God has predetermined that some kingdoms would be strong as iron and others would be weak or breakable like brittle clay. One-world empires like Babylon, Medo-Persia, Grecia and Rome will not exist again until God permits the Antichrist to rule over Earth during the Great Tribulation. Men such as Napoleon, Charlemagne, Hitler, Kaiser Wilhelm and other conquerors have vainly tried to unite the world under their rule, but their efforts could not succeed because God's Word cannot be defeated.

The sixth and last kingdom of man is represented by the toes. Remember that the toes represent a brief reign of ten kings. About two thirds of the way through the Great Tribulation, the devil himself will physically appear on Earth masquerading as God. After a successful conquest to take control of Earth, the Antichrist (Lucifer) will divide the world into ten sectors, and he will appoint ten kings to rule over these ten sectors. (Revelation 17:12-14)) During the days of *these* kings, the Rock will come out of Heaven and destroy all of the kingdoms of men. This Rock is Jesus Christ, the Rock of Ages. At the appointed time, Jesus will annihilate the wicked on Earth and establish the seventh and final world empire. His kingdom will never end. Remember, seven is God's signature. God's kingdom of righteousness will bear His likeness and He will only establish His kingdom on Earth *after* He has destroyed the kingdoms of men. Notice this text: **"In the time of those kings [the ten kings], the God of heaven will set up a kingdom that will never be destroyed, nor will it be left to another people. It will crush all those kingdoms and bring them to an end, but it will itself endure forever."** (Daniel 2:44, insertion mine)

"The Rock of Ages"

Before "The Rock of Ages" sets up His kingdom, He will destroy *all* of the kingdoms of men. Daniel told King Nebuchadnezzar, **". . . a rock was cut out, but not by human hands. It struck the statue on its feet of iron and clay and smashed them. Then the iron, the clay, the bronze, the silver and the gold were broken to pieces at the same time and became like chaff on a threshing floor in the summer. The wind swept them away without leaving a trace. But the rock that struck the statue became a huge mountain and filled the whole earth."** (Daniel 2:34,35) Three points within these verses need to be considered. First, the Bible leaves no wiggle room on the fact that the kingdom of God cannot co-exist with the kingdoms of men. Before Jesus sets up His kingdom on Earth, all previous kingdoms have to be destroyed – *swept away without a trace!* Jesus will not reign on or over a sinful Earth. Jesus will reign on Earth only *after* sin and unrepentant sinners have been annihilated. According to the final chapters of Revelation, Jesus does not begin to reign *on Earth* until there is a New Heaven and a New Earth.

Second, the sequence of events described in Daniel 2 terminates at the Second Coming. Through the years, people have asked if the Rock crushing the metal man occurs at the Second Coming or at the end of the 1,000 years mentioned in Revelation 20. The Rock crushes the kingdoms of men at the end of the Great Tribulation (at the Second Coming), when the ten kings are ruling upon Earth. (Daniel 2:44) In other words, after desolating this planet of all life (2 Thessalonians 2:8; Revelation 19:19-21) and putting the devil back in the abyss for 1,000 years (Revelation 20:1-3), Jesus has total control over Earth. However, when Jesus appears at the Second Coming, He does not touch Earth. Instead, the saints will be caught up in the sky to meet the Lord in the air. (1 Thessalonians 4:17) This gathering up of the saints occurs because they will be taken to "the Father's house" in Heaven for 1,000 years before returning to Earth in the Holy City with Jesus. (John 14:1-3; Revelation 21:1-4) During the 1,000 years, the saints will sit in court and determine the punishment that each wicked person must receive. (1 Corinthians 6:1-3; Revelation 20:4) Obviously, Daniel 2 does not address these details, but the final chapters of Revelation collaborate with Daniel 2. Using this relationship,we can determine what will occur during and after the 1,000 years of Revelation 20.

The third point concerns this phrase, **"The rock that was cut out, but not by human hands. . . ."** The Rock of Ages and His seventh kingdom are divine in origin. The kingdom of God will not be a modification of earthly kingdoms. Consider what this language meant to King Nebuchadnezzar. Ancient peoples built altars to their gods (and there were many) on mountain tops and the "high places" of Earth. They believed the gods dwelt in the lofty grandeur and vast expanses of snow capped mountains. (Jeremiah 3:6; Ezekiel 6:13; Psalm 15:1) Even among the Jews, the Mountain of Sinai was called the Mountain of God. (Exodus 4:27) Today, in the United States, the government buildings where laws are made are exalted with the title "The Capitol Building" or "Capitol Hill," even though the building itself is only slightly elevated above the surrounding area. We use this type of language to identify the place of a nation's highest authority. The same idea was used in a religious sense in ancient times.

When God gave Nebuchadnezzar this vision, He used very simple terms the king could grasp. God told the king that six kingdoms would rise and fall. God also revealed that man would not rule over Earth indefinitely. God has predetermined an end to the rule of men. A day will come when the "Rock," the Son of God, will establish

His kingdom on Earth. The idea of a rock being cut out of a mountain without human effort is language that uniquely describes God (the Mountain) and the Son of God (the Rock). The Son will come from Heaven and remove all traces of Earth's previous kingdoms before He establishes His own kingdom. The "Rock" will establish a city whose builder and maker is God. (Hebrews 11:10) Almighty God gave Nebuchadnezzar the great honor of beholding His plans. Who can prevent His coming kingdom? Who can stop Him? Who can thwart the fulfillment of this blueprint? God showed Nebuchadnezzar the climax of the ages. He saw "The Rock of Ages" utterly destroy the kingdoms of men and take possession of Earth. Thus, the ancient words of Isaiah will be fulfilled: "**. . . and the government will be on his shoulders.**" (Isaiah 9:6)

Twenty-six hundred years ago, Daniel told King Nebuchadnezzar, "**. . .The great God has shown the king what will take place in the future. The dream is true and the interpretation is trustworthy.**" (Daniel 2:45) Even though this vision has not yet been fulfilled, we have enough evidence from completed sequences within the vision to confirm the truthfulness of this vision. Apocalyptic prophecy is history written in advance and the passage of time has confirmed the accuracy of all that God said regarding the future. *Nothing proves the veracity of God's Word like the fulfillment of Bible prophecy.*

Notes and Comments on Chapter 1

The comments that follow are crucial to the concepts presented in this book, so please give the following paragraphs careful consideration. Bible students come to varied conclusions about Bible prophecy because there are many different methods of interpretation. For this reason, you may want to read and review this section from time to time as you progress through this book. I have placed these notes at the end of Chapter 1 rather than at the beginning of the book so that newcomers to the study of prophecy would not become discouraged or overwhelmed by the depth of Bible prophecy. It is all too easy to lay books aside that require thinking and processing.

Methods of interpretation is a catch-all phrase that has a lot of bearing on the interpretation of Bible prophecy. The phrase "methods of interpretation" describes a set of ideas or a particular view in a person's head *before* he starts to study and interpret prophecy. Methods of interpretation include religious views, spiritual presuppositions, scholastic assumptions and concepts about the role and authority of the Bible, the authority of prophets, and church traditions. For example, a Catholic scholar will approach the study of Bible prophecy with Catholic beliefs and traditions in mind, and his prophetic conclusions will reflect the ideas and views that were in his mind *before* he began to study. Similarly, a Baptist scholar will approach the study of Bible prophecy with methods of interpretation that are very different than his Catholic counterpart, and the Baptist scholar will arrive at very different conclusions than the Catholic scholar because their methods of interpretation are different. Obviously, no one approaches the study of prophecy without some kind of intellectual and religious baggage. This baggage is loosely called "methods of interpretation" or hermeneutics.

Faulty Interpretations until the Time of the End

The book of Daniel contains 533 sentences. While the book is very short, it contains volumes of information. Daniel was written about twenty-six centuries ago, but unlike the other 65 books in the Bible, the book of Daniel was sealed up "until the time of the end." The angel, Gabriel, said to Daniel, **". . .Go your way, Daniel, because the words are closed up and sealed until the time of the end."** (Daniel 12:9) What does "closed up and sealed until the time of the end" mean? It means that God placed certain information in the book of Daniel that remains "top secret" until the time of the end arrives. Has the time of the end arrived? On the basis of fulfilled prophecy and an understanding of God's timing, I am convinced "the time of the end" has arrived. If this is true, the time has come for the secrets in Daniel to be unveiled.

The secret information God coded into Daniel 2,600 years ago is something like the "Rosetta Stone." The Rosetta Stone was accidently unearthed in 1799 near Rosetta, Egypt, by French soldiers. The marvelous thing about this buried rock is that it bears a message written during the second century B.C. in two forms of Egyptian script – demotic and hieroglyphics. When archeologists examined the rock, they were thrilled because they were able to solve a very perplexing mystery. Prior to 1799, archeologists could not read the clay tablets bearing Egyptian hieroglyphics because no one could decipher the language. When the Rosetta Stone was discovered and translated, the demotic inscriptions enabled Thomas Young (1773-1829) and J.F. Champollion (1790-1832) to decipher the hieroglyphics of the ancient Egyptians.

In a similar way, I believe God embedded four secrets in the book of Daniel 2,600 years ago. By God's grace, I believe I have stumbled into an understanding of the four secrets that were sealed up in the book of Daniel. (Of course, the passage of time will prove or disprove the validity of my claim.) These four secrets shatter centuries of prophetic exposition, because all interpretations of Daniel are necessarily faulty and incomplete until the book of Daniel is *unsealed*. In other words, certain truths in the book of Daniel were deliberately reserved for the generation that would live "at the time of the end."

Three Levels of Information

As a person might expect, God buried His secrets in the book of Daniel very well. However, when God wants something known, He enables ordinary men and women to discover extraordinary things He has hidden. Through the ages we find this discovery process at work: *On or about the time of fulfillment, elements of prophecy are understood.* For example, when it came time to understand the timing of Christ's birth, the wise men from the East figured it out. (Matthew 2:2) The apostle Paul also noticed this phenomenon. Consider his words: **"Surely you have heard about the administration of God's grace that was given to me for you, that is, the mystery made known to me by revelation, as I have already written briefly. In reading this, then, you will be able to understand my insight into the mystery of Christ, which was not made known to men in other generations as it has now been revealed by the Spirit to God's holy apostles and prophets. This mystery is that through the gospel the Gentiles are heirs together with Israel, members together of one body, and sharers together in the promise in Christ Jesus."** (Ephesians 3:2-6)

What did God hide in the book of Daniel? The answer to this question requires a little explanation. The book of Daniel offers three levels of knowledge. They are:

1. Dramatic stories of faith
2. Visions revealing God's plans
3. Apocalyptic architecture

The first (and easiest) level of knowledge in Daniel contains dramatic stories of faith in God. These stories of faith and loyalty to God were recorded for the benefit of all generations. However, Earth's final generation will benefit the most from these stories of courage since the fiery trials in the first chapters of the book of Daniel are mini-parallels of coming events. For example, in Daniel 3 we read about Shadrach, Meshach and Abednego facing the mandatory worship of a golden *image which the king of Babylon constructed.* In Revelation 13:15, we read about the inhabitants of the world facing the mandatory worship of an *image which the king of modern Babylon will construct.* These parallels and their outcomes were put in the book of Daniel for our encouragement. (Note: I hope you will read my book, *Bible Stories With End Time Parallels,* which reveals end-time issues through the lives of certain Bible characters.)

The second (and more difficult) level of knowledge in Daniel concerns the meaning of the visions in the book of Daniel. The visions God gave to King Nebuchadnezzar and Daniel faithfully predict the passage of time and the fulfillment of all that God predestined to occur. Even more, these visions reveal what God planned to do long before He told Nebuchadnezzar or Daniel of His plans. Because students of prophecy have understood something of Daniel's visions for hundreds of years, we cannot say the visions were entirely sealed up until "the time of the end." However, something in the book of Daniel was sealed up, and that something uniquely applies to the people who *live at the end* of the world. What is it?

The Book Unsealed

The third (and deepest) level of knowledge found in Daniel is *the architecture of apocalyptic prophecy.* The prophecies in Daniel conform to a structure or pattern that controls their meaning. The exciting thing about this structure is that it is also present in Revelation! In other words, when you understand how the architecture of Daniel behaves, you will understand the architecture in Revelation because it is the same architecture! This architecture produces four rules (methods of interpretation) that govern the interpretation of Daniel and Revelation. These four rules are like combinations to a safe. When these four rules are applied to the interpretation of the prophecies in Daniel as well as Revelation, a marvelous result occurs. The prophecies make perfect sense *just as they read*! This point is extremely important. Portions of Daniel and Revelation have been a mystery for 2,600 years and then suddenly, the words make sense *just as they read!* What causes this change to occur? When the architecture of Daniel is understood, the contents of Daniel can be understood.

When the four rules found in Daniel are applied to each line of prophecy in Daniel and Revelation, a comprehensive story unfolds that is completely harmonious with everything the Bible has to say about the ways of God. Furthermore, all of the details God gave in the prophecies of Daniel and Revelation are in perfect harmony and synchrony with each other. The four rules force all of the prophecies in Daniel and Revelation into a chronological matrix of layers that are orderly in nature. To visualize this matrix, think of the seventeen* prophecies in Daniel and Revelation as a wedding cake of seventeen layers! The larger pieces are at the bottom of the stack and the smaller pieces are on top. The "toothpicks" that hold the seventeen layers together are events that unite and align the seventeen layers in Daniel and Revelation into one grand story. The toothpicks are necessary because two or more layers can describe the same prophetic event! Because the same event is described in two different ways – in two different layers – a precise alignment of the prophecies is not only possible, but essential to understanding the big picture. This feature will be examined in Chapter 3.

---

* For the past fifteen years, I have maintained there are eighteen apocalyptic prophecies in Daniel and Revelation. However, I have recently discovered that my division of Daniel 10-12 into two prophecies was unnecessary. Because Daniel 10-12 is one prophecy and not two prophecies, the total number of apocalyptic prophecies in Daniel and Revelation is seventeen – five in Daniel and twelve in Revelation.

The Value and Importance of Rules

A beginning student of Bible prophecy may not appreciate the
necessity of a valid set of rules of interpretation (or hermeneutics) at
first, so hopefully the following parallel will help you understand
why rules of interpretation are essential to prophetic study:
Scientists achieve advances in the study of genetics at the cellular
level. By studying various cells within the human body, they have
been able to determine how certain cells operate. In more and more
cases, they have been able to predict the behavior of cells under
controlled circumstances, because they now know some of the *secrets*
of proteins and the DNA structure. Scientists are constantly testing
for "consistent behavior" within their studies of cells. Once the
behavior of a specific cell is understood, cell behavior can be changed
or influenced through drugs compounded to produce the desired
results. Pharmaceutical companies spend billions of dollars on this
type of painstaking research because they know that a genuine cure
for most diseases must occur at the cellular level.

Consistent Behavior

In a similar way, the architecture in Daniel is distilled through a
careful study of Daniel's prophecies. Because the visions within
Daniel behave in a predictable way, this behavior allows us to
decipher things about the meaning of prophecy that we could not
otherwise know. For example, here is a consistent behavior that
occurs throughout the book of Daniel. Each of Daniel's prophecies
have a beginning point and an ending point in time, and the events
in each prophecy occur in the order in which they are given. This
behavior may sound simple, but it has profound ramifications.
Consider the results of violating this *self-evident* rule. If the events
given within each prophecy of Daniel do not occur in their given
order, *how,* then, is the order of events determined? This question
brings up an even greater question. Does the Bible speak for itself
or must it have an interpreter? After many years of study on this
question, I find the Bible has to speak for itself and the Bible has to
be its own interpreter. The constant and predictable architecture
within Daniel's prophecies is the basis for Rule One. This rule is:
*Each apocalyptic prophecy has a beginning point and an ending
point in time and the events within each prophecy must occur in the
order they are given.* Keep in mind, I am not inventing this rule.

Instead, I am expressing a consistent behavior that recurs without exception throughout the book of Daniel (as well as Revelation).

When the fulfilled elements of each prophecy in Daniel are aligned with widely published historical records, the validity of Rule One proves true *every time*! The prophecies in the book of Daniel cover more than 2,600 years so far. This great span of time contains everything necessary to validate the four rules that spring from the architecture of Daniel. As a bonus, the book of Daniel provides a historical foundation for certain prophecies in Revelation. Because some of the prophecies in Revelation run parallel to the prophecies in Daniel, we can link them together and establish the timing of events mentioned in both books. So, the discovery of Daniel's architecture, like the discovery of the Rosetta Stone, enables the Bible student to resolve many prophetic mysteries that would otherwise be impossible to solve.

How Can the Bible Tell Us Things We Don't Want to Believe?

Knowingly or unknowingly, every student of prophecy implements *a method of interpretation* to support his prophetic conclusions. The problem, of course, is that invalid rules will not produce valid conclusions. For example, some people believe, "A day in Bible prophecy *always* equals a year." A rule cannot have an exception, for if it does, who has the authority to determine when the rule should be applied or ignored? So, if we accept the idea that a day for a year rule is *always* true, then the 1,000 years of Revelation 20 would have to be 365,242 years in length. (365.242 days in a year x 1,000 years = 365,242 years) For many reasons, I believe the all-inclusive day-for-a-year rule is invalid. There are places in Daniel and Revelation where God measures time according to the Jubilee Calendar where a day represents a year (like the seventy weeks of Daniel 9), but there are also places in Scripture where God measures time in literal units (like the 42 months in Revelation 13:5). In fact, Rule Four tells us when God is using a day for a year and when He is using literal time. The point is that rules force the conclusions. If our rules are flawed or inadequate, our prophetic conclusions will be flawed.

Popular eschatology today is "a nose of wax" which expositors manipulate for political, religious or personal reasons. Millions of people believe things that have no truth in them. If an idea is

reasonable, then it is believable. However, we cannot ignore the
other side of the coin – that reasonableness does not ensure validity.
For thousands of years, people believed Earth stood still and the
Sun traveled in its orbit around Earth, until Copernicus came along
and ruined a very reasonable idea. Rules of interpretation are
vitally important to this study of prophecy because students of Bible
prophecy need a method whereby the Bible can tell us things that
we do not want to believe. We want a valid process whereby the
Bible can tell us things that run contrary to everything we believe so
that our understanding of God's truth can increase. Therefore, we
need rules to test our conclusions and beliefs. In short, valid rules of
interpretation allow Bible prophecy to say all that it has to say, and
they help us listen to God's truth so that we might learn of His
plans.

Private Interpretation

Any interpretation of prophecy which does not conform to a stated
set of valid rules is classified as a "private interpretation." The word
"private" in this context does not mean obscure. Millions of people
can believe and endorse a private interpretation (and they do). A
private interpretation is an interpretation which does not have an
external means of validation. In other words, a private interpretation cannot be tested and validated by an impartial jury given a
set of stated rules. This emphasizes our need to understand the
apocalyptic architecture in Daniel. *There is one architecture in
Daniel and Revelation and there is one truth.* Looking for that truth
is the joy of every Bible student. Even if we have the right rules of
interpretation, the likelihood of reaching the intended meaning is
not guaranteed, but it is greatly improved! (It is one thing to have
the right formula, but it is another to correctly solve the problem.)

The Four Rules

When the rules of interpretation are valid, the prophecies in Daniel
and Revelation will make sense *just as they read,* because the Bible
is its own interpreter. On the other hand, a private interpretation
requires an interpreter. An interpreter stands between the Bible
and its meaning; whereas, valid rules explain the meaning without a
go-between. Consider the difference. A private interpretation
prevents people from independently arriving at the same conclusion
without the coaxing of an interpreter, but a valid set of rules enables

people to arrive at similar conclusions *without* knowing one another. Many Christians believe whatever their leaders say about prophecy without actually studying the conclusions for themselves. Lay people usually "go along" because their church endorses a particular view. Because the subject of Bible prophecy is complex and complicated, and the average Christian does not study prophecy, it is easier to follow the leader. Of course, the mysteries of Bible prophecy will vanish during the Great Tribulation because everyone will see the evidence of what is predicted in Bible prophecy. However, until the Great Tribulation begins, we need a set of valid rules to guide our prophetic faith. If our rules of interpretation are valid, the books of Daniel and Revelation will form a unified story. A comprehensive explanation of God's ways will unfold in a drama that is in perfect harmony with all Scripture!

Since the following four rules will be used frequently throughout this book, you may want to bookmark this page. After several years of study and discovery, I am excited to share with you the *combination* that unlocks the books of Daniel and Revelation. The four rules are:

1. Each apocalyptic prophecy has a beginning and ending point in time and the events within each prophecy must occur in the order they are given.

2. A fulfilment of apocalyptic prophecy occurs when all of the specifications within that prophecy are met. This includes the order of events outlined in the prophecy.

3. Apocalyptic language can be literal, symbolic or analogous. To reach the intended meaning of a prophecy, the student must consider: (a) the context, (b) the use of parallel language in the Bible, and (c) relevant statements in the Bible that define that symbol if an element is thought to be symbolic.

4. God reckons apocalyptic time in two ways: (a) a day for a year, and (b) as literal time. The presence or absence of the Jubilee calendar determines how God reckons time.

By the time you finish this book, I hope you will find my conclusions to be consistent with these four rules. Test the rules to see if they are valid and test my conclusions to see if they align with the rules. Do not forget – God sealed up the book of Daniel until the time of the end because the message in Daniel and Revelation uniquely belongs to the last generation. Ours is *the* generation that will experience the Great Tribulation, and when it begins, the whole world will be caught up in a drama of unimaginable consequences. Because God's forthcoming behavior will be shocking and outrageous during the Great Tribulation, God has unsealed the book of Daniel so that the last generation might understand His ways and some of His purposes before the Great Tribulation begins. **"The knowledge of the secrets of the kingdom of God has been given to you, but to others I speak in parables, so that, 'though seeing, they may not see; though hearing, they may not understand.' "** (Luke 8:10)

Chapter 2

Daniel 3 – A Faith More Precious Than Gold

"You say, 'I am rich; I have acquired wealth and do not need a thing.' But you do not realize that you are wretched, pitiful, poor, blind and naked. I counsel you to buy from me gold refined in the fire, so you can become rich; and white clothes to wear, so you can cover your shameful nakedness; and salve to put on your eyes, so you can see. Those whom I love I rebuke and discipline. So be earnest, and repent. Here I am! I stand at the door and knock . . . ."

- Revelation 3:17-20

God's Agent of Wrath

King Nebuchadnezzar set siege to Jerusalem three times. He finally destroyed the city in 586 B.C. because Israel refused to submit to his "higher" authority. Even though the secular mind would say that Jerusalem was destroyed because of rebellion against Nebuchadnezzar, the Bible indicates that Jerusalem was destroyed because Israel refused to submit to God's "highest" authority. (See Jeremiah 25 and Ezekiel 14.) The destruction of Israel by Nebuchadnezzar teaches a profound truth: God's longsuffering with Israel and His wrath against Israel are mirrors reflecting how God deals with all nations. (Leviticus 18:28; Jeremiah 25:12; Acts 10:34) God preserved a record of His actions in the Bible so future generations could understand why *"He* sets up governments and takes them down."

In this particular setting, God selected Nebuchadnezzar to be His servant, His agent of wrath against Israel. (Jeremiah 25:9; 27:6; 43:10) God empowered and enabled the king of the north, Nebuchadnezzar, to destroy His city and His people because of their rebellion and decadence. (Daniel 9) The role of Nebuchadnezzar as *the king of the north* and the office of Nebuchadnezzar as *the king of Babylon* parallels the coming of the Antichrist. During the Great Tribulation, Lucifer will appear on Earth masquerading as God. The devil will be the "stern-faced king" from the North (Daniel 8:23;

11:36), and the devil will be the king of modern Babylon! We will examine these profound parallels in our study on Daniel 8.

Three Sins

God's patience with Israel ended because of three persistent sins: a) Israel violated God's Sabbaths, b) Israel engaged in sexual immorality, and c) Israel chose to worship idols instead of their Savior. (Do you see an end-time parallel?) Thoughtfully consider God's words as He lamented the apostasy of Israel: **"Her priests do violence to my law and profane my holy things; they do not distinguish between the holy and the common; they teach that there is no difference between the unclean and the clean; and they shut their eyes to the keeping of my Sabbaths, so that I am profaned among them."** (Ezekiel 22:26)

Also consider God's comments about the clergy of Israel: **" 'And among the prophets of Jerusalem I have seen something horrible: They commit adultery and live a lie. They strengthen the hands of evildoers, so that no one turns from his wickedness. They are all like Sodom to me; the people of Jerusalem are like Gomorrah . . . For they have done outrageous things in Israel; they have committed adultery with their neighbors' wives and in my name have spoken lies, which I did not tell them to do. I know it and am a witness to it,' declares the Lord."** (Jeremiah 23:14; 29:23) **Therefore this is what the Sovereign Lord says: 'I myself am against you, Jerusalem, and I will inflict punishment on you in the sight of the nations. Because of all your detestable idols, I will do to you what I have never done before and will never do again. Therefore in your midst fathers will eat their children, and children will eat their fathers. I will inflict punishment on you and will scatter all your survivors to the winds.' "** (Ezekiel 5:8-10)

We learn from Isaiah, Jeremiah and Ezekiel why God's anger with Israel reached a boiling point. His holy name had been profaned among the nations of Earth by Israel's decadence. As representatives of the Most High God and trustees of the everlasting gospel, Israel degenerated to such a decadent condition that God could no longer use Israel as His representative. Destruction was the only solution. Therefore, God Himself raised up a "servant-destroyer," the king of Babylon, to destroy His city and His people.

The Vanished Vision

Daniel and his three friends, Shadrach, Meshach and Abednego, were taken from Jerusalem as prisoners of war during the first siege of Nebuchadnezzar in 605 B.C. Shortly after they arrived in Babylon, God exalted Daniel and his friends before King Nebuchadnezzar through a curious turn of events. One night, God gave Nebuchadnezzar a vision that outlined the remaining course of human history. (Daniel 2) Essentially, the vision consisted of a great statue of a man that was made out of various materials. At the end of the vision, a great rock that came out of the sky smashed the statue to pieces. When the king awoke, he became agitated for two reasons. First, Nebuchadnezzar knew that he had received an important vision but he could not remember what it was. He thought it was from Marduk, the god of the Babylonians. Second, as the king fretted over his loss of memory, he realized that he had no other option than to ask the clergy of Babylon for help. The king did not have total confidence in the "wise men" of Babylon and he anticipated a skirmish with them. To stop this before it started, Nebuchadnezzar made it clear that he would not tolerate any delay or double talk on their part.

Behind the scenes, the God of Heaven was unfolding a plan to exalt His holy name throughout the world. Nebuchadnezzar's vision was from the God of Heaven, not Marduk, and it was the God of Heaven who gave the king amnesia. By doing this, God made fools of Babylon's clergy and at the same time revealed the impotence of Marduk. Even though the vanished vision agitated the king, the agitation caused by that vanished vision became the very means through which young Daniel became exalted to a position close to the king.

God Is So Clever

After rising from bed, and I am sure, pacing the floor, Nebuchadnezzar called an emergency meeting for all the wise men of the palace. Suspecting lame excuses and weasel words, Nebuchadnezzar confronted his wise men with these words: **"So the king summoned the magicians, enchanters, sorcerers and** astrologers to tell him what he had dreamed. When they came in and stood before the king, he said to them, 'I have had a dream that troubles me and I want to know what it means.' Then the astrologers answered the king in Aramaic, 'O king, live forever! Tell your servants the dream, and we will interpret it.' The king replied to the astrologers, 'This is what I have firmly decided: If you do not tell me what my dream was and interpret it, I will have you cut into pieces and your houses turned into piles of rubble. But if you tell me the dream and explain it, you will receive from me gifts and rewards and great honor. So tell me the dream and interpret it for me.' Once more they replied, 'Let the king tell his servants the dream, and we will interpret it.' Then the king answered, 'I am certain that you are trying to gain time [so that you can create another one of your incoherent riddles], because you realize that this is what I have firmly decided: If you do not [immediately] tell me the dream, there is just one penalty for you. [If you do not tell me the dream, I will know that] You have conspired to tell me misleading and wicked things [during times past], hoping the situation will [favorably] change [in each instance to fit your predictions]. So then [since you claim to have contact with the god of Babylon], tell me the dream, and I will know [beyond doubt] that you can interpret it for me.' "** (Daniel 2:2-9, insertions mine)

Nebuchadnezzar was no dummy. Consider his speech to the wise men. If the wise men proved to be a bunch of clever liars, he would destroy them. If they really did have a supernatural connection with Marduk, *as they had claimed*, they would be rewarded. The astrologers, magicians, sorcerers and enchanters represented Babylon's diverse religion and they claimed, from time to time, to have received visions from Marduk on behalf of the king. *Their claims of contact with Marduk almost led to their demise.*

False Prophets

In ancient times kings often sought out the services of clergymen as counselors and advisors. For example, Jezebel employed 450 prophets of Baal. (1 Kings 18:19) Even as late as the fourth century A.D., Constantine depended heavily upon the advice and flattery of the theologian, Eusebius. Clergymen were important because ancient rulers believed their prosperity and power depended on staying within the favor of "the gods." To earn their "salt," clergymen had to walk a fine line. They had to say things that flattered the ego of their employer and they had to utter prophecies that could not prove to be embarrassing. For this reason, "wise men" were notoriously hard to "pin down." By using carefully crafted "weasel words," they always had an "out" hidden somewhere in their riddles and prophecies.

In ancient times, the highest rank among the clergymen was that of a prophet. (Remember Balaam? See Numbers 22.) Any person who had direct connection with "the gods" was highly honored, respected and paid well. It is ironic that God's prophets in Israel received the opposite fate. God's prophets were often stoned or executed because Israel's kings did not want to hear the truth! (Matthew 23:37) Babylon's prophets were well educated and they presented their messages to Nebuchadnezzar with such slippery words that their prophecies always seemed to come true no matter how the situation unfolded. When Daniel stood before the king and repeated the forgotten vision and declared its interpretation, the king immediately recognized the veracity of Daniel's words. Daniel was a "true" prophet speaking clearly and decisively. He did not use weasel words! To keep Daniel close, Nebuchadnezzar promoted Daniel above all the prophets in Babylon.

Keep this thought in mind: A false prophet is a person who claims to speak for God when God has not spoken to that person. Every time Israel drifted away from God, she became full of false prophets and this made God angry. Men were saying "God showed this to me," or "God said this to me," when in fact God had said nothing or shown nothing. False prophets make God angry because the predictions of false prophets do not come to pass. Therefore, it is only a matter of time until God's Word is defamed and considered worthless when falsehoods are uttered in His name. God promises to destroy anyone who uses His name for the sake of credibility. (See Ezekiel 13.) Lucifer is given the title, "false prophet," in Revelation 19:20 for this very reason. The devil will speak out of his own evil imagination while masquerading as God!

So, in an effort to stay within the king's favor (and earn their keep), Babylon's prophets made up fables and riddles to please and flatter the king. But Nebuchadnezzar was smart enough to know that a dream cannot be validated or studied by other people, and although a false prophet can say that he has received a vision, no one can prove otherwise if the message is not clearly stated. (See also 1 Kings 18:22 and 2 Kings 3.) So, when Nebuchadnezzar demanded the wise men to reveal the vanished vision, he turned the tables on them. There was no room for deception. The king reasoned that if his wise men really had contact with the gods, if they received visions as he had, and if they had the ability to interpret visions from Marduk, then they *should* be able to describe and interpret the vision which Marduk had given the king.

So, the king called his wise men to his throne and he confronted them with a request that left no wiggle room. When the wise men heard the demand of the king, they knew they were in serious trouble. They would not be able to weasel their way out of this confrontation. Consider their defense: **"The astrologers answered the king, 'There is not a man on earth who can do what the king asks! No king, however great and mighty, has ever asked such a thing of any magician or enchanter or astrologer. What the king asks is too difficult. No one can reveal it to the king except the gods, and they do not live among men.' This made the king so angry and furious that he ordered the execution of all the wise men of Babylon."** (Daniel 2:10-12) Can you imagine being summoned to the palace for an emergency meeting only to discover that your execution is minutes away? In the presence of Nebuchadnezzar, all of the wise men of Babylon were forced to admit their deceitful ways and failure. How clever of the God of Heaven to have the wise men confess with their own mouths the impotence of the Babylonian religion. When the moment of truth came, the clergy of Babylon were disgraced and the king was justifiably furious with them.

Marduk Is Not a God

Before God exalted His holy name throughout the empire, He chose to demonstrate that Marduk was "not a god." It is amazing how a forgotten dream turned the world of Babylon's clergy upside down. Minutes before the vision took place, the prophets of Babylon were highly paid and widely respected as "wise men." After meeting with the king for a few minutes, the clergymen of Babylon were forced to confess their impotence and a death sentence was hung over their heads. I am reminded of Paul's words, **"But God chose the foolish things of the world to shame the wise; God chose the weak things of the world to shame the strong."** (1 Corinthians 1:27) Do you see an end-time parallel here? (Hint: Few, if any, of the 144,000 will be theologians; yet they will embarrass the clergy of the world.)

Remember, the point of this story is that God wanted to vindicate His holy name before the nations of Earth. He wanted the whole world to know that He was a God of love and salvation, a God of mercy and justice, a God of fairness and truth, a God of compassion and majesty. Unfortunately, the opposite had occurred. The Jews had made enemies of almost everyone on Earth. They had slandered and profaned the exalted name of God, trampled upon His law, and rejected every prophet He sent to them. So, God implemented a plan to restore His good name and He chose to use the mouth of a heathen king to do it! A sovereign God can make a servant out of anyone or anything.

The Death Decree

News of a sudden and unexpected death decree for all the wise men of Babylon flew from the palace of Nebuchadnezzar as fast as a horse could go. The "news media" was on this story in a heartbeat. The threat of death for all the wise men of Babylon did something that Nebuchadnezzar would later regret. The king unwittingly informed the whole world of the impotence of Babylon's wise men by putting a death decree on their heads. Even worse, the entire kingdom became eager to know the contents of a vision that had vanished from the king's memory.

Daniel Exalted

Through a series of providential events, Daniel eventually stood before the king. He not only revealed the vanished vision, but he also interpreted the vision for the king. This pleased the king more than words can express. When the king heard Daniel's testimony, he was thrilled. Notice what the king did: **"Then King Nebuchadnezzar fell prostrate before Daniel and paid him honor and ordered that an offering and incense be presented to him. The king said to Daniel, 'Surely your God is the God of gods**

and the Lord of kings and a revealer of mysteries, for you
were able to reveal this mystery.' Then the king placed
Daniel in a high position and lavished many gifts on him. He
made him ruler over the entire province of Babylon and
placed him in charge of all its wise men." (Daniel 2:46-48)

A few hours later, the king had a change of heart. He must have
grimaced as he faced three sobering truths: First, Daniel had
informed the king that Marduk did not give him the vision.
Nebuchadnezzar's vision came from the Most High God *of the Jews,*
those despicable captives from Jerusalem. How could these captives
have a God greater than the god of the Babylonians? Second, Daniel
told the king that the God *of the Jews* was sovereign over all the
kingdoms of the world, even Babylon. Nebuchadnezzar was told
that God sets up kings and He takes them down, according to *His*
sovereign authority. Nebuchadnezzar may have been somewhat
flattered to learn that it was the Most High God of Heaven who had
given *him* a throne. However, the reality of Daniel's words did not
sink in. Nevertheless, God wanted Nebuchadnezzar to know that he
had not gained the throne of Babylon by human prowess, but this
lesson would not be learned until after the king spent seven years
living among animals. (See Daniel 4:16; 5:21.) The third truth that
dawned on Nebuchadnezzar was the most chilling of all. Daniel told
the king that *his* kingdom would be destroyed in days to come and
another kingdom would rise to take its place. As the king churned
over the vanished vision and the train of events that it produced, he
must have concluded his vision was more of a nightmare than a
revelation from God.

The King Distressed

Nebuchadnezzar's impatience with the wise men had created a
political nightmare. The king had publically humiliated and
discredited the wise men of Babylon. He had tested the god of the
Babylonians and proved that Marduk was inferior to the God of the
Jews. Worst of all, he had fueled the curiosity of his subjects by
putting a death decree on the heads of Babylon's wise men.
Everyone wanted to know the contents of the forgotten vision! The
seriousness of a death decree for the exalted clergy of Babylon
indicated the forgotten vision was no trivial matter. Furthermore,
when the Jewish teenager, Daniel, was promoted above all the wise

men of Babylon, it became obvious to everyone that Daniel had successfully recalled and interpreted the vision for the king. So, now that the vision had been recalled and interpreted, what did it say?

We know the vision predicted the fall of Babylon and other world empires, but Nebuchadnezzar did not want his subjects to know that the God of the Hebrews had predestined the fall and destruction of his empire. The king knew that if this information leaked out, his government would collapse. A government cannot survive without the submission and loyalty of its subjects. If the news spread throughout his kingdom that the Most High God had decreed the fall of Babylon, Nebuchadnezzar knew he would become a king without a throne. How could anyone maintain confidence in a king that was predestined to destruction by the Most High God? Nebuchadnezzar knew that tenure on the throne was possible for as long as people *were loyal* to him and his regime. If his subjects heard that the God of Heaven had numbered his days, they would rise up in rebellion and he would perish. (Note: In ancient times, loyalty to a fallen king was usually punished by death when the next king gained dominion, so people were wary about their loyalties. The fact that Daniel remained alive and was appointed to serve in the government of Darius after Belshazzar was killed was a miracle. Daniel 5.)

Kings may conquer nations and kings may kill thousands to secure their authority, but no king can thwart the God of Heaven. The rumor began to spread that the God of the Jews had predestined the fall of Babylon. Based on Nebuchadnezzar's subsequent actions, I believe it is safe to conclude that administrators from the far reaches of the empire must have sent requests for clarification so they could deal with the rumors about the vision. As the situation worsened, Nebuchadnezzar consulted with his embarrassed wise men and they decided to dissolve the rumor by mixing error with truth. Nebuchadnezzar chose to distort the truth that was given to him in the vision for a number of practical and political purposes. The wise men owed their lives to the king (actually to Daniel and his three friends), because the king relented on the death decree. Consequently, they were very eager to help the king solve this political problem. Nebuchadnezzar and the wise men conspired to tell the world that Marduk had given the king a great vision of "a golden man." The people would be told that the golden man represented the kingdom of Babylon, *which would last forever.* Based on the course of events recorded in the Bible, Nebuchad-nezzar evidently alleged to his subjects that he "was commanded" in the vision to empty the golden coffers of Babylon to erect a great golden replica of the vision. Because the rumor had circulated that Babylon was predestined to fall, the king decided to use the golden image as a way to renew loyalty to his government. He required all of his administrators and governors to travel to the province of Babylon so that they could be present when the vision of "the golden image" would be proclaimed by the king and the image dedicated.

The construction of a 90-foot tall golden image of a man began in earnest. (It is believed that a cubit in ancient Babylon equaled 18-20 inches, so 60 cubits in height would equal about 90 feet. For comparison's sake, the Statue of Liberty is 111 feet tall, but Lady Liberty stands on a pedestal that is 194 feet high, which makes her total height 305 feet.) Due to the swiftness of rumors and the irreparable damage they can cause, there was no time for delay. Riders on horses were dispatched to the ends of Earth calling the administrators and governors to be present on the Plain of Dura at an appointed time. Because Nebuchadnezzar anticipated some resistence to his plans, he sent orders to those in charge of the giant smelting furnaces that were used to cast the metal man. They were to make sure the furnaces were burning during the dedication service. The loyalty test would be very simple. If anyone refused to bow down and worship the golden image *at the appointed time*, he would be thrown into one of the furnaces. The king calculated his loyalty test would *force* everyone back into "the fold" if any loyalties had been compromised by the rumor that Babylon was destined for destruction. The immediate death of rebels always reduces potential problems. The king was satisfied that this course of action would protect his throne.

I Did It My Way

The Bible indicates that Nebuchadnezzar had become pompous and indulgent. He erroneously believed that he had *gained* the throne through personal savvy and superior intellect. (Daniel 4:30; Daniel 7:4) He had heard Daniel's declaration, but he did not comprehend the fact that the God of Heaven *gave* him his kingdom. In short, the king was arrogant and to protect his throne, he thought a golden image and a loyalty test would bring an end to the rumor that Babylon was predestined to fall. It is possible that this is the most expensive lie ever told by a man. Consider the amount of gold and work that was required to cast a statue 90 feet tall. Consider also, the amount of travel and logistics necessary to bring thousands of administrators from the far-flung corners of the earth to the Plain of Dura. This story highlights an interesting point about the carnal heart: Power can be of greater value than money. Men will go to extremes to gain or hold on to power. (We regularly see politicians spend millions to win a government office that pays very little money.) To keep his lie covered up, Nebuchadnezzar prevented Daniel from attending the service. He had highly honored Daniel for telling the truth, but now that he was implementing a great lie, he did not want Daniel to be at the service to observe his foolishness.

A Time of Testing

When Daniel was promoted above the wise men of Babylon, Daniel asked that his friends be recognized for their contribution toward solving the mystery of the vanished vision. (Daniel 2:18,49) Their promotion almost proved to be the cause of their death. The king wanted everyone who was someone in his government to be present at the dedication of the golden image. In the political arena, the question of loyalty is paramount to everything else. *One man can exercise power over others only if the others are willing to submit.*

Daniel's friends, Meshach, Shadrach and Abednego, knew the test of loyalty was coming. What should they do? They could not run and hide because the king had given them high positions in the government of Babylon. Furthermore, the impotent wise men of Babylon were jealously eager to have Daniel and these "three Jews" removed from their high offices. Therefore, if they were to avoid the dedication of the golden image, they would show reluctance in honoring the king. Hesitation on this point could be regarded as treason. As the date approached, I am sure Daniel and his friends met together to ask the Lord for divine intervention. On the basis of their testimony during the dedication service, it is safe to say that Shadrach, Meshach and Abednego obediently went to the service expecting to be thrown into the fiery furnace. What courage! But, this is exactly what God wanted! God needed three young men who were willing to go to their death so that He could exalt His holy name. Remember, this story began because God wanted to defend His name before the nations of the world. The Jews had profaned His holy name by their degenerate behavior, and God wanted to set the record straight. In order to accomplish this, God needed an expensive golden image, a pagan king who knew the truth, a large crowd of world leaders who were confused by rumors, a very hot fiery furnace and three young men who would be faithful to their death.

The Moment of Truth

"So the satraps, prefects, governors, advisers, treasurers, judges, magistrates and all the other provincial officials assembled for the dedication of the image that King Nebuchadnezzar had set up, and they stood before it. Then the herald loudly proclaimed, 'This is what you are commanded to do, O peoples, nations and men of every language: As soon as you hear the sound of the horn, flute, zither, lyre, harp, pipes and all kinds of music, you must fall down and worship the image of gold that King Nebuchadnezzar has set up. Whoever does not fall down and worship will immediately be thrown into a blazing furnace.' Therefore, as soon as they heard the sound of the horn, flute, zither, lyre, harp and all kinds of music, all the peoples, nations and men of every language fell down and worshiped the image of gold that King Nebuchadnezzar had set up. At this time some astrologers came forward and denounced the Jews." (Daniel 3:3-8)

All of a sudden, the dedication service stopped. As far as the eye could see, all but three Jews had bowed down before the golden man. The wise men wasted no time reporting this anomaly to the king. The three Hebrews were arrested and presented to the king. The golden image was forgotten. The music stopped. Everyone stood up and turned around to see what was about to happen. Every eye focused on three young Jews who dared to rebel against the monarch of Babylon! As they approached the throne, the king must have uttered some bad Babylonian words under his breath as he said, "How did *they* get here?" The king was embarrassed and frustrated. The whole dedication service could unravel and the result could be worse than the truth he was trying to hide!

Did you notice the astrologers came forward to report the insolence of the three Hebrews? This is amazing. The wise men owed their very lives to these three young men and yet, the wise men were the first to report their disobedience to the king. (There is an end-time parallel here. The clergy will be the first to condemn God's servants!) **"They said to King Nebuchadnezzar, 'O king, live forever! You have issued a decree, O king, that everyone who hears the sound of the horn, flute, zither, lyre, harp, pipes and all kinds of music must fall down and worship the image of gold, and that whoever does not fall down and worship will be thrown into a blazing furnace. But there are some Jews whom you have set over the affairs of the province of Babylon – Shadrach, Meshach and Abednego – who pay no attention to you, O king. They neither serve your gods nor worship the image of gold you have set up.' Furious with** [embarrassment and] **rage, Nebuchadnezzar summoned Shadrach, Meshach and Abednego. So these men were brought before the king, and Nebuchadnezzar said to them, 'Is it true, Shadrach, Meshach and Abednego, that you do not serve my gods or worship the image of gold I have set up?' "** (Daniel 3:9-14, insertion mine)

The king personally knew Shadrach, Meshach and Abednego. He knew their integrity and loyalty. He knew they were close friends of Daniel, but somehow they had been overlooked in this scheme. They should not have been present. Now, he had no other option but to destroy them if he wanted to protect his throne. The king was "up the creek in a chicken wire canoe." Nebuchadnezzar, the king of Earth, had created a huge lie, but the God of Heaven had gathered everyone together to hear and see a truth that was greater than a golden lie. (The truth of God is most clearly seen when openly confronted with falsehood.) The king responded to the rebellion of Meshach, Shadrach and Abednego with feigned generosity, hoping they would humor him on this matter. The king had a big political problem on his hands (which he had created by threatening the wise men), and he did not want a showdown with the Most High God of these three men. So the king tried to appear generous: **"Now when you hear the sound of the horn, flute, zither, lyre, harp,**

pipes and all kinds of music, if you are ready to fall down
and worship the image I made, very good. But if you do not
worship it, you will be thrown immediately into a blazing
furnace. Then what god will be able to rescue you from my
hand?"** (Daniel 3:15)

The words of Nebuchadnezzar are interesting. The king honestly
knew these three lads were not rebellious toward him; after all, they
had joined with Daniel in seeking an answer to his vanished vision.
But the king was haughty enough to taunt the lads with the remark,
"Then what god will be able to rescue you from my hand?"
The king uttered these words because *he knew* of their loyalty to
their God. He may have even known about the second
commandment of their God. The action of the king reveals another
interesting fact about the carnal heart: *The performance of a miracle
does not always change the carnal heart.* (Centuries later, Jesus
raised Lazarus from the dead in the presence of many unbelievers
and some of them still refused to accept Christ as the Messiah! See
John 11.) In Nebuchadnezzar's case, he personally experienced the
vanished vision and witnessed the miracle when Daniel told him
what he had dreamed. But neither event changed the king's heart.
When confronted with the loyalty of the three Jews to the King of
kings, the king of Earth thought he had the high ground, but as it
turns out, he was on holy ground! To protect his lies, the king had to
kill those who *stood* for the truth. He knew that they knew the
truth about the vanished vision because he had promoted them for
participating with Daniel in praying for the truth! He also knew
that he could never recover from public disgrace if he showed any
sign of weakness or timidity in the presence of thousands of his
administrators. So, the king did what every carnal heart would do,
and the young men did what every born-again believer would do.
The metal in each heart was revealed.

**"Shadrach, Meshach and Abednego replied to the king, 'O
Nebuchadnezzar, we do not need to defend ourselves before
you in this matter** [because you know the truth and we know the
truth about the vanished vision]. **If we are thrown into the
blazing furnace, the God we serve is able to save us from it,
and he will rescue us from your hand, O king. But even if he
does not, we want you to know, O king, that we will not serve**

your gods or worship the image of gold you have set up.' "
(Daniel 3:16-18, insertion mine)

Shadrach, Meshach and Abednego had prepared for this moment. Through prayer and fasting, they had strengthened their resolve to stand firm for God. This event was a showdown between the gold of Babylon and the pure gold of faith in God. When the king saw that these young men were not going to acquiesce and "go along" with his plan, he became very angry. They had publically rejected his authority, and this was the very thing he was trying to protect with the creation and dedication of the golden image!

"Then was Nebuchadnezzar full of fury, and the form of his visage was changed against Shadrach, Meshach, and Abednego: therefore he spake, and commanded that they should heat the furnace one seven times more than it was wont to be [normally] heated. And he commanded the most mighty men that were in his army to bind Shadrach, Meshach, and Abednego, and to cast them into the burning fiery furnace. Then these men were bound in their coats, their hosen [trousers], and their hats, and their other garments, and were cast into the midst of the burning fiery furnace." (Daniel 3:19-21, KJV, insertions mine)

I like the way the KJV states these verses because I like the power of its language. The Bible says "the form of his visage was changed." I understand this to mean that Nebuchadnezzar's face turned fiery red (maybe his blood pressure hit 220/160). He was hotter than a firecracker on the fourth of July because his kingly ego had been hammered. Here is a mystery: *Even though the carnal heart is full of rebellion, it hates insubordination more than anything else.* When the carnal heart cannot get its way, its fury knows no limits. The king's authority was publically rejected, and no king can tolerate open rebellion. Rejection, or the fear of rejection, is the underlying basis for peer pressure and much social torment. To successfully deal with rejection, a person must receive daily injections of spiritual courage and stamina. Meshach, Shadrach and Abednego were at peace with their fate on that day because they had walked and talked with God. They had practiced obedience in small things – this was not their first test. Loyalty that can withstand the prospect of a fiery death does not come overnight. Instead, it comes in little steps.

The God of Heaven Intervenes

"The king's command was so urgent and the furnace so hot that the flames of the fire killed the soldiers who took up Shadrach, Meshach and Abednego, and these three men, firmly tied, fell into the blazing furnace. Then King Nebuchadnezzar leaped to his feet in amazement and asked his advisers, 'Weren't there three men that we tied up and threw into the fire?' They replied, 'Certainly, O king.' He said, 'Look! I see four men walking around in the fire, unbound and unharmed, and the fourth looks like a son of the gods.' Nebuchadnezzar then approached the opening of the blazing furnace and shouted, 'Shadrach, Meshach and Abednego, servants of the Most High God, come out! Come here!' So Shadrach, Meshach and Abednego came out of the fire, and the satraps, prefects, governors and royal advisers crowded around them. They saw that the fire had not harmed their bodies, nor was a hair of their heads singed; their robes were not scorched, and there was no smell of fire on them." (Daniel 3:22-27)

The death of Nebuchadnezzar's soldiers proved to the vast audience that the heat of the furnace was extreme. The soldiers who threw the three Jews into the furnace went to their death because they were loyal and obedient to their earthly king. The three Hebrews that were supposed to go to their death were obedient and loyal to their Heavenly King. (Exodus 20:4-6) In both cases, loyalty was present, but the greater question is: "Which king deserves highest loyalty?" While the three Hebrews were being bound and thrown into the furnace, the king's mind was in turmoil. He had to recover from the showdown caused by these three Jews. He watched with interest as the young men were bound and thrown into the furnace. As he observed their fate and the deaths of his own soldiers, the king was shocked! Instead of seeing their bodies consumed by fire, he saw *four* men walking around in the furnace. The king jumped to his feet and asked, **"Weren't there three men that *we* tied up and threw into the fire?"** His attendants assured him this was the case. Then the king exclaimed, **"Look! I see four men**

walking around in the fire . . ." Nebuchadnezzar immediately recognized the fiery presence of God standing in the furnace with the three Hebrews.

Nebuchadnezzar knew the golden image service was a charade. Nebuchadnezzar knew he was in the wrong when he sent Shadrach, Meshach and Abednego to the fiery furnace. In spite of knowing these things, the king moved to protect his material interests. He did this because his highest loyalties centered on himself. In this sense, Nebuchadnezzar demonstrated the carnal heart that plagues all of mankind. Nothing on Earth is more selfish and self-seeking than the carnal heart. The root of the world's problems today is selfishness and self-seeking.

"Then Nebuchadnezzar said, 'Praise be to the God of Shadrach, Meshach and Abednego, who has sent his angel and rescued his servants! They trusted in him and defied the king's command and were willing to give up their lives rather than serve or worship any god except their own God. Therefore I decree that the people of any nation or language who say anything against the God of Shadrach, Meshach and Abednego be cut into pieces and their houses be turned into piles of rubble, for no other god can save in this way.' Then the king promoted Shadrach, Meshach and Abednego in the province of Babylon." (Daniel 3:28-30)

What does a humiliated king say to an enormous gathering of world governors when his death decree upon three Jews was made null and void by a miracle? The king did not admit defeat, nor did the king offer an apology to the God of the Heaven. Instead, he turned to his impotent wise men and confused administrators and said, "If any of you speak evil about the God of Shadrach, Meshach and Abednego, you will be cut in pieces!" Wow! The king deflects his responsibility once again. The carnal heart of the king rejected another chance to be transformed. Later, the God of Heaven finally got the king's attention by exiling him to the field as an animal for seven years – but that is another story.

The End of This Story

When the administrators and governors returned to their distant homes, they had a story to tell! In a few words their story went like this, "Yes, we saw the golden image, but that was nothing! Let me tell you about the God of the Jews. He delivered three Jews out of a roaring fiery furnace. We saw it with our own eyes. The fire was so hot it killed the king's soldiers, but the flames did not hurt the Jews! That is some God the Jews have." This story, repeated by a thousand pagans all over the world, exalted the God of Heaven. As a nation, the Jews had profaned the wonderful name of God, but God found three Jews who had a faith of pure gold and He was able to exalt His holy name through their obedience and loyalty.

There are numerous important end-time parallels in this story. During the end-time, there will be "an image to the beast," and all people will be required to worship it or be killed. (Revelation 13) You and I will be players in the drama that is forthcoming. It is possible that we may have to stand before the dreaded king of Babylon (Lucifer). Will we have a faith of pure gold? **"To the angel of the church in Laodicea write: These are the words of the Amen, the faithful and true witness, the ruler of God's creation. I know your deeds, that you are neither cold nor hot. I wish you were either one or the other! So, because you are lukewarm – neither hot nor cold – I am about to spit you out of my mouth. You say, 'I am rich; I have acquired wealth and do not need a thing.' But you do not realize that you are wretched, pitiful, poor, blind and naked. I counsel you to buy from me gold refined in the fire, so you can become rich; and white clothes to wear, so you can cover your shameful nakedness; and salve to put on your eyes, so you can see. Those whom I love I rebuke and discipline. So be earnest, and repent. Here I am! I stand at the door and knock. If anyone hears my voice and opens the door, I will come in and eat with him, and he with me. To him who overcomes, I will give the right to sit with me on my throne, just as I overcame and sat down with my Father on his throne. He who has an ear, let him hear what the Spirit says to the churches."** (Revelation 3:14-22)

Chapter 3

Daniel 7 – God Is Sovereign

". . . Who foretold this long ago, who declared it from the distant past? Was it not I, the Lord? And there is no God apart from me, a righteous God and a Savior; there is none but me."

- Isaiah 45:21

Prophecy Reveals the Process of Salvation

Those who study Bible prophecy study the deeper things of God. The beauty of prophecy is that we have an opportunity to understand God's grand purposes and timeless ways, even *before* history records His actions. Unfortunately, many Christians dismiss the importance of prophecy without understanding anything about the subject. I often hear, "Prophecy has nothing to do with salvation, so why bother with it?" While it may be true that prophecy does not bring salvation, the fulfillment of prophecy has everything to do with faith in God's Word. Isn't this one of the object lessons from Noah's flood? If the study of salvation reveals the justice and mercy of God, then the study of prophecy reveals the process through which God fulfills His Word.

God Amplifies the Matrix

About fifty years after God gave King Nebuchadnezzar and Daniel the vision of the metal man, Daniel received a second vision. This second vision is important for several reasons. First, Daniel 7 is a repetition and expansion of Daniel 2. The vision in Daniel 2 is amplified in Daniel 7 so that we might better understand the ways and plans of God. Second, Daniel 7 is an important vision because God adds certain details to the prophetic matrix which later visions will build upon. Daniel 7 identifies the timing of two events upon which other prophecies depend. If the timing of these two events are overlooked or inaccurately identified, the other prophecies that depend upon this timing will not harmonize. Bible prophecy is something like a house of cards. Every new layer depends upon the strength of the layer beneath it.

The vision in Daniel 2 can be compared to "sub-flooring," that is, the first layer in our prophetic understanding. Daniel 2 describes a chronological sequence of seven kingdoms that spans more than 2,600 years (605 B.C. to the Second Coming). If the vision in Daniel 2 is sub-flooring, then the vision in Daniel 7 is the flooring. Daniel 7 lies on top of Daniel 2. (See Chart 3.1.) When bonded together, these two visions strengthen each other. Both visions are identical in length because they cover the same time period. The "nails" that hold these two visions together are the elements within them. The first four kingdoms described in Daniel 2 perfectly align with the four beasts described in Daniel 7. Thus, the four beasts in Daniel 7 are a repetition and enlargement of the first four kingdoms presented in Daniel 2. Carefully notice how repetition and enlargement is used in Chart 3.1. By amplifying the elements of each vision with information from other visions, God demonstrates the all important operation of a matrix, and this matrix makes our prophetic foundation more secure.

Timing	605 B.C.	538 B.C.	331 B.C.	168 B.C.

Daniel 7	Lion with Eagle's Wings	Bear with Three Ribs	Leopard with Four Wings	Monster with 10 Horns
(Flooring)				
Daniel 2	**Head** of Gold	**Chest** of Silver	**Thighs** of Bronze	**Legs** of Iron
(Subflooring)				
Kingdoms:	**Babylon**	**Medo-Persia**	**Grecia**	**Rome**

Chart 3.1

For at least two reasons, God implemented this architecture in Daniel so that history would produce this matrix. First, if *the same kingdom* is identified in different visions with unique specifications, the chance of misinterpretation is greatly reduced, and different views of *the same kingdom* expand our understanding of that kingdom and its duration. For example, the thighs of bronze in Daniel 2 represent the same kingdom as the leopard with four wings in Daniel 7. (Notice the kingdom of Grecia in Chart 3.1.) Second, God established the matrix in Daniel because He foreknew that He could build on it 700 years later when He gave John the visions recorded in Revelation. In other words, the matrix established in Daniel is integral to the book of Revelation.

Daniel 8 Briefly Introduced

Since we are observing the use of repetition and enlargement, allow me to jump ahead for a moment and add a few more elements to Chart 3.1 from the visions in Daniel 8 and 11. The added data may help you quickly see how the architecture in Daniel produces a historical matrix. As this matrix grows larger, it becomes more comprehensive. Eventually, every prophetic item in Daniel and Revelation will harmoniously fit within this matrix.

Two years after receiving the vision recorded in Daniel 7, God gave Daniel yet another vision. Even though Babylon had not fallen at the time of this vision, Daniel knew that another kingdom would displace Babylon. During the vision of Daniel 8, Daniel saw a great conflict between a ram with two horns and a goat that had a large horn protruding out of its head (maybe something like a unicorn horn). The angel told Daniel that the ram represented the rising kingdom of the Medes and the Persians, and the two horns of the ram represented its two kings. Also, the goat represented the future kingdom of Grecia, which would eventually destroy the kingdom of the Medes and Persians. The angel told Daniel that the great horn of the goat represented the first prominent king of the Grecian empire which proved to be Alexander the Great. (Daniel 8:20,21) With this information in mind, let us consider the first thousand years (605 B.C. - A.D. 476) of the prophetic matrix that develops in the book of Daniel.

Daniel 2, 7 and 8

Timing:	605 - 538 B.C.	538 - 331 B.C.	331 - 168 B.C.	168 B.C. - A.D. 476

Daniel 8		Ram with Two Horns	Goat with One Great Horn	
Daniel 7	Lion with Eagle's Wings	Bear with Three Ribs	Leopard with Four Wings	Monster with 10 Horns
Daniel 2	Head of Gold	Chest of Silver	Thighs of Bronze	Legs of Iron
Kingdoms:	Babylon	Medo-Persia	Grecia	Rome

Chart 3.2

Daniel 11 Briefly Introduced

Notice how the layers are adding up. The matrix is becoming more inclusive. The ram in Daniel 8, the bear in Daniel 7, and the chest of silver in Daniel 2 represent *the same entity,* Medo-Persia! This matrix provides a solid footing for all of the prophecies in Daniel and Revelation. God's use of repetition and enlargement puts our prophetic faith on solid ground. While we are discussing the expansion and development of this matrix, let us jump forward to Daniel's last vision, look at Chart 3.3, and add portions of Daniel 11 to the matrix.

Look at the top two rows on Chart 3.3. Now, review the words spoken to Daniel during the reign of Darius the Mede: **"Now then, I tell you the truth: Three more kings will appear in Persia, and then a fourth, who will be far richer than all the others. When he has gained power by his wealth, he will stir up everyone against the kingdom of Greece. Then a mighty king will appear, who will rule with great power and do as he pleases."** (Daniel 11:2,3) History confirms the rise of these four kings in Persia, and history confirms the overall progression of kingdoms presented in this matrix. God knows the future before it comes to pass and His Word cannot fail. The matrix in Chart 3.3 spans more than 1,000 years – from the rise of Babylon under

Nebuchadnezzar to the fall of civil Rome in A.D. 476. Even though the book of Daniel offers more detail than this matrix presently shows, a thousand years of history and prophecy should be sufficient to demonstrate that God's matrix conforms to a specific architecture! Remember Rule One?

Daniel 2, 7, 8 and 11

Timing:	605 - 538 B.C.	538 - 331 B.C.	331 - 168 B.C.	168 B.C. - A.D. 476

Daniel 11:2-4		Four Kings: Cambyses, False Smerdis, Darius I, Xerxes	Mighty King: Alexander the Great	
Daniel 8		Ram with Two Horns	Goat with One Great Horn	
Daniel 7	Lion with Eagle's Wings	Bear with Three Ribs	Leopard with Four Wings	Monster with 10 Horns
Daniel 2	Head of Gold	Chest of Silver	Thighs of Bronze	Legs of Iron
Kingdoms:	Babylon	Medo-Persia	Grecia	Rome

Chart 3.3

Repetition and enlargement are indispensable to the study of prophecy. *No prophecy in Daniel or Revelation tells a whole story within itself.* In fact, neither book, Daniel nor Revelation, tells the whole story! The visions in both books interconnect and depend upon each other. Many Bible teachers today offer erroneous prophetic conclusions because they lift prophetic segments out of their context and this violates the rules found in the book of Daniel. Unless the Bible student has valid rules of interpretation, truth cannot be determined. The visions of Daniel and Revelation can be manipulated in an infinite number of wrong ways. Remember this: All of the prophecies in Daniel and Revelation link to each other, and *together* they form one harmonious matrix.

The matrix teaches us two things: First, each prophetic element in Daniel can be tied to a specific time and location. Second, the intended meaning of the prophecies in Daniel and Revelation is found *after* we align all of the elements within the prophecies. A puzzle is not solved until all of its pieces are in their right places. The events described in each prophecy are the nails that hold all of the layers together. When the prophetic matrix of Daniel and Revelation is aligned correctly, a marvelous prophetic picture unfolds. Understanding the big picture is important. The prophecies of Daniel and Revelation are not limited to one nation or one church. Instead, the prophecies of Daniel and Revelation encompass *all* nations, kindred, tongues and people. God has a predetermined blueprint that affects everyone on Earth. All prophetic pieces fit together in an interlocking way so that every element in every prophecy is supported by the elements around it! This is similar to the arch over a castle's doorway. Shaped stones support the span of the arch *because* the architectural design of the doorway keeps the arch intact. In a similar way, all of the prophecies in Daniel support each other through the architectural design embedded in Daniel. God designed this feature so that at the end of time, His people could have an accurate and comprehensive understanding of His plans. Of course, people who dismiss the importance of prophecy will not have a clue as to what is going on when the next prophetic event occurs.

Daniel Saw a Lion, Bear, Leopard and Terrible Beast

Now that we have examined the concept of a prophetic matrix in the book of Daniel, we need to investigate the details in Daniel 7 and notice how they fit within the big picture. This vision, as with all the visions in Daniel, contains few words, but is full of detail. This vision is highly important because it establishes a historical footing for several other visions. *If this particular vision is misinterpreted, the intended meaning of Daniel or Revelation will be derailed.*

As the vision begins, Daniel is looking over a great body of water. From his vantage point, he sees four strange beasts rising up out of the sea. These beasts are unusual in appearance because they have strange features added to their bodies. These strange features highlight specific characteristics that help to identify the empires they represent.

1. A lion with eagle wings

2. A bear with three ribs in its mouth

3. A leopard with four wings and four heads

4. A monster or terrible beast having ten horns

To simplify this vision and its explanation, I have divided the vision and my commentary into twelve parts. I hope you will read and reread each of these parts until all of the elements are easy to identify and understand.

Part One:

"In the first year of Belshazzar king of Babylon Daniel had a dream and visions of his head upon his bed: then he wrote the dream, and told the sum of the matters. Daniel spake and said, I saw in my vision by night, and, behold, the four winds of the heaven strove upon the great sea. And four great beasts came up from the sea, diverse one from another. The first was like a lion, and had eagle's wings: I beheld till the wings thereof were plucked, and it was lifted up from the earth, and made stand upon the feet as a man, and a man's heart was given to it." (Daniel 7:1-4, KJV)

Comments on Part One: Babylon

Historians say the first year of Belshazzar was about 552 B.C. If so, this vision occurs about fifty years after the vision recorded in Daniel 2. Daniel saw four great beasts rise up from the sea and he was told these beasts represented four empires that would rise at their appointed time. (Daniel 7:15-16) The first beast to rise up was a lion, and it represents the empire of Babylon. Just as gold is the king of metals, so the lion is the king of beasts. The eagle's wings indicate a military prowess that none can escape. The ancients regarded the eagle's keen vision and its ability to swoop down on its prey as a fitting symbol of military power. (Deuteronomy 28:49) These characteristics, no doubt, prompted the founding fathers of the United States to use the Bald Eagle as a symbol of military power. As Daniel watched, the lion lost its power and ability to subdue nations. In this vision, the lion received a man's heart, a heart that is subject to vanity, arrogance, and pride. This transition uniquely describes the arrogance of the kings of Babylon. God had to humiliate King Nebuchadnezzar by taking him from the throne and giving him the mind of an animal for seven years because of pride and arrogance. (Daniel 4) Unfortunately, subsequent kings of Babylon did not learn from Nebuchadnezzar's humiliation and Babylon ultimately fell because of arrogance and vanity. (Daniel 5:22)

Consider the words of Daniel to King Belshazzar on the last night of Babylon's insolence: **"O king, the Most High God gave your father Nebuchadnezzar sovereignty and greatness and glory and splendor. Because of the high position he gave him, all the peoples and nations and men of every language dreaded and feared him. Those the king wanted to put to death, he put to death; those he wanted to spare, he spared; those he wanted to promote, he promoted; and those he wanted to humble, he humbled. But when his heart became arrogant and hardened with pride, he was deposed from his royal throne and stripped of his glory. But you his son, O Belshazzar, have not humbled yourself, though you knew all this. Instead, you have set yourself up against the Lord of heaven. You had the goblets from his temple brought to you, and you and your nobles, your wives and your concubines drank wine from them. You praised the gods of silver and gold, of bronze, iron, wood and stone, which cannot see or hear or understand. But you did not honor the God who holds in his hand your life and all your ways. Therefore he sent the hand that wrote the inscription. 'This is the inscription that was written: MENE, MENE, TEKEL, PARSIN This is what these words mean: Mene: God has numbered the days of your reign and brought it to an end. Tekel : You have been weighed on the scales and found wanting. Peres : Your kingdom is divided and given to the Medes and Persians.' "** (Daniel 5:18-28, NIV) The Bible leaves no wiggle room on the identity of the lion. Daniel 2:38 says the head of gold is Babylon, and Daniel 8 tells us the next kingdom after Babylon is that of the Medes and Persians. Therefore, the lion with a man's heart is a perfect representation of Babylon, and history agrees.

Part Two: Medo-Persia

And behold another beast, a second, like to a bear, and it raised up itself on one side, and it had three ribs in the

mouth of it between the teeth of it: and they said thus unto it, Arise, devour much flesh. (Daniel 7:5, KJV)

Comments on Part Two

Two features stand out about this ferocious bear. First, Daniel observed that one shoulder rose higher than the other. This feature corresponds with the fact that the Persians became the dominant side of the Medo-Persian empire. (An interesting parallel can be found in the metal man from Daniel 2. The chest of silver had two arms, suggesting this kingdom could have two armies.) Second, the three ribs represented the carcasses of Lydia, Egypt and Babylon. After the Medes and Persians subdued these three governments, they controlled the world. Isaiah foretold the rise of the Persians more than a hundred years before Cyrus was born. Notice this prophecy: **"This is what the Lord says to his anointed, to Cyrus, whose right hand I take hold of to subdue nations before him and to strip kings of their armor, to open doors before him so that gates will not be shut: I will go before you and will level the mountains; I will break down gates of bronze and cut through bars of iron. I will give you the treasures of darkness, riches stored in secret places, so that you may know that I am the Lord, the God of Israel, who summons you by name. For the sake of Jacob my servant, of Israel my chosen, I summon you by name and bestow on you a title of honor, though you do not acknowledge me."** (Isaiah 45:1-4)

Part Three: Grecia

After this I beheld, and lo another, like a leopard, which had upon the back of it four wings of a fowl; the beast had also four heads; and dominion was given to it. (Daniel 7:6, KJV)

Comments on Part Three

The third beast, the leopard, is a swift and cunning hunter that easily kills prey larger than itself. The leopard in this vision had four wings indicating its conquest would be incredibly swift. The leopard represented the kingdom of Grecia, the empire that swallowed up Medo-Persia. Historians marvel at the swiftness of Grecia's first king, Alexander the Great. He conquered the Medo-Persian empire in a mere ten years! When considering the geographical scope of his conquests and the fact that he did this on horseback, there is no doubt that God empowered Alexander to accomplish this military feat. At the peak of his conquests and military prowess, Alexander died of "swamp fever" (probably malaria) at the age of 33. Interestingly, his offspring did not inherit his kingdom. It was eventually divided between his four leading generals: Ptolemy, Cassander, Lysimachus and Seleucus. The four heads of the leopard represent these four kings.

Part Four: The Monster Beast

After this I saw in the night visions, and behold a fourth beast, dreadful and terrible, and strong exceedingly; and it had great iron teeth: it devoured and brake in pieces, and stamped the residue with the feet of it: and it was diverse from all the beasts that were before it; and it had ten horns. I considered the horns, and, behold, there came up among them another little horn, before whom there were three of the first horns plucked up by the roots: and, behold, in this horn were eyes like the eyes of man, and a mouth speaking great things. (Daniel 7:7,8, KJV)

Comments on Part Four

Historians generally agree that the Grecian empire ended with the battle of Pydna in 168 B.C. With this victory, the Romans finally gained control of the world. The Roman military was known for its use of iron and its scorched-earth policy. Did you notice the fourth beast has teeth of iron? This metallic feature parallels the "legs of iron" mentioned in Daniel 2. Unlike King Nebuchadnezzar who took captives to Babylon and trained them for government service, the Romans took few prisoners. (True to form, when the Romans burned Jerusalem to the ground in A.D. 70, they took everything of value, but few prisoners.) The term, "the iron age," accurately describes Rome's extensive use of this metal. The Romans were skillful manufacturers of iron weapons. Their iron-clad warriors and chariots of iron were legendary. As a world empire, Rome endured for almost 650 years (168 B.C. to A.D. 476), but like its predecessors, Rome fell. After a series of civil wars within its borders, the empire crumbled during the last half of the fifth century A.D. As the Roman empire fractured, ten ethnic nations *within* the former empire rose to power. The ten horns of the fourth beast represent these ten nations. Daniel was told, **"The ten horns are ten kings who will come from** [within] **this kingdom."** (Daniel 7:24, insertion mine) These tribal-nations have been generally identified as the Ostrogoths, Heruli, Franks, Vandals, Lombards, Visigoths, Suevi, Burgundians, Alamanni, and the Anglo-Saxons.

Conflicting Interpretation

Many prophetic commentators claim the ten horns on the fourth beast represent ten nations that will belong to a *future* European Union. (Currently, fourteen nations belong to the EU.) This interpretation is faulty because it does not satisfy *all* of the prophetic specifications given in Daniel and Revelation about the ten horns. The ten horns cannot be ten nations of a future European Union for several reasons. These reasons will be explored in Part Nine of this chapter.

Even though Daniel observed four beasts in this vision, he was particularly distressed and awed by the fourth beast, because it was different than the other three beasts. As Daniel watched this monster beast, he noticed a little horn that began to grow out of its forehead. As it grew, the little horn became great and it uprooted three of the original ten horns by their roots. This little horn had eyes and a mouth that spoke very boastful things! Even though Daniel did not comprehend the vision, he became very alarmed as he watched the ferociousness of the little horn. He could see that it was grossly evil and it wielded absolute power for a period of time, but he did not know what it represented.

Part Five:

I beheld till the thrones were cast down [arranged or set in place]**, and the Ancient of days did sit, whose garment was white as snow, and the hair of his head like the pure wool: his throne was like the fiery flame, and his wheels as burning fire. A fiery stream issued and came forth from before him: thousand thousands ministered unto him, and ten thousand times ten thousand stood before him: the judgment was set, and the books were opened.** (Daniel 7:9,10, KJV, insertion mine)

Comments on Part Five

Suddenly, while Daniel was watching the antics of the little horn on Earth, his attention was directed to a glorious scene taking place in Heaven. Daniel saw several thrones (notice that the word is plural) arranged for a great convocation. The Aramaic word *remah* means "to place or arrange" or "to set up." It can also mean "to throw," as in throwing a ball. The KJV translators may have chosen to translate the words "thrones were cast down" because they were thinking that the thrones of the beasts were "thrown down" when the Ancient of Days took His seat. The Septuagint, or the LXX, as it is sometimes called, is a Greek version of the Old Testament translated by seventy-two Jewish scholars about 280 years before Jesus was born. The translators of the LXX converted the Aramaic word *remah* to the Greek word *tithemi* which means "to set up" or "to arrange or erect." This Hebrew to Greek transition, translated two and a half centuries after Daniel's death, is very helpful. The context of this passage also gives us some additional help. Therefore, it is not surprising that many Bible translations today reflect the Greek translation of the word *remah*. The result is that Daniel saw thrones arranged or put in place. According to Revelation 4 and 5 (which also describes this scene in Daniel 7), there are a total of twenty-five thrones. Twenty-four thrones encircle the throne of the Father. As Daniel watched this scene, he saw the Father come into the previously arranged courtroom and take His seat. (The title; "The Ancient of Days," only occurs in Daniel 7 and it indicates the Father existed before time began.) A numberless multitude of angels rose to their feet as the Father entered the courtroom, and the Bible says, **"The court was seated, and the books were opened."** What is this court scene all about? When does it occur? What books were opened? What does the court scene have to do with the terror caused by the little horn on Earth?

The Pre-Advent Judgment of Mankind

Reread Daniel 7:9,10 at the beginning of Part Five. God lifted Daniel's eyes from Earth, while he was watching the little horn, to see something that would take place in Heaven's courtroom. God showed Daniel the pre-Second Coming judgment of mankind. The seriousness and importance of this great convocation can be measured by the billions of angels in attendance. According to

Revelation 4 and 5, the Father, the Son, the four living creatures, the twenty-four elders and billions of angels are all present. This convocation began in 1798, and one of the items on the agenda was the judgment of human beings. Before Jesus returns to Earth, He will judge the people of Earth and determine who will participate in His eternal kingdom. For reasons that will be presented later, this judgment began in 1844. Presently, this great convocation has been under way for more than 150 years! Can you imagine a meeting that has been in session for 150 years? Sure you can! Sessons of the United States Congress has been meeting for more than two hundred years, and Congress will continue to meet for as long as the United States exists!

Warning! Prerequisites needed: The pre-advent judgment scene described in Daniel 7:9,10 is a topic that requires a basic understanding of two Bible truths. First, you have to understand what the Bible says about the state of man in death. Therefore, I hope you have studied Chapter 13 in my companion volume, *Jesus, The Alpha and The Omega.* Second, the concept of a pre-advent judgment requires a basic understanding of the doctrine of parallel temples. This topic is covered in Chapters 11 and 12 of my companion volume. If you understand these two doctrines as I do, my comments about Daniel 7:9,10 will make a lot more sense.

The All Important Linkage

At first glance, the courtroom scene in Heaven seems out of context in a vision that concentrates on four beasts and the little horn power on Earth. God associated these disconnected elements in this vision to draw attention to their timing. In other words, the timing of certain events on Earth are associated with the timing of certain events in Heaven. As we will see, the timing of the wounding of the little horn power on Earth and Christ's pre-advent judgment are inseparably linked together. Since we cannot see events occurring in Heaven, God associated the great convocation scene *in Heaven* with the wounding of the little horn power *on Earth.* This linkage enables students of prophecy to determine the timing of the Heavenly event. God is so clever! The rise and fall of empires are historically documented and the timing of the little horn's wound is well documented. Therefore, we can date the convocation and judgment bar scene in Heaven, even though we cannot see into Heaven! God

has linked prophetic events on Earth with prophetic events in
Heaven. I like to call this linkage, "The Heaven-Earth-Linkage-
Law."

The Judgment Bar of Christ

Perhaps the easiest way to explain the pre-advent judgment process
is with a short illustration. When Cain was born, an angel was
given the responsibility to accurately record everything Cain knew,
everything Cain said, everything Cain thought, and everything Cain
did. (Perhaps the angel used a "heavenly camcorder.") Because
Heaven's technology far exceeds paper and ink, the record of Cain's
life is all inclusive. In fact, Heaven's record of every life is a true
reflection of that life. (See Ecclesiastes 12:14, Malachi 3:16; 2
Corinthians 5:10; Psalm 34:15 and 2 Chronicles 16:9.)

Even before sin began, God ordained there would be a judgment bar
imposed upon mankind to determine who will receive eternal life
and who will receive eternal death. (Acts 17:31; 24:25; Ephesians
1:4,5; 2 Corinthians 5:10) Since Jesus is the Judge of mankind (John
5:22), He alone decides the fate of each person. Even though Jesus
passes judgment upon each person, the process of judgment is
closely studied by Heaven's assembled host. The first man to die
was Abel. So, let us assume for a moment that when the books of
record were opened in 1844, Jesus began to investigate the
recording of the first man to die. Because Abel's eternal destiny will
be determined from his life's record, we can be sure the record of his
life is perfect and complete. (Ecclesiastes 12:14) Before Jesus makes
a determination on Abel, the attending host reviews Abel's life on
the equivalent of a big TV screen. Everyone hears Abel speak, and
they see Abel's motives and actions just as they happened. After the
movie of Abel's life ends, Jesus defends Abel's faith in God before the
assembly by highlighting Abel's actions. (James 2:26) Given the
evidence of Abel's faith, and the stipulation that salvation comes
through faith, Jesus declares Abel will be granted eternal life at the
first resurrection, which occurs at the Second Coming, and the gavel
comes down. (John 6:39-54; 1 Thessalonians 4:15-17) Eventually,
the life of Cain comes up in the judgment process and it is given the
same treatment. After reviewing the record of Cain on the big
screen, let us assume that Jesus has no option but to condemn Cain
for his faithless life, and Jesus *justifiably* sentences Cain to eternal

death. (Revelation 22:15) This is a brief scenario explaining how the judgment of the dead is accomplished. (The judgment of the living occurs during the Great Tribulation. The living will be tested to see who will obey God and trust in Him. People who pass the test will be sealed with a nature free from sin. See Chapter 6 in my book, *Jesus, The Alpha and The Omega*.)

After Jesus has judged everyone on Earth, the Second Coming occurs. Jesus will appear in clouds of glory and will resurrect Abel and all those determined to be righteous. He will take them to Heaven at that time along with the righteous living who are translated without seeing death. (John 14:1-3; 1 Thessalonians 4:16,17) Cain, however, will not be disturbed from his sleep at the Second Coming. In fact, billions of wicked people will sleep through the Second Coming. The wicked who are alive at the Second Coming will be destroyed by a command that comes out of Jesus' mouth and they will sleep for the next thousand years. After the 1,000 years of Revelation 20 passes, Jesus will return to Earth with all the redeemed and He will resurrect Cain and all of the wicked so that they can face their Judge and receive their sentence for the wages of sin. The wicked will be put to death by execution. (Revelation 20:5,9) After the wicked are annihilated by fire, sin and sinners will be no more.

Following the Rules

Because this study on Daniel 7 conforms to the four rules discussed at the end of Chapter 1, a few words about the timing of verses 9 and 10 are necessary. First, the position of verses 9 and 10 within Daniel 7 is important. Even though the timing of the convocation scene described in verse 9 is not explicitly stated in Daniel, Rule One provides an important clue. The courtroom scene in Heaven (verse 9) has to occur *after* the little horn has uprooted three horns in verse 8, because verse 9 occurs chronologically after verse 8. Remember, events have to occur in the order they are given. Furthermore, the courtroom scene in verse 9 has to occur *before* the monster beast is burned in the fire in verse 11 (Second Coming) because verse 9 occurs chronologically before verse 11. In other words, if the little horn uproots the three horns by A.D. 532, the judgment scene has to occur *after* A.D. 532, but before the Second Coming, because the sequence of events within the vision requires it.

Remember, Rule One states, *"Each apocalyptic prophecy has a beginning and ending point in time and the events within the prophecy must occur in the order in which they are given."* This rule is demonstrated in Chart 3.4.

Part Six:

I beheld then because of the voice of the great words which the horn spake: I beheld even till the beast was slain, and his body destroyed, and given to the burning flame. As concerning the rest of the beasts, they had their dominion taken away: yet their lives were prolonged for a season and time." (Daniel 7:11,12, KJV)

Comments on Part Six

While watching the courtroom scene unfold in Heaven's temple, Daniel's view is redirected back to Earth because he hears great words (blasphemous words) coming from the little horn. The little horn in Daniel 7 is one of the seven heads in Revelation 13:1. Because verse 11 occurs *after* verse 10 (1844) the great words spoken by the little horn in verse 11 have to occur after 1844! Rule One says the events occur in the order in which they are given. So, the little horn power will be restored to a position of authority after its fall in 1798 and Revelation 13:1 confirms this! The healing of the deadly wound will be covered in more detail later. As Daniel watched the little horn on Earth, he saw the little horn and the monster beast destroyed in a lake of fire. (Daniel 7:11) This fiery destruction represents the fact that at the Second Coming, God will destroy the little horn as well as all of the beasts in Daniel 7. (See Daniel 2 and Revelation 19:20,21.)

The Sequence Ends

Daniel 7:12 marks the end of this apocalyptic *sequence*, but it is not the end of the vision. We know this apocalyptic sequence is ended because the chronological order of events ends. According to Rule One, an apocalyptic sequence has a beginning point in time and an ending point in time and the events occur in the order in which they are given. This apocalyptic sequence began with the lion (Babylon – 605 B.C.) and ends with the beasts being destroyed in a lake of fire at the Second Coming. (See also Revelation 19:20,21.) Even though we have come to *the end* of the apocalyptic sequence in Daniel 7, the vision given to Daniel has not ended. The vision continues with commentary and details that amplify our understanding of the apocalyptic sequence. Carefully study the sequence of events in Chart 3.4:

The Apocalyptic Sequence

Verse 4	Verse 5	Verse 6	Verse 7	Verse 7	Verse 8	Verses 9 and 10	Verse 11	Verses 11 and 12
605 B.C.	538 B.C.	331 B.C.	168 B.C.	A.D. 476	A.D. 538	1798	Great Tribulation	?
						Judgment Scene		Second Coming
Lion	Bear	Leopard	Monster	10 Horns	Little Horn		Little Horn Boasting	Beasts Burned Up

Chart 3.4

Two observations should be made about Chart 3.4. First, look at the chronological order of the verses in the top row. For now, let us assume the courtroom scene described in verses 9 and 10 began in 1798. If we apply Rule One to this sequence of events, the boasting of the little horn in verse 11 has to occur *after* 1798 because verse 11 comes after verse 10. Indeed, according to Revelation 13:1-3, the boasting of the little horn in verse 11 will occur during the Great Tribulation. Second, verse 12 tells us that even though the other beasts lose their authority and dominion, they are not destroyed until the Second Coming. In other words, even though powerful kingdoms come and go, the descendants of these kingdoms remain on Earth until Jesus comes. Earth will not self-destruct before Jesus comes. Remember how the gold, silver, bronze, iron and clay were ground to powder *at the same time*. **"Then the iron, the clay, the bronze, the silver and the gold were broken to pieces *at the same time* and became like chaff on a threshing floor in the summer. The wind swept them away without leaving a trace. . . ."** (Daniel 2:35, italics mine) When Jesus returns to Earth, all of the wicked people of Earth will be annihilated by the sword (a verbal command) that comes out of His mouth, and the Antichrist and his government will be thrown into a lake of fire. (Revelation 19:15-21) This lake of fire is not to be confused with the fire that falls from Heaven at the end of the thousand years and purifies Earth. (Revelation 20:14,15)

Commentary by the Angel on the Vision

The commentary given to Daniel about verses 4 through 12 is crucial to our understanding of this vision. Before we examine the angel's explanations, we need to consider how the third rule of interpretation applies to this vision. Rule Three states, *"Apocalyptic language can be literal, symbolic or analogous. To reach the intended meaning of a prophecy, the student must consider: (a) the context; (b) the use of parallel language in the Bible and (c) relevant statements in the Bible that define that symbol if an element is thought to be symbolic."* We know the four beasts are symbols because Daniel was told the four beasts represent four kings (or kingdoms) that will appear on Earth. (Daniel 7:17) The Bible clearly defines the monster beast saying, "**. . . The fourth beast is a fourth kingdom that will appear on Earth. . . .**" (Daniel 7:23) When God uses a symbol, He tells us the meaning of the symbol within its context. Since Rule Three addresses three types of language in apocalyptic prophecy, we have to test various possibilities until all the pieces "harmoniously come together" into their rightful places.

Part Seven:

"I saw in the night visions, and, behold, one like the Son of man came with the clouds of heaven, and came to the Ancient of days, and they brought him near before him. And there was given him dominion, and glory, and a kingdom, that all people, nations, and languages, should serve him: his dominion is an everlasting dominion, which shall not pass away, and his kingdom that which shall not be destroyed." (Daniel 7:13-14, KJV)

Comments on Part Seven

Many people think these two verses occur after the Second Coming; however, this is not the case. Christ receives the kingdom of Earth from the Father before the Second Coming! This fact is confirmed in Revelation 11 and 19. Therefore, verses 11 and 12 break the chronological order of the sequence that began in verse 1 by reverting to an earlier date. Technically, because of this break in chronology, a new apocalyptic prophecy begins with verse 13, and it consists of two verses. Because this passage is so short, I prefer to say these two verses amplify the content of verses 9 and 10, because either way, the result is the same. Verse 13 tell us that Jesus approached the Father *after* the Ancient of Days took His seat in 1798.

The question, "Why did Jesus approach the Father?" cannot be answered from the details given in Daniel 7:13 and 14. No vision is complete within itself. However, the vision in Revelation 4-6 parallels this scene and John tells us more of the story. The first item of business at this great convocation is to find some worthy person who is qualified to bring the drama of sin to a successful conclusion. In John's vision, an investigation is conducted throughout the whole universe to see who is worthy to do the job. Jesus alone is found worthy because Jesus meets the necessary criteria. He lived a life of perfect obedience to God's law, a life free of sin. (1 Peter 2:22) He paid the penalty for sin with His own blood (Hebrews 9:15), and He demonstrated the depths of God's love for mankind as no one else could do. (John 13:16; 10:30) No one else in all the universe meets these qualifications, and after being found worthy by the numberless host of angels, Jesus approached the Father to be coronated as King of kings and Lord of lords.

A fiery retinue of angels (Daniel says, "the clouds of Heaven") escorted Jesus to the Father. The Father must have beamed as He bestowed upon His Son the authority and recognition necessary for the task at hand. This glorious scene is not the Second Coming. The Bible says that Jesus went before the Ancient of Days, but there is no indication that He came to Earth because this courtroom scene is conducted in Heaven's temple! After He was found worthy by Heaven's host, the Father gave every power and prerogative of God to Jesus and the Father stepped aside so that Jesus might resolve the greatest problem ever known to God: Sin. At this point in time (1798) the Father physically gave Jesus all that He had promised. The Earth became His inheritance. (See Hebrews 1:2.)

Jesus Exalted Again!

Some people have asked, "What do you mean when you say that Jesus went before the Father to receive *all* of the attributes of God." "Hasn't Jesus always had the attributes of God?" Yes, Jesus is co-eternal with the Father, and as God, He *had* all the attributes of God until sin began. A brief explanation of the humiliation and exaltation of Jesus is necessary.

When Adam and Eve sinned, Jesus generously offered to bear the penalty for sin on behalf of humanity. To receive man's punishment, Jesus had to suffer the Second Death and die in our place, and even more, He had to give up His divine prerogatives and become subject to the Father and the requirements of the plan of salvation. The humiliation of Jesus should parallel the humiliation of sinners. When a person becomes a child of God through rebirth, he joyfully submits to the authority of God. While living in our shoes, Jesus had to live a life of perfect faith and dependance upon the Father in order to be a perfect sinless substitute for man. (Hebrews 5:7,8) On the day that Jesus surrendered Himself to the Father, Jesus became known as, "The Son of God." The word "son" means "subjected one" or "one in submission." In other words, Jesus – who is fully God, co-eternal with God and equal with the Father in every way (Philippians 2:6) – willingly became subject to the Father and the plan to save sinners. (Psalm 2:7-12) To save man, Jesus had to give up His divinity in order to die. When Jesus lived on Earth, He explained His subjection to the Father on numerous occasions by saying that He came to do His Father's will – not His own. (John 6:38) Concerning His life, death and resurrection, Jesus said, **"No one takes it** [my life] **from me, but I lay it down of my own accord. I have authority to lay it down and authority to take it up again. This command I received from my Father."** (John 10:18, insertion mine)

From the day that Adam and Eve sinned until the day that Jesus was coronated (in 1798), Jesus was subject to the Father (as His Son) and to the terms and conditions set forth in the plan of salvation. When the time came to begin judging the inhabitants of Earth and exonerating the government of God against the lies of Lucifer, an investigation was conducted to see who was worthy to do such a work. Only Jesus was found worthy for the job, and the Father granted sovereign power to Jesus to conclude the drama of sin in whatever way Jesus deems best. Thus, the Father stepped aside after the coronation of the Son, and the Son took command of the universe. (Ephesians 1:9-23) Since 1798, Jesus has ruled over Heaven and Earth as King of kings and Lord of lords. At the end of sin's drama, after Jesus has destroyed death itself, Jesus does something that boggles my mind. Notice Paul's words: **"Then the end will come, when he** [Jesus] **hands over the kingdom to God the Father after he has destroyed all dominion, authority and power** [on Earth]. **For he** [Jesus] **must reign until he has put all his enemies under his feet. The last enemy to be destroyed is death. For he** [the Father] **has put everything under his feet. Now when it says that 'everything' has been put under him, it is clear that this does not include God himself, who put everything under Christ. When he** [Jesus] **has done this** [e.g., resolved the sin problem], **then the Son himself will be made subject to him who put everything under him, so that God may be all in all."** (1 Corinthians 15:24-28) With these expansive issues in mind, notice how the coronation of Jesus fits into the apocalyptic sequence in Chart 3.5:

The Apocalyptic Sequence

Verse 4	Verse 5	Verse 6	Verse 7	Verse 7	Verse 8	Verses 9 and 13	Verse 11	Verse 11
605 B.C.	538 B.C.	331 B.C.	168 B.C.	A.D. 476	A.D. 538	1798	Great Tribu-lation	?
						Judgment Scene		Second Coming
Lion	Bear	Leopard	Monster	10 Horns	Little Horn	Jesus Given the Kingdom	Little Horn Boasting	Beast Burned Up

Chart 3.5

Everything that Jesus "set aside" to redeem man was restored to Him at this convocation. The exaltation of Jesus in 1798 was based on His infinite love for man and His superior achievements on behalf of the Father and the plan of salvation. Therefore, Jesus was given everything the Father could give. Additionally, the Father gave Earth to Jesus as His personal inheritance in 1798. (Psalm 2:7-12; Hebrews 1:1,2)

Even though Daniel did not understand the promotion of Jesus, this awesome scene was embedded in this particular prophecy because of its timing. No one living on Earth in 1798 saw the exaltation of Jesus, but we can see into Heaven through the eye of prophetic faith. Few people understand the coronation of Jesus in 1798, not to mention the humiliation Jesus experienced to save the human race. Even though Jesus was coronated as King of kings at the beginning of the convocation in 1798, Jesus does not take possession of Earth until two additional events occur. First, Jesus has to determine who will live in His kingdom. This is the reason the judgment was set and books were opened. Second, Jesus will not inherit an Earth that groans under the curse of sin. Only after Jesus annihilates the wicked and purifies the Earth with fire, will He create a new Heaven and a new Earth. Earth will then become the headquarters of His kingdom. After being found worthy to receive the authority of the Father, Jesus began several processes in Heaven's courtroom. He began breaking the seven seals, and after the third seal was broken, Jesus began to pass judgment upon humanity. (The seven seals will be presented in our study on Revelation 4-6.)

All Authority?

Notice Daniel 7:14 again: **"And there was given him dominion, and glory, and a kingdom, that all people, nations, and languages, should serve him: his dominion is an everlasting dominion, which shall not pass away, and his kingdom that which shall not be destroyed."** (KJV) This verse confuses a lot of people. How can Jesus be given complete dominion (or sovereign power, NIV) more than once? According to Webster, the word "sovereign" means "having all authority." At face value this verse in Daniel 7 seems to contradict the words of Jesus in Matthew 28. Notice the following text: **"Then Jesus came to them** [His disciples] **and said, 'All authority in heaven and on Earth has been given to me. Therefore go and make disciples of all nations, baptizing them in the name of the Father and of the Son and of the Holy Spirit, and teaching them to obey everything I have commanded you. And surely I am with you always, to the very end of the age.' "** (Matthew 28:18-20, insertion mine) How can Jesus say in Matthew 28 that He has *all* authority in Heaven and on Earth when Daniel 7 indicates that Jesus is given dominion (and sovereign authority) *after* the Ancient of Days takes His seat? The answer to this apparent conflict is found in the *scope* of authority.

On Resurrection Sunday, Jesus returned to Heaven, and with the help of His angels, drove Lucifer, the prince of this world, out of Heaven. (Revelation 12:7-9; John 12:31) Lucifer lost his seat as Earth's governor at the table of God's government. On the basis of His shed blood and the power of an indestructible life (Hebrews 7:16), Jesus physically removed Lucifer from Heaven and cast him to Earth. (Revelation 12:13) The kingdom that was stolen from Jesus by Lucifer (the deceitful prince of this world, John 12:31) was returned to Jesus by right of redemption. (John 16:33; Revelation 12:10) As the Crown Prince of Earth, Jesus has been Earth's representative at the table of God's government ever since Resurrection Sunday. After Jesus ascended to Heaven on that Sunday morning and cast Lucifer out, He was given authority over all matters in Heaven pertaining to Earth. Forty days later, at the time of His ascension, He declared this authority to His disciples in His parting words recorded in Matthew 28:18-20.

Daniel saw an even higher exaltation of Jesus than the exaltation given on Resurrection Sunday. In 1798, Jesus was ceremoniously exalted to a position equal to that of the Father. Jesus was found worthy to receive power over all of God's creation. The Father transferred His authority to Jesus so that Jesus could righteously conclude the sin problem. The Ancient of Days convened this convocation so that the actions of Jesus could be observed by all the angels. The Father wanted all the angels to know that Jesus was equal to the Father in every way. (John 5:23) Of course, the Son is not greater than the Father, but neither is the Father greater than the Son! Jesus was exalted before the angels and the elders because He did something that no one else in the universe could do. He paid the penalty of sin for man. After He was found worthy to take over the universe, He took the scroll sealed with seven seals. In His new role as Commander-In-Chief of the Universe, Jesus began the process of deciding who will participate in His kingdom. He also began a process that will fully vindicate the government of God against the false claims of Lucifer. At the end of the 1,000 years, everyone will behold that God is love, that God's laws are righteous and His government is based on the principle of love. We have already examined 1 Corinthians 15:24-28, where Paul says that at the end of sin's drama, an exalted Jesus will return all that the Father has given Him. Jesus will return the authority and throne to the Father because He wants to be free to live among this creation as one of us! What Gods of grace and love!

Part Eight:

"I Daniel was grieved in my spirit in the midst of my body, and the visions of my head troubled me. I came near unto one of them that stood by, and asked him the truth of all this. So he told me, and made me know the interpretation of the things. These great beasts, which are four, are four kings, which shall arise out of the earth. But the saints of the most High shall take the kingdom, and possess the kingdom for ever, even for ever and ever." (Daniel 7:15-18, KJV)

Comments on Part Eight

Daniel wanted to know the meaning of everything he had seen, so he asked for an explanation. A nearby angel informed Daniel that these great beasts are four kingdoms. Some translations like the LXX say "four kingdoms" while others say "four kings." But, verse 23 removes any doubt about the intended meaning because it says, **"the fourth beast is the fourth kingdom that will appear on Earth."** Then, in the same breath, the angel asserts, **"But, the saints of the Most High shall take the kingdom, and possess the kingdom for ever, even for ever and ever."** The angel chose deliberate language to make this statement. The angel is emphasizing a profound point to those who suffer for their faith. This world was created for the children of God. Temporarily, the devil has gained control of Earth, BUT at an appointed time, there will be an end to sin and the devil. The saints will inherit the Earth. God has decreed it! (Matthew 5:5)

Part Nine:

"Then I would know the truth of the fourth beast, which was diverse from all the others, exceeding dreadful, whose teeth were of iron, and his nails of brass; which devoured, brake in pieces, and stamped the residue with his feet; And of the ten horns that were in his head, and of the other which came up, and before whom three fell; even of that horn that had eyes, and a mouth that spake very great things, whose look was more stout than his fellows." (Daniel 7:19,20, KJV)

Daniel wanted to know *the truth* about the fourth beast, the ten horns, and the little horn. If we are going to determine the truth about the fourth beast and the little horn, we must consider all of the specifications given to Daniel because the Bible is about to identify a world power that is corrupt and offensive in God's sight. This is a good time to apply Rule Two which states, *"A fulfilment of apocalyptic prophecy occurs when all of the specifications within that prophecy are met. This includes the order of events outlined in the prophecy."*

The truth that will unfold from this prophecy is neither pleasant nor politically correct. In fact, people have denied the *truth* about the fourth beast, the ten horns, and the little horn for centuries, because the truth is offensive. The actions of the little horn have been offensive to God for centuries! God is the author of prophecy, and people who love truth, regardless of what the truth says or where it leads, are the kind of people whom God loves. (John 4:23) Daniel provides a dozen specifications about the fourth beast, the ten horns, and the little horn that grew out of the fourth beast. Look at these specifications:

1. The monster beast is the fourth world empire.

2. The monster beast has unusual strength and it stomps its enemies.

3. The monster beast is different; it has crushing teeth of iron.

4. Out of the monster beast, ten horns (or kings/ kingdoms) arise.

5. After the ten horns appear, a little horn rises. As it rises to power, it uproots three of the original ten kings leaving a total of eight.

6. As the little horn grows and becomes great, it exhibits the same fierce qualities of its parent, the monster beast.

7. Eventually, the little horn dominates the other seven horns.

8. The little horn blasphemes God by usurping His authority.

9. The little horn wars against the saints of the Most High for a specified period of time.

10. The little horn "thinks" it can change God's times and laws.

11. The little horn endures until the end of the world; in fact, it speaks boastfully during the time of the end.

12. The monster beast and the little horn are burned in the fire at the Second Coming.

History allows no wiggle room regarding the identity of the monster beast. The fourth beast represents the empire of Rome, which followed the fall of Grecia in 168 B.C. History allows no wiggle room on the identity of the ten horns or the little horn power that came out of Rome. The ten horns represent the ten ethnic nations that caused the breakup of the Roman empire. The little horn represents the powerful entity that grew out of the empire of Rome, namely, the Roman Catholic Church.

History has faithfully documented the course of the Catholic Church through the centuries. The following is a brief summary of what happened to Christians as they moved farther and farther away from following God's Word. The history of the Christian church is a parallel to that of ancient Israel. Both religious systems displaced God's Word with manmade traditions and doctrines and ended up in apostasy. Many wonderful people can be found within Judaism and Catholicism. Both groups love God and their religion, and they faithfully adhere to their respective beliefs. Many Jews and Catholics have not had an opportunity or sufficient reason to consider the Protestant view of Church history. Even further, many Catholics have little or no knowledge concerning the origins of Church doctrines or teachings. Upon close examination, many Catholics are shocked to learn that many of their doctrines have no biblical basis or authority whatsoever.

The Monster Beast Is the Roman Empire

Protestants have identified the Roman Catholic Church as the little horn of Daniel 7 for more than 700 years. This conclusion was reached by comparing Scripture with history. History says Rome is the fourth kingdom from Babylon to appear on Earth. The prophetic matrix and abundant historical records indicate the lineage of kingdoms is Babylon, Medo-Persia, Grecia and Rome. History confirms that the fall of Rome is not like the fall of the other nations before it. For example, in Daniel 2 the head of gold is *displaced* by a different metal, the chest of silver. However, the legs of iron of the fourth kingdom are displaced by feet of iron *and* clay. Look at this transition from Daniel 7's perspective. The lion is *displaced* by the leopard, but the monster beast is not displaced by another beast. Rome does not disappear like Babylon disappeared. Instead, the ten kings that brought down civil Rome in A.D. 476 grew out of the Roman empire. History says the ten horns pulled the Roman empire apart from within. Rome disintegrated into ten kingdoms, some of which were strong (like iron) and others which were breakable or weak (like clay).

Two Sets of Ten Horns

Many commentators teach that the ten horns of Daniel 7 are a *future* union of ten kings who are yet to rise out of a revived Roman empire (thought to be the European Union). This conclusion is contrary to several statements given in Scripture and the prophetic matrix. The prophetic matrix reveals the ten horns in Daniel 7 have come and gone, and history confirms the ten horns of Daniel 7 have come and gone! History also confirms the little horn ruled over the nations of Europe for 1,260 years before it was wounded in 1798.

Some people make the mistake of thinking the ten horns of Daniel 7 are the *same* ten horns found in Revelation 13 and 17! The ten horns in Daniel 7 appeared around A.D. 476 at the fall of the Roman empire, and three of the original ten horns were uprooted within 60 years of A.D. 476 by the Church of Rome over a religious dispute on the eternal co-existence of Jesus with the Father.

The ten horns in Revelation 13 and 17 have not yet appeared. They will appear during the very last days of Earth's history and will be empowered for a very short time just before the Second Coming.

(Revelation 17:12) There are two sets of ten horns in Bible prophecy, because there is an important parallel between them. The ten horns in Daniel 7 were reduced to seven horns after three were uprooted. Then, the little horn of Daniel 7 dominated the remaining seven horns as the *eighth* king. In Revelation13, there is a beast that rises out of the sea having seven heads and ten horns. This beast is not the Roman empire of Daniel 7, as some suppose. This beast will be a diverse world empire made up of seven heads (seven religious systems) and ten horns (ten political powers) during the Great Tribulation. When the devil appears on Earth masquerading as God, he will rule over the seven heads as an eighth king! (Revelation 17:11) The parallel here is obvious. The devil will rule with absolute power over the seven religious systems of the world just like the papacy (the little horn) ruled over the seven kings (the seven horns) it dominated. The devil will divide the Earth into ten sectors and he will appoint ten kings to rule as "puppet kings" of his kingdom. Daniel 2:44 says during the time of *these* kings, that is, the ten kings, the God of Heaven will set up His kingdom! Study Chart 3.6 and observe two things: First, notice that both kingdoms – the kingdom of the *feet* and the kingdom of the *toes* – have ten horns. Second, notice that the ten horns in the kingdom of the *feet* become seven horns, with the little horn ruling over them. Then notice the kingdom of the *toes*. During the kingdom of the [ten] *toes,* the Second Coming occurs while ten kings are ruling over Earth! (Daniel 2:44, Revelation 17:14)

Reviewing the Ten Horns

History identifies the ten horns that caused the disintegration of Rome as the kings of the Ostrogoths, Heruli, Franks, Vandals, Lombards, Visigoths, Suevi, Burgundians, Alamanni and the Anglo-Saxons. The infrastructure of the Roman empire finally fell in A.D. 476, because powerful warlords brought the emperor, Romulus, the Roman senate and the empire to an end. The city of Rome was sacked and burned. These warlords included Alaric the Goth, Attila the Hun, Genseric the Vandal, Theodoric the Ostrogoth, Odoacer, and others who contributed to the collapse of Rome. These kings originated within the ethnic nations that constituted the bulk of the Roman empire. Geographically, they came from northern Africa, Asia Minor, the Middle East and Europe. These warlords broke the iron fist of Caesar. A new order for world government came into

The Ten Horns in Daniel 7 Are Not the Same As the Ten Horns in Revelation 13 and 17

Daniel 7	Verse 7	Verse 7	Verse 8	Verses 9 and 13	Verse 11	Verses 11 and 12
Time	168 B.C.	A.D. 476	A.D. 538	1798	Great Tribulation	?
Revelation 17					Sea Beast: 7 Heads and 10 Horns	
Revelation 13					Sea Beast: 7 Heads and 10 Horns	
			Little Horn	Judgment Scene		Second Coming
Daniel 7	Monster Beast	10 Horns	3 Horns Uprooted Leaving 7 Horns	Jesus Given the Kingdom	Little Horn Boasting	The Four Beasts Are Burned Up
Daniel 2	Legs of Iron	Feet			Toes	Rock

Chart 3.6

existence after A.D. 476. During the centuries of Babylon, Medo-Persia, Grecia and Rome, there had been one universal empire. After A.D. 476, the world was broken into diverse ethnic nations. When civil Rome fell, the distinction between the nations of the East and the nations of the West became separate and prominent. Perhaps the two legs and the two feet in Daniel 2 reflect the East-West division of Earth. Regardless, one simple fact from Daniel 2 has held true for the past 1,600 years: No man has been able to merge the world back into a single empire since A.D. 476. Would-be conquerors have tried and failed. Nations have come and gone. Some nations have become strong and others have become weak. The continual presence of weak nations is a sociological mystery because the law of the jungle mandates that only the strong survive.

Who Is the Little Horn?

According to Daniel 7, the little horn appears on the world stage *after* the ten horns rise to power, because the little horn power uproots three of the ten horns when it appears. Christianity, of course, began in Jerusalem at the time of Christ and was dispersed throughout the world by the Romans in A.D. 70 when they destroyed Jerusalem. The Christian Church in Rome started during the time of the apostle Paul, but grew to become a substantial political force by the beginning of the fourth century A.D. It was then that Constantine determined to make Christianity the defacto religion of the Roman empire. Constantine was not timid about giving his religious views the force of law. According to Daniel 7, the *little* horn power would start small, but would grow and become stronger than any of the kingdoms represented by the remaining horns! The timing in this vision is important: *After* Rome was broken up by the ten horns, the Church of Rome rose to power and, in so doing, it had to uproot three nations to consolidate its dominion over a new *Holy Roman Empire*.

The church was instrumental in uprooting the Ostrogoths, Vandals and Heruli, three of the original ten nations, for religious and political reasons. These kingdoms were destroyed because of a long-standing theological dispute over the deity of Christ. This dispute is well documented in history and is called the Arian Controversy. Arius, a theologian from Alexandria, Egypt, taught that Jesus was not co-eternal and not equal with the Father. The church at Rome countered Arius' teachings by saying they were heresy and blasphemy, and a power struggle began. This particular controversy raged for about 200 years between Christians in Rome and Christians in Alexandria. Constantine called a general council at Nicaea in A.D. 325 to settle the conflict, but the dispute could not be resolved. Looking at the controversy from our vantage point today, the real issue was theological control. The real issue was not the deity of Christ, but who would define Christian doctrine – the Church in Rome or the Church in Alexandria. By A.D. 508, the Church in Rome had gained enough political support to silence the opposition in Alexandria. For political and religious reasons, Clovis, King of the Salian Franks, destroyed the Ostrogoths, Vandals and Heruli. When the Arian influence was eliminated, the Church in Rome established herself as the guardian and defender of the universal (or catholic) Christian faith. About 25 years after the victories of Clovis, Emperor Justinian consolidated supreme authority in the pope in matters of faith and religion. Justinian bequeathed the title, "Corrector of Heretics," upon the pope in A.D. 533 even though the pope was not in a position to wield complete authority over the nations. However, just five years later in A.D. 538, after Belisarius (Justinian's general) subdued Italy, the pope had the posture and dominion he sought. He ruled over the Christian church and Christian states with absolute power.

Little Horn Wages War on the Saints

According to Daniel 7, the little horn power had the same fierce qualities as its parent, the monster beast. It was predicted the little horn would become "stouter" than the other seven horns. It would have a "mouth" that spoke great words against the Most High and it would have "eyes" like a man. The mouth on the little horn indicates that the church would "speak;" that is, it would dictate orders (laws and rules) which people must *obey* if they wanted to receive eternal life. The church blackmailed the laity into obedience with the threat of excommunication. The eyes on the little horn indicated the church would have insight into matters which would allow it to "see" things that political rulers would not understand. In short, the little horn would be religious and it would use the power of religion to control the ways and thoughts of rulers. The power of religion uniquely made the little horn of Daniel 7 much stronger than all of the other horns put together.

In ancient times, religion attracted the best minds, much like science does today. Priests were considered God's representatives on Earth, and whatever they said was "the Word of God." When Justinian surrendered the state to the *higher* power of the church, the church became lord over the nations of Europe. The church approved, appointed and coronated the kings and queens of Europe. The church controlled political issues, as well as religious matters. The church manipulated its members out of fear of hell and eternal death. The church claimed that its priests had the authority to determine eternal life or eternal death, and since few Bibles were available, king and peasant alike believed whatever the priests said. There was no "approved" source of knowledge about God except through the church. In effect, the clergy of the church became God for 1,260 long years (A.D. 538-1798). History rightly calls this period, "The Dark Ages."

The church became as determined and cruel in conquering her foes as she had been treated in her early years by Romans and Jews. To gain power and dominion, popes bribed people with forgiveness for all sins – past, present and future – if they were willing to fight for the expansion of the *Holy* Roman Empire. Millions of people perished in the crusades, which, ironically, were fought in the name of God. Popes ruled over Christianity with an iron fist for 1,260 years. The light of truth was extinguished, and religious freedom and the right to worship God according to the dictates of conscience were non-existent. For centuries, the church prohibited ownership of the Bible. The authority of the church knew no bounds. Kings, fearful of losing eternal life, could not overthrow the authority of the pope and his prelates, but as powerful as the church was, God predetermined a limit to the reign of terror. The church would receive an almost fatal wound in 1798.

Little Horn Persecutes Saints 1,260 Years

The angel said to Daniel, **"And he** [the little horn] **shall speak great words against the most High, and shall wear out the saints of the most High, and think to change times and laws: and they** [the saints] **shall be given into his hand until a time and times and the dividing of time."** (Daniel 7:25, KJV, insertions mine) This verse says so much. To appreciate the depths of apostasy to which the Christian church fell, the reader is encouraged to review the writings of reformers like Martin Luther and John Knox.

It should not surprise you to learn that the conflict between popes and protestors (the beginning of Protestantism) centered on the question of religious authority. The Roman Catholic Church claims that it alone possesses all authority from God in matters pertaining to salvation. This authority, the church claims, has been passed down to each pope from the apostle Peter. (Matthew 16:18,19) Historians on this time period say millions of protestors perished at the stake for disagreeing with the church over this point. (See also *Foxe's Book of Martyrs,* written by John Foxe, 1516-1587) Protestors claimed that everyone had the right to own a Bible and to determine what was truth. Protestants believed that obeying God according to the dictates of one's conscience was a matter of personal choice. The following statements may help you to see the great chasm between Catholics and Protestants on matters pertaining to religious authority:

Statement #1

"That a person with no other equipment than a knowledge of the English language and a seventeenth century English translation of the Bible in his hands is qualified to decide all matters of eternal consequence for himself and the rest of mankind, is the ridiculous conclusion to which the principle of private judgment can finally be brought. In such a process, the countless generations of devout people who have lived and died according to other beliefs simply count for nothing. The centuries of thought and prayer that have gone into the interpretation of the Bible for all these generations likewise count for nothing." [*Some Bible Beliefs Have to Be Wrong!*, Booklet #68, page 5, (1963), Imprimatur: Most Reverend John F. Whealon, Archbishop of Hartford, Knights of Columbus.]

Statement #2

"Since the Catholic Church holds that the Bible is not sufficient in itself, it naturally teaches that the Bible needs an interpreter. The reason the Catholic Church so teaches is twofold: first, because Christ established a living church to teach with His authority. He did not simply give His disciples a Bible, whole and entire, and tell them to go out and make copies of it for mass distribution and allow people to come to whatever interpretation they may. Second, the Bible itself states that it needs an interpreter. . . . The Holy Spirit was given to the Church by Jesus Christ, and it is exactly this same Spirit who protects the Church's visible head, the Pope, and the teaching authority of the Church by never permitting him or it to lapse into error." [*Scripture Alone? 21 Reasons to Reject Sola Scriptura,* pages 21, 26, (1999), Joel Peters, Tan Books and Publishers, Inc., Rockford, Il.]

Statement #3

"We teach and define it to be a dogma divinely revealed that the Roman Pontiff, when he speaks *ex cathedra*, that is, when acting in his office as pastor and teacher of all Christians, by his supreme Apostolic authority, he defines a doctrine concerning faith or morals to be held by the whole Church through the divine assistance promised him in Blessed Peter, he enjoys that infallibility with which the divine Redeemer willed His Church to be endowed in defining doctrine concerning faith and morals; and therefore such definitions of the said Roman Pontiff are irreformable of themselves, and not from the consent of the Church." [*The Papacy, Expression of God's Love,* page 29, (undated), Imprimatur: Most Reverend John J. Carberry, Archbishop of St. Louis, Knights of Columbus.]

These three statements summarize the bedrock of Catholic doctrine and they reflect the nonnegotiable themes that have divided Protestants from Catholics for more than 700 years.

Three and a Half Times

Daniel 7:25 also says the little horn would "wear out the saints of God (through persecution)." In fact, the Bible says "**they** [the saints] **shall be given into his hand** [e.g., the hand of the little horn] **for a time, times and half a time!**" (insertions mine) This single verse should cause every believer in a pre-tribulation rapture to think about his position, because this verse indicates that God Himself handed His saints over to the little horn to be persecuted for a prescribed length of time! If God subjected His saints to persecution in times past, why should the last generation expect to escape from the coming tribulation? Instead of delivering the saints *from* persecution, God did the opposite by handing His people over to the little horn for 1,260 years! Why would an all wise God do this? I can offer two possible reasons:

First, persecution keeps the saints on their knees and their focus on the Word of God. When life is easy, faith in God evaporates. Moses warned Israel: **"Be careful that you do not forget the Lord your God, failing to observe his commands, his laws and his decrees that I am giving you this day. Otherwise, when you eat and are satisfied, when you build fine houses and settle down, and when your herds and flocks grow large and your silver and gold increase and all you have is multiplied, then your heart will become proud and you will forget the Lord your God, who brought you out of Egypt, out of the land of slavery."** (Deuteronomy 8:11-14) When we contrast the Church at Rome (the little horn) with the Church in the Wilderness (the persecuted saints), we clearly see what prosperity and persecution produces. Prosperity produces decadence. Persecution, on the other hand, pushes people into a life of dynamic faith, clinging to Jesus as their hope and salvation. Persecution made God's Word extremely precious to the Church in the Wilderness. Many Bibles, or portions of the Bible, were laboriously copied by hand so that people could have the Word of God to study. Meanwhile, back in prosperous Rome, the Bible was not important. The Bible was chained to the walls of monasteries and libraries because the authority of the church rested in its clergy, not the Word of God! The Church in the Wilderness hungered for every word that proceeded out of the mouth of God, while the Church in Rome preferred the authority of the popes and priests who spoke boastful things. For the saints, a plain "thus saith the Lord" was more important than any papal bull. The saints loved and honored the Word of God and held it in much higher esteem than life itself. In summary, the persecution of God's people kept the Word of God alive.

The second reason God handed His saints over to the little horn is this: Persecution keeps faith in Christ alive. This is ironic. The very circumstances that cause faith to grow are the very circumstances that human nature hates the most! The selfish desires of the carnal nature include pleasure, prosperity, power, unchallenged authority, limitless amounts of money, fame and respect. Faith during times of persecution means trusting God for survival of life itself. Furthermore, as the Holy Spirit led the saints into a greater understanding of truth, the Church in the Wilderness proceeded to follow God's Word without regard for social and financial consequences. This is the essence of faith – obeying God at any cost. When the Church in Rome rose to power, the word, "faith," was changed. Faith came to mean a religious view, not a religious experience. Even today, people typically ask, "What faith do you belong to?" So, the second reason God wisely gave the saints over to persecution was to keep faith in *Jesus* alive!

What Is a Time?

We do not need to review the atrocities of the Roman Catholic Church or those of her enemies during centuries past. (Historians have devoted thousands of pages to this topic and these works can be found in public libraries.) However, we do need to consider a specification about the Roman Catholic Church that is profound.

Daniel 7:25 says the saints would be given over to the little horn for a time, times and half a time. According to Rule Four, this time-period amounts to 1,260 years in length. It began in A.D. 538 and ended in 1798.

You may recall that, until the sixteenth century A.D., men believed the Earth stood still and the Sun orbited our planet. For purposes of computing time, the ancients used 360 degrees of arc to represent a completed *circle* or *cycle* of the Sun. The Jews did not count a year as 365 days because the number of days in their year is either 354 or 384. God gave Israel a solar/lunar calendar to measure time and the cycles of the Sun and Moon determine the number of days in a year. (Exodus 12) Since the Sun moves about one degree of arc per day in a year, the use of 360 degrees of arc (the number of degrees in a circle) to represent the length of a year was a practical method for measuring "a time." This type of averaging was also done for the length of a month. Even though a month is actually 29.53 days, the ancients counted a month (or a moon) as 30 days for purposes of calculation.

The Aramaic word, *'hiddan,* translated "a time" in Daniel 7:25 (and used elsewhere in Daniel), refers to "a set time" or "a turning." The word, *'hiddan,* indicates the beginning or turning of a year at its appointed time. Revelation 12:14 also contains the phrase "a time, times and a half a time," and according to Revelation 12:6, this phrase represents 1,260 days. Some people question if the word "times" means two times or more than two times. First, Revelation 12 reveals that 1,260 days are "a time, times and half a time." (Revelation 12:6,14) Second, at a minimum, the plural of "a time" is two times. If there are more than two times, the time period cannot be measured because no one knows how many times to count. Last, historical evidence confirms that God had 1,260 years in mind when He defined this time-period. The number of days in "a time, times and half a time" is determined by the following formula:

1. One **time** of the Sun equals one circle of 360 degrees of arc.

2. Two **times** of the Sun equals two circles of 360 degrees of arc or 720 degrees.

3. **Half a time** equals half a circle or 180 degrees of arc.

4. Total: 1,260 degrees of arc
     (360 + 720 + 180 = 1,260 degrees)

It is widely known that God gave the Jews a calendar in which a day of the week represents a year, e.g., a week of seven days equals seven years. (See Leviticus 25; Numbers 14:34; Ezekiel 4:5,6.) Many Bible students understand the 70 weeks mentioned in Daniel to be 490 years (that is, 70 weeks times seven days equals 490 days, and each day represents a year). Therefore, if God used the Jubilee Calendar to measure the 70 weeks in Daniel 9, then it is possible that He used the Jubilee Calendar to define the 1,260 days in Daniel 7 as 1,260 years. This is a good place to repeat Rule Four which states: *"God reckons apocalyptic time in two ways: (a) a day for a year, and (b) as literal time. The presence or absence of the Jubilee calender determines how God reckons time."* Even though it is essential to understand the Jubilee Calendar when applying this rule, for now just consider this fact: History confirms the duration of the little horn's power was 1,260 years – to the very month! The Roman Catholic Church persecuted the saints for 1,260 years. Even though Protestants in centuries past did not properly understand the operation of the Jubilee Calendar, they did conclude that history and prophecy are in perfect harmony, and many Protestants predicted a "wounding" of papal power prior to 1798. In short, Daniel was told the Roman Catholic Church would persecute God's saints for 1,260 years – and history confirms this to be the case.

Part Ten:

I beheld, and the same horn made war with the saints, and prevailed against them; Until the Ancient of days came, and [a favorable] **judgment was given to the saints of the most High; and the time came that the saints possessed the kingdom. Thus he said, The fourth beast shall be the fourth kingdom upon earth, which shall be diverse from all kingdoms, and shall devour the whole earth, and shall tread it down, and break it in pieces.** (Daniel 7:21-23, KJV, insertion mine)

Comments on Part Ten

History leaves no wiggle room about the identity of the fourth beast or the little horn. The fourth beast is Rome and the little horn is the

religious entity that grew out of Rome, the *Roman* Catholic Church.
Daniel 7:25 does not explicitly say when the 1,260 years of perse-
cution would begin or end. However, we can determine these dates
with a brief review of history. The Bible says the little horn would
prevail against the saints *until* the Ancient of Days took His seat in
Heaven's courtroom and pronounced judgment in favor of the saints!
Remember the Heaven-Earth-Linkage-Law? Here's how it works:
When the Roman Catholic Church was removed from power so that
it could no longer persecute the saints *on Earth*, we know the
Ancient of Days had taken His seat in Heaven and pronounced
judgment in their favor. In other words, God put a temporary
restraining order on the Church of Rome! Daniel 7:20 aligns these
two events for us, "**the same horn made war with the saints,
and prevailed against them;** *until* **the Ancient of days came**
[to the convocation and took His seat]**. . . .**" (insertion mine) So, the
Bible indicates the 1,260 years ended shortly after the Ancient of
Days took His seat in verse 9. Historical records show that the
power of the church was broken in February 1798.

Several prominent Protestants predicted the 1,260 years of papal
dominion would end during the eighteenth century. Writers such as
Thomas Parker, 1646; Increase Mather, President of Harvard
University, 1723; William Burnet, 1724; Richard Clark, 1759, and
others anticipated the Roman church would collapse before year
1800 arrived. Sure enough, French Generals Berthier and Waller
fulfilled this specification of prophecy during the French Revolution.
They captured the pope and put him in exile in February 1798. By
counting backwards from 1798, we arrive at year A.D. 538 which is
the date that papal dominion began. (Remember Justinian's decree
in A.D. 533 and the victory of Belisarious over the Italians in A.D.
538?) This timing is not coincidence. Clearly, God measures a time,
a times and half a time in Daniel 7 as 1,260 days using the day-for-
a-year principle, and God emphasizes this time-period again in
Revelation 12! The wounding of the papacy occurred at the end of
1,260 years when judgment was pronounced in favor of the Church
in the Wilderness. With God, timing is everything.

There Is More to the Story

This is not the end of the story for the little horn of Daniel 7. The
Bible predicts the little horn will return to power in the future.

Revelation 13 indicates that one of the seven heads, the head that received a deadly wound, will be healed. Also, do not forget, Daniel heard boastful words coming from the little horn *after* viewing the courtroom scene in Heaven. Daniel 7 predicts the Catholic Church will return to a position of great power. This will climax when the Great Tribulation begins. Watch for it. The Roman church will lead a coalition of the world's religions in persecuting the saints of God! Notice how these verses predict a return to power: **"I beheld, and the same horn made war with the saints, and prevailed against them; until [A] the Ancient of days came, and judgment was given to the saints of the most High; and [B] the time came that the saints possessed the kingdom."** (Daniel 7:21,22, KJV, insertions mine) I have inserted "A" and "B" in these verses because Daniel indicates there are two persecutions of the saints. The first persecution, "A," lasted 1,260 years (a time, times and half a time) and it ended in 1798. The second persecution, "B," lasts for 42 months and it ends with the 1,305th day of the Great Tribulation. (See Revelation 13:1-8) No wonder the angel reminded Daniel that the saints are going to possess the kingdom! The course of human history indicates that the saints are always under attack. So, keep this promise in your mind and do not forget it, no matter how discouraging circumstances may appear in days ahead: *The saints will inherit the Earth.* (Matthew 5:5)

Part Eleven:

"And the ten horns out of this kingdom are ten kings that shall arise: and another shall rise after them; and he shall be diverse from the first, and he shall subdue three kings. And he shall speak great words against the most High, and shall wear out the saints of the most High, and think to change times and laws: and they shall be given into his hand until a time and times and the dividing of time." (Daniel 7:24,25, KJV)

Comments on Part Eleven

To make sense of this prophecy, we have already discussed the specifications given in these verses. However, one specification has not been covered. Daniel was told the little horn power would "think" to change times and laws. This language describes how the little horn would blaspheme God. The little horn would presume (or think it has authority) to displace the laws of God with its own laws!

In A.D. 787, at the Second Nicean Council, Catholic leaders removed the second commandment from the Ten Commandments, and the tenth commandment was divided into two separate commandments so that ten would remain. The reason for this change was to reduce questions about the use of images or icons in worship. In addition to this, church leaders reduced the fourth commandment to just a few words so the laity would not raise questions about *which day* of the week was God's holy day. Compare the Ten Commandments (Exodus 20:3-17) as written in a Catholic Bible with the Catholic Catechism and notice these blatant deviations.

The "Anti" Christ

For almost 700 years, Protestants have claimed the Roman Catholic Church was the little horn power of Daniel 7. Even though there is growing debate within Protestantism today as to who the little horn power is, if we use valid rules of interpretation, the chronological and historical harmony of Daniel 7 leaves no room for doubt. The tragic point in this prophecy is that Satan succeeded. He was able to corrupt the Christian church so that it eventually became "anti" Christ. In fact, the war cry of Protestantism through centuries past is that the Roman Catholic Church is the beast, the Antichrist, the great whore, etc. These claims are false. The Bible says all religions are "anti" Christ. The Moslem is no less anti-Christ than the Jew, Hindu or Catholic! Revelation teaches that all of the religious systems of the world are corrupt because the devil has infiltrated them. The devil is the original antichrist, and Revelation's story climaxes with a powerful contest between a physical Jesus and a physical Lucifer. The devil is very clever and he transformed the institution that Jesus established to save souls into a machine for torturing the people of God! Some researchers have estimated that the Catholic Church killed some fifty million people during its millennial reign for refusing to receive its doctrines. During those dark centuries, the devil was overjoyed – he loves to see people suffering in the name of God. The devil hates God and does everything possible to ruin the work of God on Earth.

Part Twelve:

"But the judgment shall sit, and they shall take away his dominion, to consume and to destroy it unto the end. And

the kingdom and dominion, and the greatness of the kingdom under the whole heaven, shall be given to the people of the saints of the most High, whose kingdom is an everlasting kingdom, and all dominions shall serve and obey him. Hitherto is the end of the matter. As for me Daniel, my cogitations much troubled me, and my countenance changed in me: but I kept the matter in my heart." (Daniel 7:26-28, KJV)

Comments on Part Twelve

This vision brought Daniel indescribable agony. The Lord revealed to Daniel that the saints would inherit the Earth, but he became ill when he saw the travail of the ages that must first occur. The angel closed this vision, reminding Daniel that the judgment would sit, and Jesus will ultimately remove the dominion of the little horn, destroying it with fire. Then, God will give the kingdom to the saints forever and ever!

This chapter has been lengthy because there are many important details in Daniel 7. Remember, if Daniel 7 is not interpreted correctly, the remainder of Daniel's prophecies, as well as Revelation's prophecies, will not make much sense, nor will they align properly within the matrix that history confirms. God tells us many important things in Daniel 7 and if we fail to organize these pieces correctly, our prophetic conclusions in other areas of Daniel and Revelation will miss the mark. In conclusion, we can summarize Daniel 7 with the following seven thoughts:

1. Daniel 7 harmoniously builds upon the progression of nations described in Daniel 2.

2. The sequential order of apocalyptic events forms a historical matrix.

3. Daniel 7 and history leave no wiggle room on the identity of the fourth beast or the little horn.

4. The wounding of the little horn is directly connected to the timing of the courtroom scene in Heaven.

5. The little horn will eventually return to power and speak boastful words against God.

6. At the appointed time, Jesus was exalted and given sovereign authority over the universe and He has been judging the dead to determine who will participate in His coming kingdom.

7. God is sovereign over the kings of Earth. He sets up kings and takes them down.

Chapter 4

Daniel 8 – The Antichrist

"Dear children, this is the last hour; and as you have heard that the Antichrist is coming, even now many antichrists have come. This is how we know it is the last hour."

– 1 John 2:18

Section I - The Symbols

As we proceed through the book of Daniel, the prophetic matrix will continue to unfold, and our understanding of God's Word will become clearer. Daniel 8 adds several important elements to the prophetic matrix. God can say so much with very few words! To make this chapter easier to digest, I have sub-divided it into seven segments. If you make sure that you understand the issues in each segment as you proceed, you should end up with a deeper appreciation for God's Word at the end of this study. Before we examine Daniel 8, there are four points from the previous chapter that need to be restated:

1. History confirms the identity of the fourth beast in Daniel 7 to be the empire of Rome.

2. History confirms the identity of the little horn that uprooted three of the ten horns to be the *Roman* Catholic Church.

3. The timing of the convocation in Heaven (Daniel 7:9) is *linked* to the wounding of the little horn power on Earth. (Daniel 7:21,22) The time, times and half a time (the 1,260 years of persecution) mentioned in Daniel 7:25 came to an end in February 1798, when French soldiers captured the pope and put him in exile. The downfall of

the papacy occurred because the allotted time of 1,260 years ended, and the Ancient of Days pronounced a restraining order in favor of the saints. As a result, the persecution of God's people ended. The linkage between the wounding of the papacy in 1798 (on Earth) and the issuance of the restraining order (in Heaven) is a key point. Because the event on Earth is linked to an event in Heaven, we can determine when the convocation in Heaven began.

4. Daniel 7:11 (and Revelation 13:3) indicates the Roman Catholic Church will return to a position of world preeminence *after* 1798. Daniel heard boastful words from the little horn *after* he observed the courtroom scene in Heaven. (Compare Daniel 7:11 with Revelation 13:3.)

Now that these four points have been reviewed, consider the following points that will rise from this study on Daniel 8:

1. Babylon will fall and the Medo-Persian empire will rise to power.

2. The Medo-Persian empire will fall and the Grecian empire will rise to power.

3. The cleansing of Heaven's temple begins after 2,300 years.

4. During the Great Tribulation, Lucifer, the Antichrist, will physically appear and masquerade as God. He will gain control over Earth for a short period of time and kill a large number of people.

Look over the matrix in Chart 4.1, and notice that it contains some repetition and enlargement of the matrix presented in Chapter 3. Especially notice the placement and order of the items located in the rows for Daniel 7 and Daniel 8.

Remember from Chapter 1 that "no prophecy is complete within itself," and Daniel 8 is no exception. As we will see, Daniel 8 cannot be accurately interpreted without using the developing matrix which the four rules produce. Even with a valid set of rules, we have to be careful that we put each element in its intended place. All of the prophetic pieces have to fit together in a harmonious matrix, for God

Prophetic Matrix Including Daniel 2, 7, 8, and 11

Timing:	605 B.C.	538 B.C.	331 B.C.	168 B.C.	A.D. 476	A.D. 538	1798 1844	Great Tribulation	
Daniel 11:2-4		Four Kings	Mighty King						
		Cambyses, False Smerdis, Darius 1, Xerxes	Alex the Great then Four Generals						
Daniel 8		Ram with Two Horns	Goat with a Great Horn then Four Horns				Judgment of the Dead	Judgment of the Living	Horn Power: The Stern Faced King
Daniel 7	Lion with Eagle's Wings	Bear with Three Ribs	Leopard with Four Heads	Monster	10 Horns	Little Horn Rises	Little Horn Wounded	Little Horn Heard Boasting	
Daniel 2	Head of Gold	Chest of Silver	Thighs of Bronze	Legs of Iron		Feet			10 Toes
						Iron and Clay			Iron/ Clay
	Babylon	Medo-Persia	Grecia	Rome		Many Kings			10 Kings

Chart 4.1

is the Author and Designer of prophecy. Remember, each prophetic element is like a piece of a puzzle that has several sides. The puzzle is solved when *all* the pieces are positioned in such a way that they harmoniously align with the surrounding pieces.

The Apocalyptic Sequence

God gave the vision in Daniel 8 to Daniel about 550 B.C. Daniel 8 follows the *same* order found in Daniel 2 and 7. In other words, this vision contains an orderly sequence of events which is followed by commentary that explains the sequence. Carefully study the apocalyptic sequence:

"In the third year of the reign of king Belshazzar a vision appeared unto me, even unto me Daniel, after that which appeared unto me at the first. And I saw in a vision; and it came to pass, when I saw, that I was at Shushan in the palace, which is in the province of Elam; and I saw in a vision, and I was by the river of Ulai. Then I lifted up mine eyes, and saw, and, behold, there stood before the river a ram which had two horns: and the two horns were high; but one was higher than the other, and the higher came up last. I saw the ram pushing westward, and northward, and southward; so that no beasts might stand before him, neither was there any that could deliver out of his hand; but he did according to his will, and became great.

"And as I was considering, behold, an he goat came from the west on the face of the whole Earth, and touched not the ground: and the goat had a notable horn between his eyes. And he came to the ram that had two horns, which I had seen standing before the river, and ran unto him in the fury of his power. And I saw him come close unto the ram, and he was moved with choler against him, and smote the ram, and brake his two horns: and there was no power in the ram to stand before him, but he cast him down to the ground, and stamped upon him: and there was none that could deliver the ram out of his hand. Therefore the he goat waxed very great: and when he was strong, the great horn was broken; and for it came up four notable ones toward the four winds of heaven.

"And out of one of them came forth a little horn, which waxed exceeding great, toward the south, and toward the east, and toward the pleasant land. And it waxed great, even to the host of heaven; and it cast down some of the host and of the stars to the ground, and stamped upon them. Yea, he magnified himself even to the prince of the host, and by him the daily sacrifice was taken away, and the place of his sanctuary was cast down. And an host was given him against the daily sacrifice by reason of transgression, and it cast

down the truth to the ground; and it practiced, and prospered." (Daniel 8:1-12, KJV)

Comments

These twelve verses focus on three symbols: a ram, a goat and a horn power. Because the Bible is its own interpreter, it provides the meaning of these symbols. The ram represents the kingdom of Medo-Persia. (Daniel 5:28; 8:20). The two horns of the ram represent the co-regent reign of two kings, the king of the Medes and the king of the Persians. The higher horn (the greater king) represents the Persian side of this kingdom. The higher horn of the ram in Daniel 8:3 also aligns with the "higher shoulder" of the bear in Daniel 7:5. (See Chart 4.1.)

The second symbol, the goat, represents the kingdom of Grecia. (Daniel 8:21) The great horn represents the first prominent king of the Grecian empire. History reveals this king was Alexander the Great, who died in the prime of his life. The four horns that replaced the great horn represent four generals that eventually gained control of Alexander's empire. Historians identify these generals as Cassander, Lysimachus, Ptolemy and Seleucus.

We know the identity of the ram and goat, but what does the third symbol, the horn power, represent? Until the twentieth century, a majority of Protestants claimed the little horn in Daniel 7 and the horn power in Daniel 8 represented the papacy. True, both horns have important similarities, but they are not the same entity. We will see that the horn power in Daniel 8 is many times more powerful than the Roman Catholic Church.

Beasts Are Kingdoms – Horns Are Kings

In Daniel 8, the two beasts represent empires, but the horns of the ram and of the goat represent *kings*. This distinction is important, because the horn power in this vision is not attached to a beast (a world empire). Further, the Bible says this horn power is a king. (Daniel 8:23) Daniel was told this king will exalt himself to be as great as the Prince of the host, Jesus Christ! (Daniel 8:11) The horn power in Daniel 8 is a stern-faced king that will rule over Earth during the Great Tribulation. (Daniel 11:36) This coming king is the Antichrist, Lucifer, who will dazzle the world with his power, authority and ability to perform incredible miracles. He will gain

control of Earth and do more evil than Hitler, Stalin and Pol Pot
combined. In short, the dreaded Antichrist will not be a mere man.
The coming Antichrist will be Lucifer, appearing in the flesh,
masquerading as an angel of light, and claiming to be Almighty God.
(2 Corinthians 11:14; Daniel 11:36; Revelation 9; Revelation 13:11-18)

Timing Is Everything

The vision in Daniel 8 almost covers the same 2,600 years described
in Daniel 2 and 7. The only difference is that the Daniel 8 vision
starts with the Medo-Persian empire (538 B.C.) instead of the
Babylonian empire (605 B.C.). The sequence in this vision ends
when Jesus destroys "the stern-faced king" at the Second Coming.
Daniel 8:25 indicates the horn power will be destroyed by God:
"**. . . he will be destroyed, but not by human power.**" (See
Daniel 2:44, Daniel 7:11 and Revelation 19:11-21.) This is an
important specification. Men will not be able to destroy the
Antichrist. Lucifer will do whatever he wants and no one will be
able to stop him. Jesus does not lay hands on His enemies at the
Second Coming; He simply commands the wicked to die. The sharp
sword that comes out of His mouth represents His ability to speak
the command and people drop dead. (See Revelation 19:15-21.) It is
interesting to note that the voice that calls the righteous dead to life
(1 Thessalonians 4:16) is the *same* voice that commands the wicked
to die. (Revelation 19:21)

Because God is the Creator of apocalyptic prophecy, we know Daniel
8 will harmonize with the matrix established in Daniel 2 and Daniel
7. Pay close attention to the words of Gabriel, as he speaks to
Daniel about the sequence of events: "**And I heard a man's voice
from the Ulai calling, 'Gabriel, tell this man the meaning of
the vision.' As he came near the place where I was standing, I
was terrified and fell prostrate. 'Son of man,' he said to me,
'understand that the vision concerns *the time of the end.*'
While he was speaking to me, I was in a deep sleep, with my
face to the ground. Then he touched me and raised me to my
feet. He said: 'I am going to tell you what will happen later *in
the time of wrath*, because the vision concerns *the appointed
time of the end.*' **" (Daniel 8:16-19, italics mine)

Look at the words which have been italicized. Gabriel twice
emphasized the point that this vision concerns "the time of the end"

or "the *appointed* time of the end." The word "appointed" means the time of the end was set or predetermined long ago. This is why Gabriel calls it "the *appointed* time of the end." God has set a date for the Great Tribulation to begin. The Father has also set a date for the Second Coming. (Matthew 24:36) So, ready or not, believe it or not, God's great clock is counting the days to the appointed time of the end. (Read Revelation 9:15 and notice how the date for the sixth trumpet has been predetermined down to the very hour.)

The Time of Wrath

Gabriel said the appointed time of the end will be a time of wrath. A time of wrath means that everyone will suffer wrath during the appointed time of the end. The wicked will receive God's wrath for their rebellion and insolence (Colossians 3:5,6; Revelation 16), and the saints will receive the wrath of their governments when they refuse to obey the dictates of Babylon and the Antichrist! (Revelation 13:7-10) Everyone will suffer wrath.

How does the horn power in Daniel 8 connect to the appointed time of the end? The connection is quite simple because the ram and the goat are not end-time players. History says these world empires disappeared more than two thousand years ago. However, the horn power, or "the stern-faced king," has not yet appeared. He is the *only* item left in this vision that relates to the *appointed* time of the end. As we will see, the horn power in Daniel 8 is the coming Antichrist. He will appear "out of nowhere" during the Great Tribulation. He does not rise out of a nation or a kingdom like the little horn of Daniel 7. Lucifer will suddenly appear in clouds of light with his angels, and through counterfeit miracles, signs, wonders, deceit and lies, he will deceive the whole world. He will gain control of Earth during the *appointed* time of the end.

First Question

After hearing that the horn power is the *only* part of this vision that applies to the time of the end, one of the first questions people ask is this: "Why did God put two ancient kingdoms in this vision if they have nothing to do with the end-time?" There are at least three reasons for placing these ancient kingdoms in a prophecy that points to the appointed time of the end:

1. God placed the ram and goat in the vision of Daniel 8 so that we could identify *by name* the two empires that followed Babylon. The Bible says the ram and the goat represent the kingdoms of the Medes and Persians and the Grecians, respectively. (Daniel 8:20,21) By stating their names, God eliminated any wiggle room about the identity of the first three empires in Daniel's historical matrix, namely, Babylon, Medo-Persia and Grecia. Furthermore, the identity of these three kingdoms leaves no question about the identity of the fourth beast in Daniel 7 (Rome) nor the identity of the little horn power in Daniel 7 that rose out of Rome (the *Roman* Catholic Church).

2. The second reason God put two ancient kingdoms in this end-time vision is linkage. The ram is connected by the 2,300 days to an event that occurs in Heaven. Because we cannot see into Heaven with the naked eye, God has linked events in Heaven with well known events on Earth. The result is simple. Students of apocalyptic prophecy can determine the timing of several heavenly events which no one can see.

3. Last, God put two ancient kingdoms in this end-time vision because God wants everyone to know the horn power *in Daniel 8 does not rise* out of an ancient empire like the little horn of Daniel 7. The horn power in Daniel 8 is not an extension of the Roman empire nor any world empire. The point here is *separation*. The horn power in Daniel 8 is separate and isolated from earthly kingdoms. This was not the case in Daniel 7. We know the little horn in Daniel 7 rose out of the fourth beast and it derived its name from its powerful host. For seventeen centuries, the little horn of Daniel 7 has been called the *Roman* Catholic Church. To keep us from misidentifying the horn power of Daniel 8, God inserted more than 2,000 years between the ancient kingdoms and the appearing of the horn power. God wants the world to understand that the horn power in Daniel 8 does not have an earthly origin. Instead, he will have a supernatural one.

Revelation 9 indicates that Lucifer will come down *out of the sky* attended by millions of angels.

Antichrist Will Not be Human

The books of Isaiah, Ezekiel, 2 Thessalonians, 2 Corinthians, Daniel and Revelation harmonize because they are the Word of God. They present a rather startling picture of the coming Antichrist by adding valuable pieces to the puzzle. The following comments are a brief synthesis of what these books say about the Antichrist:

The coming Antichrist will not be a mere mortal. The coming Antichrist will not be born to a woman. The coming Antichrist cannot be killed by men. The coming Antichrist will have supernatural powers that far exceed anything men can do. The coming Antichrist will be evil and destructive beyond comprehension. The coming Antichrist will be dazzling and commanding in appearance, but deadly in his manipulation. The coming Antichrist will be a stern-faced king, that is, he will not show mercy unless temporal mercy facilitates his evil schemes. Billions of powerful demons serve him. The coming Antichrist is the ancient foe of Christ. In fact, Lucifer is the most powerful and greatest angel that God ever created. He was the first being to become anti-Christ. The Bible predicts that God will allow Lucifer and his angels to appear in physical form visible to the human race. Just as Jesus became a man to save the world, Lucifer will be granted authority to masquerade as God so that he can quickly lead the wicked to their destruction. Lucifer will mimic Christ's return and appear with clouds of angels. You can be sure the appearing of the devil will be the most spectacular event ever viewed by human eyes (Revelation 17:8) – only to be eclipsed by the brighter and more glorious appearing of Jesus. (Revelation 1:7, 19:11-21)

Horn Power Not Antiochus Epiphanes IV Nor the Papacy

Most Christians believe the horn power in Daniel 8 is either Antiochus Epiphanes IV, an ancient king who ruled with Rome's permission over a tiny Syrian state (175-164 B.C.), or they say this horn power is the Roman Catholic Church. Of course, the only way we can determine the true identity of this horn power is by satisfying *all* of the specifications given to Daniel. We will find in this presentation that both interpretations share the same deficiency. Neither conclusion satisfies *all* of the specifications given in Daniel 8.

Even though Bible students and scholars have studied the book of Daniel for centuries, it was impossible for them to know the truth about Daniel 8 because the knowledge of the architecture of Daniel was sealed up until the time of the end. (Daniel 12:4,9) Because the end of the age is here and the Great Tribulation is about to begin, the book of Daniel has been unsealed and God's Word now speaks with a clarity and precision that it did not have before. When Daniel 8 is integrated into the historical matrix which the four rules of interpretation produce, the horn power in Daniel 8 cannot be Antiochus IV or the papacy! The horn power in Daniel 8 is something far more powerful and far more sinister. The horn power in Daniel 8 is the great enemy of God and man. He is the coming Antichrist.

Section II - Antichrist as King of the North

All Specifications Have to Be Fulfilled

Rule Two says, *"A fulfilment of apocalyptic prophecy occurs when all of the specifications within that prophecy are met. This includes the order of events outlined in the prophecy."* With this rule in mind, we will carefully examine *all* of the specifications of the horn power in Daniel 8. We will begin with the origin of the Horn Power. **"The goat** [Grecia] **became very great, but at the height of his power his large horn** [Alexander the Great] **was broken off, and in its place four prominent horns grew up toward the four winds of heaven** [North, East, West, South]**. Out of one of them** [the four winds] **came another horn, which started small but grew in power to the south and to the east and toward** [the west] **the Beautiful Land."** (Daniel 8:8,9, insertions mine) The Bible says the large or prominent horn of the goat was broken off at the height of its power. This seems odd. A person would not expect a powerful horn to "break off" at the peak of its strength, but remember, this horn represents a king, not an empire. Alexander the Great died at the peak of his military power. His kingdom was divided between his four generals which are represented by the four horns. Gabriel told Daniel, **"The four horns that replaced the one that was broken off represent four** [kings or] **kingdoms that will emerge from his nation but will not have the same power."** (Daniel 8:22, insertion mine) It is interesting to observe that prophecy is history written in advance. History confirms Gabriel's words. None of Alexander's generals were strong enough to reunite the Grecian kingdom.

God used beasts in Daniel 7 and Daniel 8 to represent *empires*, but He consistently used horns to represent *kings*. The Hebrew word for horn, *malkuwth,* can mean king, ruler or kingdom. Most translators treat *malkuwth* in Daniel 8:22 as "four kingdoms," however, in this context *malkuwth* is better translated "four kings." Because horns represent kings in Daniel 8, this consistency forces the horn power in Daniel 8 to also be a king. In fact, the Bible emphasizes this point by indicating the horn power in Daniel 8 will be a stern-faced "king" who appears during the appointed time of the end! (See Daniel 8:19,23.)

The Horn Power Comes out of the North

"And out of one of them [the four winds] **came forth a little horn, which waxed exceeding great, toward the south, and toward the east, and toward the** [west] **pleasant land."** (Daniel 8:9, KJV, insertions mine) From the evidence that follows, we will discover that the horn power (the stern-faced king) does not originate within an earthly kingdom. Actually, the Antichrist *just appears* out of nowhere. The Bible reveals he comes from the north, out of one of the four *winds*. There is more to this direction than one might think at first. As we proceed, notice how the horn power in Daniel 8 does not have its roots in ancient kingdoms such as Medo-Persia, Grecia or Rome!

Daniel 8:9 says, **"And out of one of *them* came another horn. . . ."** To understand this phrase we have to examine the grammar. To what noun does the pronoun "them" refer? The Hebrew pronoun "them" (*hem*) is masculine, and the Hebrew word for "winds" (*ruwach*) can be masculine or feminine, but the Hebrew word for "horns" (*qeren*) is feminine. Therefore, a gender agreement (masculine "them" and masculine "winds") is possible if we say, "Out of one of the four winds. . . ." But if we say, "Out of one of the four horns. . .," the gender in the grammar does not agree. Even though grammar suggests the horn power comes out of one of the four winds, grammar alone does not make this conclusion air-tight. So, let us see if there is stronger evidence.

Daniel was standing on the banks of the Ulai River when he received this vision. From his point of reference, the horn power started out small, but became "exceeding great" as it grew toward the south, east and "toward the beautiful land." Daniel refers to his homeland as "the beautiful land" without explicitly saying "west." (See Jeremiah 3:19.) Maps of this region show Jerusalem to be due west of the province of Elam where Daniel was located. So, after analyzing verse 9, we discover the horn power comes out of the north and grows toward the south, east and west.

The direction of north is very significant. The ancients thought the world was flat, and north was "up" and south was "down." Two thousand six hundred years later, while we know the world is not flat, we still follow this tradition. Most people think the North Pole is on the *top* of the world and the South Pole is at the bottom. The ancients believed that God's throne was above the world, so they concluded that divine judgments came *down* from the north. Carefully study the following seven texts and notice how the direction of north is associated with divine destruction (italics and insertions mine):

1. **"This is what the Lord says** [to Israel]: **'Look, an army is coming from the land of the *north*** [to destroy you]; **a great nation is being stirred up from the ends of the Earth. They are armed with bow and spear; they are cruel and show no mercy. They sound like the roaring sea as they ride on their horses; they come like men in battle formation to attack you, O Daughter of Zion.' "** (Jeremiah 6:22,23)

2. **" 'I will summon all the peoples of the *north* and my servant Nebuchadnezzar king of Babylon,' declares the Lord, 'and I will bring them against this land and its inhabitants and against all the surrounding nations. I will completely destroy them** [the inhabitants of Judah] **and make them an object of horror and scorn, and an everlasting ruin.' "** (Jeremiah 25:9)

3. "This is the message the Lord spoke to Jeremiah the prophet about the coming of Nebuchadnezzar king of Babylon to attack Egypt. . . Egypt is a beautiful heifer, but a gadfly is coming against her from the *north*. The mercenaries in her ranks are like fattened calves. They too will turn and flee together, they will not stand their ground, for the day of disaster is coming upon them, the time for them to be punished." (Jeremiah 46:13,20,21)

4. "Announce and proclaim among the nations, lift up a banner and proclaim it; keep nothing back, but say, 'Babylon will be captured; Bel will be put to shame, Marduk filled with terror. Her images will be put to shame and her idols filled with terror.' A nation from the *North* [the Medes] will attack her and lay waste her land. No one will live in it; both men and animals will flee away." (Jeremiah 50:2,3)

5. "Therefore, son of man, prophesy and say to Gog [Lucifer]: 'This is what the Sovereign Lord says: In that day, when my people Israel are living in safety, will you not take notice of it? You will come from your place in the far *north*, you and many nations with you, all of them riding on horses, a great horde, a mighty army. You will advance against my people Israel like a cloud that covers the land. In days to come, O Gog [Lucifer], I will bring you against my land, so that the nations may know me when I show myself holy through you before their eyes.' " (Ezekiel 38:14-16)

6. The horn power in Daniel 8 descends from the *north* because north is a meaningful direction. God deliberately embedded this seemingly insignificant detail in Daniel 8 because He can say profound things with very few words through figurative speech. (Remember, no copy machines or printing presses existed in those days. Hand copied books were scarce and extremely expensive, so books with fewer words were easier to preserve.) The direction of "north" became a significant direction when Lucifer began

campaigning against Christ in Heaven. Speaking about Lucifer's blasphemy, the Lord said, **"For thou hast said in thine heart, I will ascend into Heaven, I will exalt my throne above the stars of God: I will sit also upon the mount of the congregation, in *the sides of the north*: I will ascend above the heights of the clouds; I will be like the most High."** (Isaiah 14:13,14, KJV) The phrase, "the sides of the north," refers to the location of God's throne. God's throne was located on the "higher side" or the north side of Heaven's temple! (The Table of Showbread, which represented God's throne, was placed on the north side of the earthly temple.) This knowledge and God's consistent use of the direction of "north" in the Old Testament indicate that divine authority or judgment originates on "the sides of the north."

7. One more text highlighting the importance of the direction north which the reader should consider. In the book of Job, Elihu speaks for God. He addresses a number of false arguments which Job's friends had made against God. (I am convinced that Elihu was Jesus, who physically appeared before Job and his friends, much like the Lord appeared before Abraham. Genesis 18:22) Elihu said, **"Be assured that my words are not false; one perfect in knowledge is with you. . . . Out of the *north* he comes in golden splendor; God comes in awesome majesty."** (Job 36:4; 37:22, italics mine) In the context of Job 36 and 37, the sovereign authority and awesome wisdom of God comes out of the north. This makes perfect sense because God's throne is located "on the sides of the north" in Heaven's temple. (See Exodus 26:35 and Exodus 40:22 for the location of the Table of Showbread which represented God's throne.)

Intermediate Review

1. The horn power comes out of one of the four winds.

2. The horn power comes out of the north and grows toward the south, east and west.

3. Divine authority and divine destruction come out of the north.

4. God's throne is located on the north side of Heaven's temple.

The King of the North in Daniel 11

Even though Daniel 8 indicates the horn power comes out of the north, Daniel 11 offers more details about the king who comes out of the north. Let us jump ahead for a moment to Daniel 11:36 and notice a few verses. These verses may help you see more clearly how the architecture of Daniel influences my conclusion that the horn power in Daniel 8 is the Antichrist. First, consider these verses: **"Some of the wise will stumble, so that they may be refined, purified and made spotless** *until the time of the end***, for it will still come at the appointed time.** [However, at the appointed time of the end] **The** [stern-faced] **king will do as he pleases. He will exalt and magnify himself above every god and will say unheard-of things against the God of gods. He will be successful until the time of wrath** [the Great Tribulation] **is completed, for what has been determined must take place."** (Daniel 11:35,36, italics and insertions mine) These two verses speak about the time of the end. Now we will jump forward to verses 40 and 41. **"At** *the time of the end* **the king of the south will** [rebel and] **engage him in battle, and the king of the north** [the Antichrist] **will storm out against him with chariots and cavalry and a great fleet of ships. He will invade many countries and sweep through them like a flood. He will also invade the Beautiful Land. . . ."** (Daniel 11:40,41, insertions mine)

After Lucifer appears on Earth, Revelation 13:8 indicates most wicked people will receive him as God, but many of them will reject him and rebel against his claims of authority. Daniel 11 reveals the wicked king of the south will rise up and oppose the arrogant and pompous claims of Lucifer, the king of the north. Lucifer will wage war against the king of the south, and will destroy him and his followers. In fact, this destruction amounts to one-third of the wicked! The remaining two-thirds of the wicked will gladly submit to the devil as though he were Almighty God. As horrendous as this battle is, the sixth-trumpet war is not the battle of Armageddon.

The battle of Armageddon occurs as Jesus appears. (Revelation 16:12-21)

The war described in Daniel 11:40,41 is also described in Revelation 9:13-21. Daniel and Revelation perfectly harmonize on this matter. The point is that the horn power of Daniel 8 is the king from the north. Study over Chart 4.2 and notice how the king from the north in Daniel 11:36 and the horn power of Daniel 8 appear *at the appointed time of the end.* The architecture of apocalyptic prophecy is amazing! (**Note:** To keep the size of this growing matrix within the physical constraints of the pages within this book, the column for Babylon has been removed.)

Summarizing His Origin

The horn power in Daniel 8 does not arise from a nation on Earth. This king will come out of the north during the appointed time of the end. God uses the point of origin to make a profound statement. The Antichrist will arrive on a divine mission of destruction! God will send the stern-faced king to rule over the wicked. God will send him because the wicked rejected His truth and rebelled against His generous offer of salvation. Paul talked about this, "**. . . They** [the wicked] **perish because** *they refused to love the truth* **and so be saved. For this reason God sends them a powerful delusion so that they will believe the lie and so that all will be condemned who have not believed the truth but have delighted in wickedness.**" (2 Thessalonians 2:10-12, italics mine)

Consider God's consistent ways. He sent armies to destroy the Caananites, the Israelites, the Egyptians, the Babylonians, the Medes and Persians, the Grecians, and the Romans. When nations go beyond the point of redemption, God raises up a destroyer king. The reason God places the Antichrist in the end time story is because He sets up kings and He takes them down *with other kings.* During the Great Tribulation, God will send the stern-faced king of Daniel 8 (the Antichrist) to destroy much of the world. The devil will kill one-third of mankind, leaving two groups of survivors. When Jesus appears, one group will obey the commandments of the Lamb (Revelation 12:17) and the other group will obey the lamb-like beast (the Antichrist).

Prophecy Matrix With the King of the North

Timing:	538 B.C.	331 B.C.	168 B.C.	A.D. 476	A.D. 538	1798	1844	Great Tribulation
Daniel 11:36								King of the North Appears
Daniel 11:2-35	Four Kings Cambyses, False Smerdis, Darius I, Artexerxes	Mighty King Alex the Great Plus Four Generals	Kingdoms to the North and South of Israel at War. Israel Caught in the Middle. Jerusalem Destroyed A.D. 70.					God's People Caught Between Kings of the North and the South
	|---457 B.C. ----------- 2,300 Day/Years ------------ 1844---|							The Time of the End
Daniel 8	Ram with Two Horns	Goat with One Great Horn -- Then Four Horns				Judgment of the Dead	Judgment of the Living	Horn Power from the North: Stern Faced King
Daniel 7	Bear with Three Ribs	Leopard with Four Heads	Monster	10 Horns at First	1,260 Day/Years A.D. 538 to 1798 — Little Horn Rises Uproots 3 Horns — Court Seated Little Horn Falls	Books of Record Opened	Little Horn Heard Boasting	Beasts Are Burned Up in the Fire at the End
Daniel 2	Chest of	Thighs of	Legs of	Feet				10 Toes 10 Kings
	Silver	Bronze	Iron	Iron and Clay				Iron/Clay
	Medo Persia	Grecia	Rome	Many Kings				10 Kings

Chart 4.2

I know this explanation of the horn power goes beyond the evidence presented thus far in Daniel 8, but my purpose is to help you behold a very large picture that will continue to unfold if the apocalyptic rules are followed!

Section III - Antichrist Will Oppose All Religions

The Horn Power Grows Until. . . .

"It grew until it reached the host of the heavens, and it threw some of the starry host down to the earth and trampled on them." (Daniel 8:10) The horn power from the north starts small, but it grows until it reaches the starry host of the heavens, then it throws them down and tramples them. This language indicates the stern-faced king will *grow* in recognition and authority among the inhabitants of Earth until he is exalted above all gods! The book of Revelation reveals more about this process than Daniel. Revelation indicates the devil will begin his physical work on Earth with *local* appearances. The devil, along with his enormous host of angels, will come down out of the sky in blinding clouds of light at specific locations on Earth. He will imitate Christ's Second Coming with two obvious differences. First, God will not permit the devil to be visible to the whole world *at one time*. So, the people of Earth will not be introduced to the Antichrist at one event. He will grow in popularity as he appears in the skies over the populated cities of Earth. Great cities of the world such as Mexico City, Jerusalem, Washington D.C., Moscow, Sydney, Beijing, Calcutta, Houston and others, will see magnificent displays of power and glory. Lucifer will appear in various places and he will exercise miracle-working powers to convince people that *he* is God. (Revelation 13:14,15) Even though his display of power will be amazing, the saints will not be deceived. They know who lives behind the mask. (Revelation 14:9,10)

To understand the meaning of "the starry hosts" in Daniel 8, we have to examine the language and ways of people who lived in ancient times. Polytheism was popular. The ancients worshiped various gods who lived among the stars of the heavens. (Daniel 2:11,28) They used the stars, like dots on a drawing pad, to draw pictures of their gods. These mythical gods belonged to a collection called "the starry hosts." Idols of gold, silver, wood and stone *were representations* of these various gods. These five texts help us understand who the starry hosts were (italics mine):

1. **"They [Israel] forsook all the commands of the Lord their God and made for themselves two idols cast in the shape of calves, and an Asherah pole. They bowed down to all the *starry hosts,* and they worshiped Baal."** (2 Kings 17:16, insertion mine)

2. **"He [King Manasseh] rebuilt the high places his father Hezekiah had destroyed; he also erected altars to Baal and made an Asherah pole, as Ahab king of Israel had done. He bowed down to all the starry hosts and worshiped them. He built altars in the temple of the Lord, of which the Lord had said, 'In Jerusalem I will put my Name.' In both courts of the temple of the Lord, he built altars to all the *starry hosts.* . . ."** (2 Kings 21:3-5, insertion mine)

3. **"He [King Josiah] did away with the pagan priests appointed by the kings of Judah to burn incense on the high places of the towns of Judah and on those around Jerusalem – those who burned incense to Baal, to the sun and moon, to the constellations and to all the *starry hosts.*"** (2 Kings 23:5, insertion mine)

4. **"You alone are the Lord. You made the heavens, even the highest heavens, and all their *starry host,* the earth and all that is on it, the seas and all that is in them. You give life to everything, and the multitudes of heaven worship you."** (Nehemiah 9:6)

5. **"And when you look up to the sky and see the sun, the moon and the stars – all the heavenly array – do not be enticed into bowing down**

> to them and worshiping things the Lord your
> God has apportioned to all the nations under
> heaven." (Deuteronomy 4:19)

If we allow the Bible to be its own interpreter, the term "starry
hosts" represents pagan deities. The ancients gave them names such
as Baal, Mercury, Zeus, Hermes, Venus, Ra, Sol and others. (Acts
14:12) With this setting in mind, Daniel 8:10 indicates the
Antichrist will grow in authority and recognition until he is honored
above all gods worshiped by men. The stern-faced king *will prove*
himself greater than the gods of all religions because he can perform
great signs and miracles at will. No other false god will be able to
match his glory or prowess. Even King Nebuchadnezzar admitted
that Daniel's God was greater than his own god when Daniel
interpreted the king's vision! So, when the time comes, the
Antichrist will call fire down out of Heaven to destroy rebellious
groups of people, and his actions will convince onlookers that they
are in the presence of Almighty God. (Revelation 13:13,14; 2 Thessalonians 2:9) In this way, the devil will trample down (show
inferior) all of the gods of this world and the religions of men. Now
that you have an idea of what the horn power from the north will do
to the nations and religions of the world, notice these two texts:

1. **"The** [stern-faced] **king** [of the North] **will do as he
   pleases. He will exalt and magnify himself above
   every god and will say unheard-of things against
   the God of gods. He will be successful** *until the time
   of wrath* **is completed, for what has been determined must take place. He will show no regard for
   the gods of his fathers** [the traditional gods of religions]
   or for the one desired by women [Jesus Christ*], **nor
   will he regard any god, but will exalt himself above
   them all."** (Daniel 11:36,37, italics and insertion mine.

2. **"Let no man deceive you by any means: for that day**
   [the Second Coming] **shall not come, except there
   come a falling away** [from the truth] **first, and that**

---

* Most virgins in Israel hoped they would be the one through whom the
Deliverer would be born. See how Mary's good fortune is described in
Luke 1:34,35.

man of sin be revealed, the son of perdition
[destruction]; **Who opposeth and exalteth himself
above all that is called God, or that is worshipped;
so that he as God sitteth in the temple of God,
showing himself that he is God.**"
(2 Thessalonians 2:3,4, KJV, insertions mine)

Do not forget each of these specifications. The details regarding the
horn power of Daniel 8 are creating a tall order – in fact, no ordinary
person can meet these specifications.

Section IV - Horn Power Cannot Be Antiochus
Epiphanes IV

Daily Services in Heaven

It is regrettable that millions of Christians believe that Antiochus
Epiphanes IV (175-164 B.C.) is the horn power of Daniel 8. We will
investigate this claim by comparing the specifications given in the
Bible with historical facts about Antiochus IV. Beginning with
Daniel 8:11, the angel said, **"It** [the horn power] **set itself up to be
as great as the Prince of the host** [The Lord Jesus]; **it** [the horn
power] **took away the daily** *sacrifice* **from him, and the place
of his sanctuary was brought low."** (Daniel 8:11, insertions and
italics mine) Verse 11 will make a lot more sense if you understand
God's use of parallel temples. (See * below.) Daniel 8:11 is not
describing the cessation of daily sacrifices in Jerusalem's temple in
167 B.C. Instead, we will see that this verse describes the cessation
of daily services *in Heaven's temple* which during "the appointed
time of the end."

The word "sacrifice" in verse 11 has been added by translators and is
not found in the original manuscripts. This fact is important
because Gabriel is not talking about the cessation of animal
sacrifices on Earth. He is talking about the cessation of the *daily*

---

*   If you have not investigated the doctrine of parallel sanctuaries,
     please review Chapters 11 and 12 in my companion volume,
     Jesus, The Alpha and The Omega.

services in Heaven's temple. The word "daily" comes from a perpetual round of services that occurred evening and morning in the earthly temple. The daily services on Earth shadow similar services in Heaven's temple. (Hebrews 8:1-5) During the appointed time of the end, the Antichrist will cause the daily services *in Heaven's* temple to end and the Antichrist will cause the place of Christ's sanctuary to be brought low (treated with disdain and contempt).

History reveals that Antiochus IV ended the daily services in Jerusalem's temple for a three year period. However, the cessation of the daily in 167 B.C. is not a fulfillment of Daniel 8, nor does this make Antiochus IV the horn power of Daniel 8. *Antiochus IV was not the only king that terminated the daily services at the temple in Jerusalem.* For example, Nebuchadnezzar destroyed the temple in 586 B.C. and ended the daily services for more than seventy years. The Roman general, Titus, destroyed the temple in A.D. 70, and the daily services of the temple have not resumed to this day because there is no temple in Jerusalem. However, the primary question begging for an answer is whether Antiochus IV was powerful enough to take the daily away from the Prince of the host, Jesus! Review verse 11 again: **"It** [the horn power] **set itself up to be as great as the Prince of the host** [the Lord Jesus]**; it took away the daily** *sacrifice* **from him, and the place of his sanctuary was brought low."**

The History of Antiochus IV

A brief history of Antiochus Epiphanes IV may be helpful because millions of people believe Antiochus IV is a fulfillment of the horn power in Daniel 8. Let us closely examine the logic that produces this conclusion.

1. The Bible says the goat in Daniel 8 represents Grecia.

2. The Bible says the great horn represents the first king of Grecia, Alexander the Great.

3. The Bible says the four horns represent the four generals that gained control of Alexander's empire.

4. One of the four generals was Seleucus. He was the first in a long line of succeeding kings.

5. Just before the Grecian empire fell to Rome, Antiochus IV came to power as the king of Syria (175-164 B.C.). After his father, Antiochus the Great, died, the Romans, who controlled the Middle East at this time, *allowed* Antiochus IV to become the eighth king in a line of kings whose lineage dates back to Seleucus. Antiochus IV exalted himself by adding "Epiphany" to his name. An epiphany is "a great manifestation of God." The Romans mocked the pompous little king by calling him Antiochus Epimanes IV. Epimanes sounds similar to Epiphany, but it means "mad man."

6. About 168 B.C., Antiochus sent his army to Egypt to steal some wealth. He desperately needed to replenish his empty treasury. Antiochus had squandered the assets of his kingdom on foolish endeavors and Syria was near the point of bankruptcy. He defeated the cowardly Ptolemee, king of Egypt, but Rome sent an envoy to inform Antiochus IV that he could not rule over Egypt. Antiochus knew that any sign of rebellion against Rome was fatal. Thwarted and humiliated, but happy with the loot he had stolen, he returned home.

7. Meanwhile, in Jerusalem, the high priest, Jason, had initiated a rebellion against the rigid control of conservative Jews. He wanted to adopt some of the more liberal Hellenistic ways of the Greeks and build a Greek gymnasium where nude body-building and sensual exercises could be conducted. While this conflict was unfolding, Menelaus, a wealthy Jew, offered Antiochus IV a large bribe if he would send soldiers to overthrow Jerusalem's leadership and appoint Menelaus as high priest. This bribe gave Antiochus a "golden" opportunity to quell Jason's rebellion and plunder the Jewish temple of its gold and silver. Gold and silver from the Jewish temple would help replenish his ever-empty treasury.

8. Antiochus loved the decadent and sensual ways of the Greeks. When the king arrived in Jerusalem, he showed contempt for the conservative Jews by erecting a statue of the Greek god, Zeus, on the Altar of Burnt Offering on

Chislev 15, 167 B.C. Ten days later, on Chislev 25, Antiochus ended daily services (including the daily sacrifices) at the temple when he offered a pig (or some unclean animal) on the Altar of Burnt Offering. This abominable act led to a series of wars between Antiochus' forces and conservative Jews. This series of wars became known as the Maccabean revolt because a conservative priest, Judas Maccabeus, led the Jews against the forces of Antiochus IV.

9. A year or so later, Antiochus ran out of money *again*. This time he decided to raid portions of Persia to finance his excessive spending habits. So he turned the management of his kingdom over to his friend, Lysais, instructing him to destroy the Jews and Jerusalem as quickly as possible. However, Judas Maccabeus and the Jews eventually defeated Lysais and his generals. The victory over Lysais did not end the wars between the Jews and their enemies. Three years after offering a pig on the altar, to the very day, on Chislev 25, 164 B.C., a new altar was installed and dedicated in the temple at Jerusalem and daily services resumed. The Jews have celebrated the restoration of temple services on this day ever since. (See John 10:22,23.) It is called Hannukkah, which means "the dedication."

10. Meanwhile, in Persia, Antiochus IV experienced a number of sound defeats, and when he learned that the Jews had defeated Lysais and robbed him of his armament, Antiochus IV became heartsick. After a period of suffering from illness (perhaps from too much drinking), Antiochus uttered these words, "I perish through great grief in a strange land." (1 Maccabees 6:13) After giving his close friend, Philip, his crown, robe, and signet, he gave instructions that he was to raise his son, Antiochus V, to take his throne. Then, Antiochus IV died.

What Is Wrong with the Antiochus Interpretation?

Because there are valid rules of interpretation, no prophecy stands alone. Daniel 8 is not isolated from the historical matrix that unfolds in the book of Daniel. Because there are so many variables in the study of prophecy, we have to follow a set of valid rules if we want to know the intended meaning of prophecy. If we do not follow a valid set of rules, the outcome will be a private interpretation. Even though a private interpretation may be exciting and very reasonable, and even though millions of people may accept it as truth, a private interpretation *never* produces God's intended meaning in apocalyptic prophecy. (2 Peter 1:20)

Because God sealed the book of Daniel until the time of the end, the intended meaning of Daniel's visions could not be known until the time of the end arrives. (Daniel 12:4,9) *When it comes to apocalyptic prophecy, there is one fulfillment of prophecy. There is one meaning and there is one time-line.* Apocalyptic events do not occur more than once. Rule One prohibits multiple fulfillments because there is a beginning point in time and an ending point in time for each prophecy and the events within the prophecy occur in the order in which are they given. God's foreknowledge is perfect. A fulfillment is the full-filling of *all* that God has said would come to pass. If *all* of the specifications of a prophecy are not met in an interpretation, the student has two options: (a) ignore the specifications and accept an interpretation that merely sounds good, or (b) reject the interpretation because it does not satisfy all of the specifications. Given these two choices, let us compare some of the supporting arguments for Antiochus IV with Scripture:

1. Gabriel said, **"It** [the horn power] **set itself up to be as great as the Prince of the host** [Jesus Christ]**; it took away the daily sacrifice from him** [Jesus Christ]**, and the place of his sanctuary was brought low."** (Daniel 8:11, insertions mine) History indicates that whatever Antiochus lacked in intelligence, he compensated with insolence and arrogance. No doubt, his ego was so delirious that he believed he was greater than the Prince of the host, Jesus Christ. Remember, Antiochus IV claimed to be an epiphany, but history reveals he was anything but an epiphany. Antiochus IV caused the daily services at the temple in Jerusalem to stop for a period of three years when he desecrated the Altar of Burnt Offering, but Antiochus was neither the first nor the last to defile the temple. Nebuchadnezzar (586 B.C.) and Titus (A.D. 70) did the same thing. Consider the

specifications in the text. Verse 11 requires Antiochus IV
to take the daily services away from Jesus Christ, the
Prince of the host. Did Antiochus take the daily away
from the Jews or from the Prince of the host? The answer
to this question is obvious. Antiochus took the daily away
from "the Jews." The daily ceased in Jerusalem for three
years, but Antiochus did not take away the daily
intercession of our High Priest in Heaven's temple.
(Hebrews 7:25-27) The termination of the daily in Heaven
does not occur until *the appointed time of the end* arrives!
(Daniel 12:11,12; Revelation 8:2-5)

2. Gabriel said, **"The four horns that replaced the one
    that was broken off represent four kingdoms that
    will emerge from his nation but will not have the
    same power. In the latter part of their reign, when
    rebels have become completely wicked, a stern-
    faced king, a master of intrigue, will arise."** (Daniel
    8:22,23) Many advocates of the Antiochus theory say
    these two verses describe Antiochus IV because he rose to
    power during the fading years of the Grecian empire. The
    Bible says, **"In the latter part of *their* reign, when
    rebels have become completely wicked. . ."** People
    defending Antiochus IV claim "the latter part of *their*
    reign" applies to the final days of the four divisions of the
    Grecian empire because Antiochus IV came to power with
    Rome's permission in 175 B.C. and Grecia fell about seven
    years later in 168 B.C. Does the phrase "the latter part of
    their reign" point to the final days of the Grecian empire
    or does it point to the reign of those kings who will be
    ruling at "the appointed time of the end?" Does the stern-
    faced king arise while Grecia is falling or at the end of the
    world? These are pivotal questions that need answers.

In an effort to give Antiochus every advantage to fulfill
this prophecy, let us apply the phrase, "In the latter part
of their reign..." to the last days of Grecia, so that
Antiochus might be able to satisfy this specification. If
we do this, the next phrase, **". . . when rebels have
become completely wicked,"** would have to apply to
the rebels in Jerusalem who, like Jason and the renegade

Jews, wanted to adopt the sensual ways of Antiochus IV and the Greeks.

The next specification reveals: **". . . a stern-faced king, a master of intrigue will arise."** Historians say that Antiochus IV was a hoodlum, basically a leader of bandits, not a stern faced king and a master of intrigue. History says he was a self-indulgent and tempermental nit wit. If he had not inherited the kingdom from his father, historians are confident that he would not have been able to build one. Because Antiochus IV was inept as a king (remember, even the Romans called him a madman), advocates of Antiochus IV claim he was perhaps more stern-faced (as in pouting) than a master of evil manipulation. They claim that Antiochus IV has to be the fulfillment of the horn power of Daniel 8 because he rose to power at the end of the Grecian period and he caused the daily sacrifices in Jerusalem to cease for three years. This claim may sound convincing for people who have not examined Daniel 8, but obviously Antiochus could neither take the daily away from the Prince of the host (Jesus) nor did Antiochus live at the appointed time of the end.

3. Gabriel said, **"He** [the horn power] **will become very strong, but not by his own power. He** [will be empowered by God as a destroyer and he] **will cause astounding devastation and will succeed in whatever he does. He will destroy the mighty men** [who stand in opposition] **and the holy people** [the saints of God]. [Because he is an evil despot and totally lawless] **He will cause deceit to prosper, and he will consider himself superior** [above every god]. **When they** [the wicked] **feel secure** [with him], **he will destroy many** [of his own people] **and take his stand against the Prince of princes** [Jesus Christ]. **Yet he** [this invincible and awesome being] **will be destroyed, but not by human power."** (Daniel 8:24,25, insertions mine) Paul explains how Lucifer will be destroyed, **"And then the lawless one will be revealed, whom the Lord Jesus will overthrow with the breath of his**

mouth and destroy by the splendor of his coming."
(2 Thessalonians 2:8) These verses bring the Antiochus
interpretation to an abrupt halt. Antiochus never became
a strong king. He did not cause astounding devastation
during his nine years on the throne. In fact, Antiochus
had very few successes. We have to put Antiochus within
the confines of historical perspective. At best, he ruled
over a tiny "state" kingdom with Rome's permission. Did
Antiochus cause deceit to prosper throughout the world
more than any other pagan king? Did Antiochus take his
stand against the Prince of princes (the Lord Jesus)
during the appointed time of the end? If so, when did this
battle occur? Who won the battle? Did the Lord Jesus
destroy Antiochus with the brightness of His coming or
did he die in Persia from too much liquor? The Antiochus
interpretation does not come close to meeting *all* of the
specifications given in Daniel 8. If any doubt remains
about Antiochus IV fulfilling the specifications given in
Daniel 8, the next specification should remove it.

4. **"Then I heard a holy one speaking, and another
    holy one said to him, 'How long will it take for the
    vision to be fulfilled – the vision concerning the
    daily sacrifice, the rebellion that causes desolation,
    and the surrender of the sanctuary and of the host
    that will be trampled underfoot?' He said to me, 'It
    will take 2,300 evenings and mornings; then the
    sanctuary will be reconsecrated.' "** (Daniel 8:13,14)
    The 2,300 evenings and mornings of Daniel 8 have proven
    to be an insurmountable mystery for thousands of years,
    and rightly so. Without valid rules of interpretation and
    an understanding of the doctrine of God's use of parallel
    temples, the purpose, the meaning and the timing of the
    2,300 days cannot be accurately determined!   Because
    many Christian scholars believe the horn power of Daniel
    8 is Antiochus IV, consider how they explain the 2,300
    evenings and mornings.

Scofield's Explanation of the 2,300 Days

Cyrus I. Scofield (1843-1921), was a writer whose theological and prophetic views dramatically influenced Protestants during the twentieth century. Dr. Scofield was not the first to suggest that Antiochus IV was the horn power of Daniel 8, but he was arguably the best. To prove that Antiochus IV was the horn power, Dr. Scofield claimed the 2,300 days in Daniel 8:14 began with the desecration of the temple in Jerusalem (Kislev 15, 167 B.C.; 1 Maccabees 1:57) and terminated with the death of General Nicanor on March 27, 160 B.C. According to 1 Maccabees 3, Nicanor was one of the generals that Lysais appointed to destroy the Jews while Antiochus was looking for someone to plunder in Persia. According to 1 Maccabees 4:52-54, the temple was cleansed and services resumed three years and ten days after its desecration. (See also 2 Maccabees 10:1-8.) In other words, the number of days between the defilement of the temple by Antiochus IV and the reconsecration of the temple by Judas Maccabeus was 1,096 days, less than half of the needed 2,300 days. Because Daniel 8:14 specifies 2,300 days, Scofield realized there was a problem, so he began searching for some event that occurred 2,300 days after Antiochus desecrated the temple in Jerusalem. The death of a nondescript general was the only thing that Scofield could find that even came close to 2,300 days. Rather than abandon the Antiochus IV interpretation for a better interpretation of the horn power, Scofield declared the 2,300 days were fulfilled by two events that do not have 2,300 days between them. No doubt Dr. Scofield was a sincere man, but if a person does not use valid rules of interpretation, eventually he will end up in a corner where he has no choice but to twist or distort the Word of God to make the pieces fit. God said there would be 2,300 evenings and mornings – not more, not less – before the sanctuary would be cleansed.

During the last half of the twentieth century, defenders of Scofield's position have been forced to acknowledge that temple services resumed long before the 2,300 days expired. So, they argue with weasel words that temple services were only free of "destructive threat" after General Nicanor died. The problem with this claim is that God says nothing about the temple being free of threat or about the Jews enjoying freedom from destruction in Daniel 8:14. The King James Version of Daniel 8:14 simply states, **"Unto two** thousand three hundred days, *then shall* the sanctuary be cleansed." (or *reconsecrated,* NIV) The following chart shows how Scofield defined the 2,300 days. The dates are taken from 1 Maccabees 1:57; 4:52 and 7:43.

Scofield's Understanding of the 2,300 Days

167 B.C.	166 B.C.	165 B.C.	164 B.C.	163 B.C.	162 B.C.	161 B.C.	160 B.C.	159 B.C.
x			y				z	

Chart 4.3

x = December 6, 167 B.C. Antiochus IV desecrated temple.

y = December 16, 164 B.C. Temple cleansed and services resume.

z = March 27, 160 B.C. General Nicanor killed.

The 2,300 days are calculated as follows:

$$360 + 360 + 360 + 360 + 360 + 360 + 110 = 2{,}270$$

add 30 days per seven years for calendar adjustment   30

Total time   **2,300 days**

Here are five major problems with Scofield's interpretation:

Problem 1: 1 Maccabees 4:52 says the temple in Jerusalem was cleansed and services restored years before General Nicanor was killed. So, Nicanor's death has nothing to do with the cleansing of the temple!

Problem 2: The calendar presented in Chart 4.3 is based on the supposition that the Jews observed a 360-day year. Advocates of this dating scheme calculate the time between December 6, 167, and March 27, 160 B.C., to be 2,270 days. Then they add one month of 30 days for calendar adjustment because a solar year is 365.242 days in length. The total time, according to this formula, adds up to 2,300 days.

This view of the 2,300 days has no merit. First, there is no historical evidence showing the Jews ever *observed* a 360-day year. The Jewish year is either 354 or 384 days in length depending on the cycles of the moon – never 360 days. Even if the Jews did observe a 360-day year, the adjustment of 30 days every seven years does not resolve the problem of solar alignment which is critical for planting crops. In seven years, a proper alignment with the arrival of Spring requires an adjustment of 36.7 days, not 30 days if one is using a 360 day calendar. If the Jews used a 360-day calendar with a 30-day correction every seven years, their calendar would be 27 days out of alignment with the sun in 28 years. No agricultural nation could survive this kind of error in their calendar.

Problem 3: Dr. Scofield knew the time-frame between the desecration of the temple and the death of General Nicanor was not precisely 2,300 days, so he declared God's prophetic time-periods to be "indeterminate" (not very precise). Scofield, commenting on the seventy weeks of Daniel 9:24, wrote these words: "In this connection it should be remembered that, in the grand sweep of prophecy, prophetic time is invariably so near as to give full warning, so indeterminate as to give no satisfaction to mere curiosity." (See the Scofield Reference Bible, commentary on Daniel 9:24.) Does Scofield mean that once we find something "close enough" to fit within a prophetic time-period, we can declare a prophetic mystery solved? How can an omniscient God not know the actual number of days between two events? In Daniel 12, God mentions two specific time periods having 1,290 days and 1,335 days. Revelation 20 speaks of 1,000 years. Revelation 13:5 speaks of 42 months and Revelation 11:9 speaks of 3.5 days. Does God regard these time-periods as indeterminate? Of course not! Scofield "imposed" a bad interpretation onto Daniel 8:14 and then justified a poor fit for the 2,300 days by declaring God's Word to be "indeterminate." If God can number the hairs of our heads, if God can number the stars of the sky, if God created the precise pulses of atomic energy in billionths of a second, surely He can accurately count the span of days between two events.

Problem 4: An issue affecting the 2,300 days in Daniel 8:14 exists which Scofield did not resolve. We know that the "time, times and half a time" in Daniel 7:25 represents 1,260 years. The Bible confirms this point. (See Revelation 12:6,14.) Bible history confirms that God sometimes translates a day for a year so that 1,260 days would represent 1,260 years. This is not unusual. Most scholars agree that the "seventy weeks" in Daniel 9:24 have to be translated as 490 years because of the day/year principle found in the Jubilee Calendar. Because the 2,300 days in Daniel 8 and the seventy weeks in Daniel 9 begin at the same time (this point will be demonstrated in our study on Daniel 9), they share the same translation. In other words, the 2,300 days represent 2,300 years because the seventy weeks represent 490 years. In fact, the seventy weeks of Daniel 9 are "cut off" from the 2,300 days in Daniel 8! The matrix is at work and the timing in Daniel and Revelation fits together like hand and glove. God measures the time-periods in Daniel 7, Daniel 8 and Daniel 9 according to the day/year operation of the Jubilee Calendar. (Leviticus 25) This is why Rule Four states: *"God measures apocalyptic time according to the presence or absence of the Jubilee Calendar."* Scofield should have translated the 2,300 days as 2,300 years.

Problem 5: Scofield claims the bitter persecution of the Jews under Antiochus IV ended with the death of General Nicanor. History says just the opposite. In fact, life for the Jews only became worse after Nicanor was killed. For example, King Demetrius killed Judas Maccabeus (1 Maccabees 9:18) about 2 months after Nicanor died. Then, about a year after the death of Nicanor in May, 159 B.C., "Alcimus ordered the wall of the inner court of the sanctuary to be torn down, thus destroying the work of the prophets." (1 Maccabees 9:54) The book of 1 Maccabees records that many wars were inflicted on Israel after Nicanor's death. Thus, the persecution of the Jews did not cease with the death of General Nicanor. History discredits Scofield's explanation of the 2,300 days.

Given the evidence presented thus far, advocates of Antiochus face insurmountable issues: The temple in Jerusalem was not free from threat after the death of Nicanor. The length of time between the Antiochus' desecration of the temple and Nicanor's death was not 2,300 days. Jewish persecution did not end after Nicanor died. The 2,300 days of Daniel 8:14 cannot begin with the conduct of Antiochus IV and end with the death of General Nicanor. Nicanor's death does not have anything to do with the cleansing of the temple in Jerusalem. When the "interpretation" of Antiochus is closely examined, claims of fulfillment do not even come close to meeting *all* of the specifications given in Daniel 8. Given the specifications in Daniel 8, it is amazing that millions of Christians accept Scofield's position without question.

Section V - Heaven and Earth Linked Together with 2,300 Days

With God Timing Is Everything

God created the orbit of the electrons spinning around the nucleus of the cesium atom. This demonstrates that He is very capable of measuring time. If the cesium atom can be used to create an atomic clock that does not vary by more than one second in a hundred million years, surely God can measure time! I make this point because when it comes to timing and punctuality, no one in the universe is more precise than God! The God who said there would be 2,300 evenings and mornings before the sanctuary would be cleansed is the same God who said seventy weeks would be granted to Israel in Daniel 9. Surely the Lord God knows what He is talking about! Look at His punctuality with Israel at the Exodus: **"At the end of the 430 years, *to the very day,* all the Lord's divisions left Egypt. Because the Lord kept vigil that night to bring them out of Egypt, on this night all the Israelites are to keep vigil to honor the Lord for the generations to come."** (Exodus 12:41,42, italics mine) Consider the timing of the birth of Jesus: **"But when *the time had fully come,* God sent his Son, born of a woman, born under law, to redeem those under law, that we might receive the full rights of sons."** (Galatians 4:4, italics mine) God is never late. God is never wrong. With God, timing is everything!

Look up! The Event Is Not on Earth

The 2,300 days is placed in Daniel 8 for a very good reason, if you are aware of two prerequisites. First, you need to know about the historical matrix which the four rules produce. Second, you have to understand the essential doctrine that explains God's use of parallel temple services. (See Chapters 11 and 12 in *Jesus, The Alpha and The Omega*.) When these two prerequisites are combined, we can

determine *when* Jesus began to cleanse Heaven's temple and *why* it
must be cleansed. God connected the cleansing of Heaven's temple
with the ram (the kingdom of the Medes and Persians). The
connection between the ram and the cleansing of Heaven's temple is
precisely 2,300 years in length. The countdown of 2,300 years began
when the Persian, King Artaxerxes, issued a decree to restore and
rebuild Jerusalem in 457 B.C. (Ezra 7) Because God tied the decree
of Artaxerxes to a yardstick that was 2,300 years in length, we can
easily calculate the date when the cleansing of God's temple began
in Heaven. Even though we cannot see the event taking place in
Heaven, we know it began in 1844. We will also see, when we
examine the seventy weeks of Daniel 9 and the seven seals in
Revelation, that the dates of 1798 and 1844 are highly important
dates in Heaven's sequence of events.

1,150 Days?

Some people have tried to divide the 2,300 evenings and mornings
so that this time-period is 1,150 literal days (1,150 evenings + 1,150
mornings = 2,300 evenings and mornings), but, this timing scheme
does not work for several reasons. First, the Hebrew words *'erab* and
boqer go together to form one unit of time. They literally mean
"evening and morning," as in one day. Notice how *'erab* and *boqer*
are used on the first page of the Bible: **"And God called the light
Day, and the darkness he called Night. And the evening**
['erab] **and the morning** [boqer] **were the first day."** (Genesis 1:5,
KJV) According to God's method for measuring time, a "day" has an
evening and a morning. A day begins at sundown (evening) and the
midway point through the day is sunrise (morning). (Leviticus
23:32) Translators of the King James Version recognized this fact
and they translated the 2,300 evenings and mornings of Daniel 8:14
as 2,300 *days*. New International Version translators were more
literal with the text, translating it as "2,300 evenings and
mornings."

Unfortunately, most Christians do not understand the doctrine of
God's use of parallel temples. If a person does not understand the
cleansing of Earth's temple, he cannot understand the cleansing of
Heaven's temple. If a person does not understand God's purpose in
cleansing Heaven's temple, then the timing of this event is of no

value. If God's use of parallel temples was better understood, Christians could understand that the temple to be cleansed is not on Earth, but in Heaven! Bible students tend to interpret Bible prophecy as though Earth was the center of prophecy, but this is not the case. Daniel was directed to view a great convocation in Heaven. He saw a service when the Ancient of Days took His seat and billions of angels were in attendance. This heavenly meeting is profoundly important because it marks the beginning of services in Heaven's temple that lead up to the end of the world. The services in Heaven's temple *are directly linked* to the final events that occur on Earth. Remember the Heaven-Earth-Linkage-Law?

Five clues in the Bible indicate the temple to be cleansed in Daniel 8:14 is in Heaven:

First, the doctrine of parallel temples teaches there were two temples. The one on Earth was a shadow of the real temple in Heaven where our Jesus serves as our High Priest. (Hebrews 8:1-5) We know the earthly temple was destroyed by the Romans in A.D. 70. The only temple remaining is in Heaven.

Second, the cleansing of the earthly temple occurred at an appointed time every year – on the Day of Atonement (Leviticus 16), but the heavenly temple is cleansed only once – at the appointed time of the end! (Hebrews 9:24-26)

Third, the 2,300 evenings and mornings must be translated as 2,300 years because God uses the Jubilee Calendar to translate a day into a year. (This point and the Jubilee Calendar will be discussed at length when we examine the seventy weeks of Daniel 9.) The 2,300 years began in the Spring of 457 B.C. and they ended in the Spring of 1844.

Fourth, the cleansing of Heaven's temple began in 1844. This date aligns with 1798 which marks the year the great convocation in Heaven's temple began. (See Chart 4.4.) In fact, the timing of the great convocation in Daniel 7 (1798) and the cleansing of the sanctuary in Daniel 8 (1844), aligns with the seventy weeks in Daniel 9 (457 B.C.), and these three events align with the opening of the third seal in Revelation 6. The matrix is building!

The 2,300 Days of Daniel 8:14

		<--457 B.C. ---------------2300 Day/Years----------------1844 -->					The Time of the End
Daniel 8	Ram with Two Horns Artaxerxes Issues Decree in 457 B.C.	Goat with One Great Horn -- then Four Horns				Temple Cleansing Begins in Heaven	Judgment of the Living	Horn Power from the North Stern Faced King
Daniel 7	Medo Persia Bear with Three Ribs	Grecia Leopard with Four Heads	Rome Monster	10 Horns at First	1,260 Day/Years A.D. 538 to 1798	Books Opened Guilt Assigned to Guilt Bearer	Little Horn Recovers and is Heard Boasting	Beasts are Destroyed in the Fire at the End
					Little Horn Rises, Uproots 3 Horns	Court Seated in Heaven Little Horn Falls on Earth			

Chart 4.4

Fifth, the remarks that follow do not begin to cover the scope and breadth of the subject of parallel temples (Hebrews 8:1-5), but a few words may be necessary about the annual service of cleansing the earthly temple, so you can understand the marvelous parallel that exists between the earthly temple and the heavenly temple. Again, the doctrine of parallel temples is a prerequisite doctrine for understanding Daniel 8.

The angel said, ". . .**Unto two thousand three hundred days, then shall the sanctuary be cleansed.**" (Daniel 8:14, KJV) Why does the sanctuary in Heaven need cleansing? The answer to this question is found in the cleansing of the earthly temple. The cleansing of the earthly temple was an annual event that occurred on the tenth day of the seventh month. This day was called the Day of Atonement. Jews today call it Yom Kippur, which means Day of Judgment. The cleansing of the earthly temple was necessary because it was defiled by sinners bringing sin offerings to the temple. The sinner, standing at the Altar of Burnt Offering, confessed his sins over the head of his sacrifice. Then, he cut the jugular vein of the sacrificial animal with his own hands. The priest then captured some of the lamb's blood and sprinkled this blood on the horns of the altar. This procedure shadows a divine truth. The sinner's guilt *was transferred* away from himself and his family to the Altar of Burnt Offering by the blood of the Lamb.

This earthly process was a shadow or pantomime of a reality that was coming. The guilt of sinners could be transferred to Heaven's temple through the death of Jesus (the Lamb of God). When the blood was applied to the horns of the altar, the altar became defiled because the guilt of the sinner had been transferred to it. *The process of setting sinners free of the guilt of sin defiles the temple because the sinner's guilt is transferred to the altar.* Because the altars of the temple were depositories of guilt, the earthly temple was defiled until the Day for Cleansing (the Day of Atonement) arrived. For a single day, the earthly temple was restored to an undefiled state. (Leviticus 16) Then, on the following day, sacrifices resumed and the temple was defiled because the annual cycle started over.

How Jesus Cleanses the Temple in Heaven

Unlike the earthly temple, which was cleansed annually, Heaven's temple is cleansed once, at the end of the age. (Hebrews 9:24-26) This cleansing began in 1844, which is 2,300 years after the decree to restore and rebuild Jerusalem given by Artaxerxes in 457 B.C. (457 B.C. also marks the beginning of the seventy weeks in Daniel 9.) The Day of Atonement service in the earthly temple was a shadow of the plan of salvation. Notice what the shadow reveals:

Two animals, a bull and a goat, were sacrificed in this service. (Leviticus 16) The service began right after day break with the slaying of a bull that belonged to the high priest. This bull (a very expensive sacrifice) represents the sacrifice which the Father made in order to redeem mankind. **"For God so loved the world that He gave His only begotten Son . . ."** (John 3:16, KJV) The Father gave up the most valuable asset He could provide so fallen man could have the offer of salvation. After the bull was slain, the high priest carried some of the bull's blood behind the veil into the Most Holy Place where he met with God. The high priest had to be found worthy to cleanse the temple before he could conduct the service. The slaying of the bull and the worthiness of the high priest shadows the sacrifice which the Father made and the qualifying process which Jesus our High Priest underwent before He could conclude the sin problem. (See Revelation 4 and 5.)

The next event on the Day of Atonement was the casting of lots to determine which goat should die. After the lots were cast, the Lord's goat was slain. The Lord's goat represents the death which Jesus was willing to experience in order to save man. A goat was used for this sacrifice because a goat has a free spirit. Jesus freely gave up His life for sinners. After the Lord's goat was slain, its blood was mixed with the bull's blood. Then, the high priest went behind the veil a second time to begin the cleansing of the temple. The first item to be cleansed was the Ark of the Covenant. The second item was the Altar of Incense and the last item to be cleansed was the Altar of Burnt Offering. These items were cleansed in this order and they became free of sin (cleansed, reconsecrated, restored) when the mixed blood of the bull and goat was sprinkled on them.

The last event in this service was the laying of hands on the head of the scapegoat. The scapegoat represents Lucifer, the author of sin, who freely exercised his power of choice to commit sin. After the temple furniture had been made holy with the sprinkling of blood, the high priest placed his hands on the head of the scapegoat. Through the placement of hands on the scapegoat, the sins of the people (which had been stored on the temple's altars) were *transferred* onto the head of the scapegoat. Then, the scapegoat was led out into the wilderness to slowly starve to death.

This may come as a shock, but in God's economy, sin is never forgiven because someone other than God is responsible for sin. The beauty of salvation is that sinners can escape the penalty of sin through faith. If a sinner makes restitution for his sin and confesses his sin to God, he transfers his guilt to Heaven's temple. At the end of the 1,000 years in Revelation 20, Lucifer, the scapegoat, will receive all of the guilt transferred into Heaven's temple because he is responsible for the presence of sin. On the other hand, if a sinner does not transfer his sin to the temple, his sins remain upon his own head and in God's economy, the wages of sin is eternal death. (Romans 6:23) At the end of the 1,000 years, God will execute justice on the scapegoat and the wicked and they will suffer in proportion to their guilt until they are annihilated. This is the meaning of divine justice.

The Temple to be Cleansed Is in Heaven

The cleansing of the earthly temple shadows a process that began in Heaven in 1844. It is interesting to notice that 1844 is exactly forty-six years after 1798. When Jesus began His ministry on Earth, His first action after returning from fasting in the desert was the cleansing of a temple that took forty-six years to restore! (John 2:13-21) The parallel is that Jesus began cleansing the heavenly temple forty-six years after the twenty-five thrones had been arranged and the convocation in Heaven began!

Before the cleansing of Heaven's temple could begin, someone had to be found worthy to conduct the process. Jesus was found worthy to cleanse Heaven's temple. After Jesus was found worthy, both Daniel (Daniel 7:13,14) and John (Revelation 4 and 5) saw Jesus highly exalted. Daniel 7 and Revelation 4 and 5 describe the same scene from slightly different angles. After Jesus was found worthy to cleanse Heaven's temple, He began passing judgment on the records of the dead. Since the Spring of 1844, Jesus has been going through the books of record – one sinner at a time. Standing before the hosts of Heaven, Jesus has been deciding who will be a part of His eternal kingdom and who will not. When Jesus determines a person will be saved, Jesus removes the record of sin from Heaven's book and He transfers the guilt of the sinner to the head of Lucifer. When Jesus determines a person cannot be saved, Jesus places the guilt of that sinner on the sinner's head. The point is that the temple in Heaven is cleansed as the guilt of sin is *removed* and placed on the appropriate party. (Leviticus 20; Ezekiel 11:21; 22:31; 18:1-24)

When the time comes for the destruction of sinners at the end of the 1,000 years, every wicked person will suffer the appropriate penalty for his sins. God will see that every condemned sinner gets their due reward: **"For we know him who said, 'It is mine to avenge; I will repay,' and again, 'The Lord will judge his people.' It is a dreadful thing to fall into the hands of the living God."** (Hebrews 10:30,31)

Jesus will complete the task of judging mankind during the Great Tribulation. People living during the Great Tribulation will not be judged in the same way as those who have died. The faith of people living at that time will be tested with persecution. In this way, they will choose and determine their eternal destiny. At the sounding of the seventh trumpet (Revelation 11:15-19) the cleansing of Heaven's temple will be finished and the temple will at last, be free of sin. (Revelation 15:1-8) The book of Revelation reveals much more about this process, but this synopsis is intended to give you a general overview of the judgment process. Consider these comments by Bible writers:

"Now all has been heard; here is the conclusion of the matter: Fear God and keep his commandments, for this is the whole duty of man. For *God will bring every deed into judgment*, including every hidden thing, whether it is good or evil." (Ecclesiastes 12:13,14, italics mine)

"Moreover, the Father judges no one, but has *entrusted all judgment to the Son*, that all may honor the Son just as they honor the Father. He who does not honor the Son does not honor the Father, who sent him." (John 5:22,23, italics mine)

"For we must all appear before *the judgment seat of Christ*, that each one may receive what is due him for the things done while in the body, whether good or bad." (2 Corinthains 5:10)

"For he [the Father] *has set a day* when he will judge the world with justice by the man he has appointed. He has given proof of this to all men by raising him from the dead." (Acts 17:31, insertion and italics mine)

"As Paul discoursed on righteousness, self-control *and the judgment to come*, Felix was afraid and said, 'That's enough for now! You may leave. When I find it convenient, I will send for you.'" (Acts 24:25, italics mine)

"Behold, I am coming soon! My reward is with me, and I will give to everyone according to what he has done." (Revelation 22:12)

Remember that the 2,300 days in Daniel 8:14 have been a great mystery for most Bible students. The reason for the mystery is quite simple. *The event to which this prophecy points is not on Earth, but in Heaven.* God uses the Heaven-Earth-Linkage-Law again to inform us of the timing of something we cannot see. God put the kingdoms of Medo-Persia and Grecia in Daniel 8 because the

2,300 days began during the time of Medo-Persia. Then, God linked the decree of a Persian king (Artaxerxes, Ezra 7) with the cleansing of Heaven's temple in 1844 by inserting a 2,300 year time-period in the prophecy of Daniel 8. (Review Chart 4.4 and notice how Daniel 7 and Daniel 8 align.)

A starting date for the 2,300 years is not mentioned in Daniel 8 because the starting date is given in Daniel 9. To make matters more mysterious, the cleansing of the temple is in Heaven and not on Earth! No wonder this time-period has been a great mystery for nearly twenty-six centuries! Fortunately, God has revealed the architecture of Daniel and we can determine when the 2,300 evenings and mornings began. We will find in our study on Daniel 9 that the seventy weeks and 2,300 days start together and we will find that Daniel 7, Daniel 8, Daniel 9 and Revelation 4 and 5 perfectly align. I hope you will be patient enough to allow the prophetic matrix to build. My frustration, as the author of this book, is in trying to explain why each piece of prophecy belongs in a certain place (according to the rules) before all the pieces that belong to the story have been identified! Therefore, all I can ask at the present is that you allow the matrix to place each new piece in its place.

Section VI - The Horn Power in Daniel 8 Cannot be the Papacy

The Time of Wrath

The Reformation Christians believed the horn power of Daniel 8 represented the papacy and some Christians today believe the same thing. Let us briefly examine this view. Gabriel told Daniel, "**. . . I am going to tell you what will happen later in the time of wrath, because the vision concerns the appointed time of the end.**" (Daniel 8:19) Since the ram and goat represent ancient empires, this leaves the horn power as the only element in this vision that can appear at "the appointed time of the end." This vision includes a prophetic span of 2,300 evenings and mornings, so the appointed time of the end has to occur *after* 1844! In other words, the horn power described in Daniel 8 *does not* appear prior to 1844. This simple fact eliminates the Roman Catholic Church as a possible candidate for the horn power of Daniel 8 because the Roman Catholic Church achieved absolute power in A.D. 538. The little horn of Daniel 7 and the horn power of Daniel 8 cannot be the same entity for the following reasons:

1. The little horn of Daniel 7 rises out of the Roman empire. The horn power of Daniel 8 does not derive its strength from Rome or any nation. The horn power in Daniel 8 is a power unto itself. It appears out of one of the four winds, specifically, the north.

2. The little horn of Daniel 7 arises in A.D. 538 after the ten horns have broken the Roman empire. The horn power of Daniel 8 has to appear *after* 1844 because it appears during the appointed time of the end.

3. The little horn of Daniel 7 represents a diverse or different type of kingdom (Daniel 7:8) that wars against the saints for a very long time (1,260 years). The little horn in Daniel 7 was unlike the remaining seven horns in that it had eyes and a mouth. The horn power of Daniel 8 represents a man, a stern-faced king who will take "the daily" away from Jesus during the appointed time of the end. As we will see, taking the daily away from Jesus is something that no ordinary mortal can do, not even a pope!

4. Daniel 7 predicts the papacy will recover from its wound and speak boastfully against the Most High. Revelation 13:1-5 confirms the deadly wound will be healed at the time of the end, but Daniel 8 reveals that the Antichrist will destroy the authority of the papacy by casting all religions to the ground and trampling on them. The Antichrist **"will exalt himself over everything that is called God"** by means of the miracles he has power to do. (2 Thessalonians 2:4; Revelation 13:14) The Antichrist will abolish all religious systems, including the papacy, to establish his global religion. The stern-faced king in Daniel 8 will lead the world to war against the King of kings, and the prince of darkness will take his stand

against the Prince of Heaven's hosts (Jesus, King of kings) at the Second Coming.

5. The horn power in Daniel 8 cannot be destroyed by human power. This feature stands in contrast to the fact that the little horn in Daniel 7 is subject to mortality. The papacy was almost destroyed by the sword (war) in 1798.

6. Daniel 11:36-12:3 contributes several important points to the apocalyptic matrix. Even though we have not studied Daniel 10-12, this prophecy amplifies the works and activities of the horn power in Daniel 8. The king of the north in Daniel 11:36 and the stern-faced king that comes out of the north in Daniel 8 are the *same* entity. The papacy cannot meet *all* of the specifications that go with the horn power of Daniel 8. A study of Revelation 9 and Revelation 13:11-18, will show the Antichrist, the physical appearing of Lucifer with millions of his angels, to be the only solution that satisfies all of the specifications for this power in the books of Daniel and Revelation.

Section VII - The Termination of the Daily

The Antichrist Will Take the Daily Away from Jesus

The wording of Daniel 8:13 is difficult to understand at first: **"Then I heard a holy one** [angel] **speaking, and another holy one** [angel] **said to him, 'How long will it take for the vision to be fulfilled – the vision concerning the** [cessation of the] **daily sacrifice, the** [vision concerning a great] **rebellion that causes desolation, and the surrender of the sanctuary and of the host** [of saints] **that will be trampled underfoot?' "** (Insertions mine) To help you understand this question better, here is a paraphrase of Daniel 8:13: "Daniel heard one angel speak to another angel. The first angel said, 'How long will it take for this vision of the ram, the goat, and the horn power to be fulfilled?" When the question is phrased this way, the answer that follows makes sense. Daniel writes, **"And I heard a man's voice from** the Ulai [canal] **calling, 'Gabriel, tell this man the meaning of the vision.' As he came near the place where I was standing, I was terrified and fell prostrate. 'Son of man,' he said to me, 'understand that the vision concerns** *the time of the end.'* " (Daniel 8:16,17, insertion and italics mine) It is clear that the question in verse 13 is finally answered in verses 16 and 17. You may wonder why the actual question in verse 13 is worded in such a complex way. God is both deliberate and purposeful in everything He does. With one question and one answer God informs us that the appointed time of the end involves four great issues:

1. The termination of the daily

2. A rebellion that causes desolation

3. The surrender of Heaven's sanctuary

4. God's people will be trampled underfoot

We have examined Daniel 8:11 within the context of Antiochus IV. Let us examine it again, this time within the context of the Antichrist and the appointed time of the end. This approach will yield a much better fulfillment of Scripture. Gabriel said, **"It** [the horn power will] **set itself up to be as great as the Prince of the host** [Jesus]**; it took away the daily sacrifice from him** [Jesus]**, and the place of his** [Jesus'] **sanctuary was brought low."** (Daniel 8:11, insertions mine) The word "daily" is a term that describes the daily cycle of services that occurred in the earthly temple. Every day, evening and morning, a lamb was slain on the Altar of Burnt Offering and its blood was sprinkled on the Altar of Incense. Every day, sinners presented their sacrifices at the Altar of Burnt Offering. These rituals, and many other services became known as the "daily" or the "continual." They shadowed the intercession that Jesus began making on behalf of humanity *the day sin occurred* as well as His death on Calvary. The immediate intercession of Jesus spared Adam and Eve from sudden death the day they sinned. (Genesis 2:17) The Father allowed Adam and Eve (and their offspring) to live because of Christ's intercession on their behalf. (Genesis 2:17; Hebrews 7:25) Gabriel indicates the coming Antichrist will take away Jesus' daily intercession in Heaven's temple. Christ's intercession for man is terminated in one of four ways. Notice how two ways concern the individual and two ways concern corporate bodies of people:

1. When a person dies, life terminates. The dead know nothing. There is no need for further intercession. (Ecclesiastes 9:5,6)

2. If a person commits the unpardonable sin, intercession for that person ends because there is nothing more that God can do to bring a person to repentance. There is no forgiveness for the unpardonable sin. (Hebrews 10:26, Matthew 12:31,32)

3. When a decadent nation exhausts the limits of God's patience, corporate intercession ends and that nation is destroyed. (Genesis 15:16; Leviticus 4:13,14; 18:24-28; Jeremiah 25)

4. When God's patience with the decadence of the world reaches its limit, He sends destruction. (Genesis 6; Matthew 24:37)

Corporate and Personal Intercession Ends

You may wonder how the Antichrist can take away the daily intercession from Jesus during the appointed time of the end. The termination of the daily happens *twice* because daily services in Heaven's temple involves atonement at two altars. The corporate altar is called the Altar of Incense and its services will be concluded first. (Daniel 12:11; Revelation 8:2-5) The individual altar is called the Altar of Burnt Offering and its services will be terminated at the seventh trumpet. (Daniel 8:11-13; Revelation 11:15-19). The corporate daily ends when the *majority* of the world stands in rebellion against the authority of God. As it was in the days of Noah; God's patience will come to an end. We know His patience can come to an end *with a city of people* (e.g., Sodom and Gomorrah) *or with the whole world* as it did in Noah's day. When this happens, He sends a series of judgments to destroy those who have exhausted His grace. (Genesis 6; Revelation 7:1-4 and 8:2-13) On the individual level, the termination of the daily is similar: When the devil leads a person to finally commit the unpardonable sin (persistently rejecting the demands of the Holy Spirit) God's patience with that person comes to an end and God turns that person over to be subject to the devil. (Matthew 12:31,32; Hebrews 10:26) When a person, a nation, or the whole world refuses to surrender to the clearest evidences of God's will, Jesus will no longer offer intercession for them. Why should He? For this reason, Jesus' corporate intercession for Babylon, Medo-Persia, Grecia, and Rome ended and the kingdoms fell. (See Daniel 5.)

We see a parallel on the individual level as well. During the Great Tribulation, God will empower His servants, the 144,000, to proclaim the terms and conditions of salvation to every nation, kindred, tongue and people. The Antichrist will lead the wicked of Earth into committing the unpardonable sin. He will lead them to rebel against the authority of God and despise the generous offer of salvation from Jesus. (2 Thessalonians 2:11,12; Romans 1:18-32; Hebrews 10:29) Thus, the daily intercession of Jesus on behalf of the world and individuals will be taken away.

Some people will not voluntarily go along with the devil's schemes. God knows this and He empowers the Antichrist to bring an end to Christ's intercession by forcing people to make a hard choice. There will be no middle ground. The devil will require worship (obedience) and all who refuse to submit to his assumed authority are to be killed. (Revelation 13:15) The "salvation" which the Antichrist offers will be the temporal privilege of obtaining the necessities of life during the final days of the Great Tribulation. In other words, if a person chooses to join forces with the devil and receive the mark of the beast, that person will be able to buy and sell so that he can survive. If a person refuses the mark of the beast, that person will be shut off from all earthly means of survival to starve or be killed. When every decision for or against salvation has been made, the Jesus' intercession for that person ends.

Gabriel also said, "**. . . and the place of his** [Jesus'] **sanctuary was brought low.**" The exalted ministry of man's Savior in Heaven's temple will become a matter of mockery (brought low through contempt). During the Great Tribulation, a majority of people will be convinced the devil is God! (2 Thessalonians 2) In other words, the unseen ministry and temple of Jesus in Heaven will not be able to compete with the dazzling show of miracles which the Antichrist conducts. However, the heavenly temple will be physically displayed to everyone living on Earth after the daily has ended. (Revelation 11:19)

Rebellion Will Overtake the World

Consider this next verse: **"Because of rebellion, the host of the saints and the daily sacrifice were given over to it** [the Antichrist]. **It prospered in everything it did, and truth was thrown to the ground."** (Daniel 8:12, insertion) This verse aligns with many details in Revelation. The following is a short scenario of this verse:

When the Great Tribulation begins, the Holy Spirit will be poured out on all nations and people. The purpose of the Spirit's influence is to pry open every heart to receive the gospel message that God's servants, the 144,000, will present. Jesus will send the Holy Spirit for one purpose, to save as many people as possible. Sadly, billions of people will refuse to submit to the demands of the Holy Spirit, and they will choose rebellion (lawlessness) against God. When the advance of the gospel stalls, God allows "the stern-face king," the destroyer, to physically appear. The mission of the Antichrist is to deceive and destroy. As the devil's popularity grows (it starts out small), the wicked people of Earth will be divided into two camps. One camp will be the "religious wicked" and the other camp will consist of wicked people who want nothing to do with the devil. They just want him to go away and leave them alone. The "religious wicked" will be people like the Pharisees in Christ's day who stubbornly hang on to false religion. These people would rather believe that Lucifer is God than to submit to the authority of Jesus Christ. These people appear to be religious, but they do not love truth. They do not even love God. These are people who chase miraculous signs instead of searching for truth. The other camp, the "non-religious wicked," consists of people like Hitler and Stalin who have no use for God and they detest Lucifer's heavy handed ways. They will not accept the authority and dominion of the Antichrist. The "non-religious wicked" are represented in Daniel 11:36-12:3 as the kingdom of the South. In other words, the kingdom of the South is poles apart from the kingdom of the North. The Antichrist will use their rebellion against his authority to justify their destruction. Of course, the devil will destroy many saints for the same reason. The war described in the sixth trumpet (Revelation 9) is conducted to establish Lucifer's undisputed dominion over Earth. (Revelation 9:13-21) Revelation says the devil and his angels will kill one-third of mankind (the non-religious wicked). When he has gained control of Earth, the devil will divide up the spoils of Earth and he will appoint ten kings to rule over ten sectors. His puppet kings will control Earth. The surviving saints will run for their lives and hide in the desolate places of Earth. God will feed and sustain them just as He did Elijah. (1 Kings 17:6) With this setting in mind, consider Daniel's words again. I have inserted phrases that complete the ideas already presented: "[At the time of the end] **It** [the horn power, the Antichrist will] **set itself up to be as great as the Prince of the host** [Jesus]**; it took away the** [need for the] **daily sacrifice from him, and the** [exalted purpose or] **place of his** [intercession for sinners in Heaven's] **sanctuary was brought low** [ridiculed]. **Because of** [extensive] **rebellion, the host of the saints** [*were defeated] **and the daily sacrifice were given over to it** [brought to an end]**. It** [the Antichrist] **prospered in everything it did, and truth was thrown to the ground** [because truth was despised]**."** (Daniel 8:11,12, insertions mine.)

Arrogance and Blasphemy

"**He** [the Antichrist] **will cause deceit to prosper, and he will consider himself superior** [above the gods of all religions]**. When they** [his followers] **feel secure** [in his lies]**, he will destroy many** [the non-religious-wicked] **and take his stand against the Prince of princes** [Jesus]**. Yet he will be destroyed** [by the sword that comes out of the mouth of Jesus]**, but not by human power."** (Daniel 8:25, insertions mine) The following specification about the horn power cannot be overlooked: "**The king** [of the North] **will do as he pleases. He will exalt and magnify himself above every god and will say unheard-of things against the God of gods. He will be successful until** *the time of wrath* **is completed, for what has been** [pre-]**determined must take place. . . . He** [the Antichrist] **will pitch his royal tents between the seas at the beautiful holy mountain. Yet he will come to his end, and no one will help him."** (Daniel 11:36,45)

Four elements stand out in these verses.

1. Jesus Himself destroys the horn power in Daniel 8. (Daniel 8:25; 2 Thessalonians 2:8)

---

*   See Revelation 13:7.

2. The horn power of Daniel 8 will lead the whole
    world into a great deception. (Daniel 8:25;
    Revelation 13:14)

3. The horn power of Daniel 8 will exalt himself
    above all of the gods that people worship. (Daniel
    8:25, 11:36; 2 Thessalonians 2:4)

4. The Antichrist will pitch his royal tents "between
    the seas at the beautiful holy mountain."

Daniel indicates the devil will establish a throne in Jerusalem.
What better way to stop the controversies between Christians,
Arabs and Jews? The term "holy mountain" is used several times in
the Old Testament as a reference to Jerusalem (the city of God,
Mount Zion, Mount Moriah, etc.). It is well known that Jews,
Muslims and Christians have roots in this ancient city. Perhaps the
best reason for interpreting this specification just as it reads is that
at the end, two kings will take their stand against each other. The
stern-faced king of Daniel 8 establishes his kingdom and rules from
ancient Jerusalem. The King of kings, however, will rule from His
city, New Jerusalem. This is good news! The stern-faced king will
come to his end and no one among the wicked will be left to help
him!

Gabriel's Final Words

**"The vision of the evenings and mornings that has been
given you is true, but seal up the vision, for it concerns the
distant future."** (Daniel 8:26) With these words, Gabriel left
Daniel. It is interesting that Gabriel gave this vision a title. While
the prophetic sequence concerns a ram, a goat, the appointed time of
the end and a stern-faced king, Gabriel called it "The vision of the
[2,300] evenings and mornings." Evidently, Gabriel used this title to
highlight the critical element within this vision. The most
important element in Daniel 8 is the daily services in Heaven's
temple. The daily intercession of Jesus is the *only* thing that
protects mankind from God's wrath and the wrath of the destroyer!
Even the words, 2,300 evenings and mornings reflects the time of
day when *daily* temple services were conducted. The date for
cleansing Heaven's temple was given in temple language! The
bottom line in Daniel 8 is that a time is coming when the stern-faced

king (the Antichrist) will cause Jesus' daily intercession to cease. This is the worst possible thing that can happen to Earth's inhabitants, because when Jesus terminates His intercession on behalf of sinners, the seven bowls of God's wrath will be poured out without mercy. (Revelation 15 and 16)

Daniel was deeply distressed and very disturbed after seeing this vision. He did not understand what he had seen, but he did recognize enough to know the world would continue to spiral downward until Lucifer himself would be released upon humanity. The thought of this must have made him sick. Daniel writes, " **I, Daniel, was exhausted and lay ill for several days. Then I got up and went about the king's business. I was appalled by the vision; it was beyond understanding.**" (Daniel 8:27)

Conclusion

This chapter has been lengthy because Daniel 8 contains several critical building blocks in the matrix that is unfolding. If you still have questions, please review this chapter to make sure you understand how the apocalyptic rules work and the results they produce. If the apocalyptic foundations in Daniel 2, Daniel 7 and Daniel 8 are not laid properly, the remaining prophecies in Daniel and Revelation cannot yield their intended meaning. If the foundation of a skyscraper is not solid, no amount of paint or ornamentation will compensate for it. We have seen all four rules at work in this chapter. The four rules have produced these conclusions for us:

Rule One. Daniel 8 is a prophecy that has a beginning point in time (538 B.C.) and an ending point in time (the destruction of the Antichrist at the Second Coming). The events in this prophecy occur in the order they were given: Ram – Goat – Horn Power.

Rule Two. The appearing of the Antichrist during the appointed time of the end is the *only* interpretation that meets *all* of the specifications given in this prophecy.

Rule Three. The Bible uses various types of language in this prophecy. For example, by reviewing seven Bible texts we found the direction of "north" to be very significant for the origin of the horn power. We also found "the starry hosts" to be used in five texts as a broad definition for false religions.

Rule Four. God measures the 2,300 days as years because God measures time according to the presence or absence of the Jubilee Calendar. This point will be amplified in our study of Daniel 9.

Note: The Origin of the Antiochus IV Interpretation

From the 1500's to the 1900's, Protestants widely agreed the horn power of Daniel 8 was the papacy because Protestantism struggled against the Roman Catholic Church in much the same way that Christians struggled against Judaism. If history teaches anything, it is this: Religious institutions place loyalty and allegiance above the importance of truth. The reason behind this is simple. Over time, religious organizations embrace a collection of doctrines or teachings which they believe to be God's will and any significant deviation from that body of knowledge is considered divisive and/or heretical.

During the 1,260 years of papal dominion, "the protesters" as they were first called, suffered imprisonment or death for challenging the authority of the church. Protesters claimed the Bible was the final authority in matters of faith. Church leaders were convinced that ecclesiastical authority and traditions were higher authority. This simple difference became the all important distinction between Protestants and Catholics. As Protestants began to see that the church was unwilling to change, a number of "protester" preachers began to conclude that the church was anti-Christ. The Protestant position was bolstered by the prophetic fact that the little horn of Daniel 7 *is* the papacy. Protesters traced the history and power of the church (the little horn) back to its Roman origin. Because there is some similarity between the little horn of Daniel 7 and the horn power of Daniel 8, Protestants *assumed* that Daniel 8 was a repetition and enlargement of Daniel 7.

About the turn of the seventeenth century, two Jesuit scholars from Spain, Francisco Ribera and Luis de Alcasar, introduced counter-reformation theories to refute the claims of Protestants. Their objective was to use the Bible to defeat Protestants by openly refuting their prophetic interpretations with Scripture! As a result of their endeavors, two conflicting prophetic schemes emerged within the Catholic Church. Ribera's findings, published in 1590, claimed that the Antichrist was a single male individual who would appear just before the Second Coming of Jesus. By showing the Antichrist to be a single individual, Ribera thought he could defeat a principal argument of the Protestants. Most sixteenth century Protestants believed the popes occupied *the seat* of the Antichrist. In other words, Protestants did not believe the Antichrist was a single individual (the little horn of Daniel 7 is not a single individual). Ribera claimed that the Antichrist would bitterly persecute the saints during the last days of Earth, and he would abolish the Christian religion and rebuild the temple in Jerusalem. Ribera also claimed that the Jews would receive the Antichrist as Messiah because of his miracles and then he would conquer the world in three and one half years.

Alcasar's preterist position, published in 1614 was just the opposite. Alcasar's position was based on the supposition that Revelation's story was essentially fulfilled during the first century A.D. Alcasar concluded that Revelation described the victory of early Christians over the Jewish nation and the overthrow of pagan Rome in A.D. 476. He concluded that Nero was the Antichrist of Revelation. He also concluded that Antiochus Epiphanes IV was the horn power of Daniel 8.

When these opposing views were presented to the Protestants, they were not moved or impressed. For about two hundred years, Protestants stood firm and united on their prophetic position that the Roman Catholic Church was the Babylon of Revelation and the Antichrist was a succession of popes. In the early part of the nineteenth century, Protestantism began to change its mind because it became apparent to some Protestants that the Roman Catholic Church could not meet all of the specifications about the Antichrist in Daniel and Revelation. A survey of prophetic literature written by Protestants since 1826 shows how Protestant expositors began to drift away from their long standing claim that the Roman Catholic Church was the Antichrist. Today, most Protestant expositors do not believe the Roman Catholic Church is Babylon and they do not believe the succession of popes is the Antichrist. It is ironic that three hundred years after Ribera published his works, the Protestant, C.I. Scofield, endorsed a modified version of Ribera's counter-reformation claim and, as a result, most Protestants today accept the ideas advanced by Ribera.

Chapter 5

Daniel 6 – The Question of Loyalty

"I issue a decree that in every part of my kingdom people must fear and reverence the God of Daniel. 'For he is the living God and he endures forever; his kingdom will not be destroyed, his dominion will never end. He rescues and he saves; he performs signs and wonders in the heavens and on the earth. He has rescued Daniel from the power of the lions.'"

– Daniel 6:26,27

Someone once said that loyalty is like the juice of an orange – the flavor cannot be determined until the orange is squeezed beyond the breaking point. The Bible testifies to the truthfulness of this statement. Loyalty is one of the most powerful forces within the human heart. Loyalty can produce good results, and misplaced loyalty can produce evil results. For example: Judas Iscariot was loyal to his dreams of self-importance, power and wealth. When he realized that following Jesus would not fulfill *his* dreams, he betrayed Jesus for the equivalent of $12.60 (thirty pieces of silver). King David was loyal to *his* passions for Bathsheba. To cover up their illicit affair and the resulting pregnancy, the king killed her husband. David's crime was especially heinous because Bathsheba's husband, Uriah, was one of the thirty-seven gallant men who defended David during his days of hiding from King Saul. Peter swore loyalty to Jesus in the garden, but when he learned that he might have to share a martyr's death with Jesus, he denied that he knew The Master. The Philippian jailer was loyal to his job until an earthquake destroyed his jail. When he realized his life was in jeopardy, he suddenly experienced a change of heart. Saul was loyal to his religion. He faithfully persecuted Christians until Jesus confronted him on the road to Damascus. Afterwards, Paul maintained unwavering loyalty to Jesus and he suffered persecution from Jews and Romans alike for preaching salvation through Jesus

Christ. Legend says that Nero sentenced Paul to death because Paul refused to renounce his loyalty to Jesus and worship Caesar. Shadrach, Meshach and Abednego chose to be loyal to the God of Heaven rather than worship the golden image, and King Nebuchadnezzar threw them into a fiery furnace. John the Baptist was loyal to God's righteousness when he told King Herod that living with his brother's wife was a sin. John's remarks cost him his life. Jonathan was loyal to David instead of his father, King Saul. Jonathan was almost killed because of his loyalty to David. Jeremiah was loyal to the Lord when he told Israel all that the Lord had said about their apostasy. The Jews threw Jeremiah into a cistern to die. Job's loyalty to God was tested with some of the harshest suffering ever recorded, but Job was more blessed in the end than at the beginning. Noah was loyal to God's command and he suffered an incredible amount of ridicule, but his loyalty and faith saved his family. Ruth was loyal to Naomi and chose to suffer poverty with her, but Ruth's loyalty to Naomi made her an ancestor of Jesus. Because she feared God, Rahab, the prostitute, was loyal to the spies that entered Jericho and she saved her family. Queen Esther was loyal to her people and ultimately saved them from destruction. The prophet Daniel chose to defy the decree of the king by openly praying toward Jerusalem, and for this act of rebellion, he was thrown into the lions' den. Webster says that loyalty means being constant and faithful, bearing true allegiance to something. Every human being has loyalties, but the essential question is, "To what or whom are we loyal?" *Our deepest loyalties are revealed when we are forced into making a decision that favors one loyalty and harms others.* Until we are put to the test, it is impossible to say where our deepest loyalties really lie. This is the sobering point that Peter learned after the rooster crowed the third time.

Daniel: A Prisoner of War

For centuries, Christians have repeated the story of Daniel's escape from the lions' den, but few people know the whole story that surrounds this incident. As we will see, Daniel's loyalty to God had a profound impact on two nations! I would like to present this story with the necessary background information so that (a) you can "stand in Daniel's sandals" and consider the importance of loyalty to God, and (b) Daniel 9 will make a lot more sense.

Daniel was taken to Babylon as a prisoner of war as a result of Nebuchadnezzar's first siege on Jerusalem in 605 B.C. It is believed that Daniel was about 17 or 18 years of age. It was King Nebuchadnezzar's policy to take the brightest captives and enroll them in an academy to prepare them for government service. The king had wisely established a school to train captives from various tribal nations, so the captives could return to their homeland and serve the empire of Babylon as rulers *loyal* to the interests of the king of Babylon. This is why Daniel and some of his friends were inducted into the king's academy. The book of Daniel begins with Daniel and his closest friends asking the king's steward if they could be excused from eating at the king's table. They wanted to maintain a more simple, vegetarian diet, but the steward refused this first request. He was sure that Daniel and his friends would become sick and feeble if they ate nothing but vegetables and water. If they became sick on his watch, he could lose his job or possibly his head! Daniel persisted and the steward gave in. When it came time for the king to test the trainees, Daniel and his friends were found to be at the top of their class. In fact, the Bible says their knowledge was ten times better than their fellow students. (Daniel 1:20) Do you think the success of Daniel and his friends had anything to do with their diet and their loyalty to God?

A short time later, Daniel gained world-wide recognition when God used him to interpret a dream that God gave to Nebuchadnezzar. (Daniel 2) As a result of that incident, Nebuchadnezzar promoted Daniel to a very high government position and all the *wise* men of Babylon reported to him. Do you think Daniel's lofty promotion had anything to do with his loyalty to God?

Why Was Daniel Sent to Babylon?

Historians tell us that Nebuchadnezzar set siege to Jerusalem three times. He finally destroyed the city in 586 B.C., because Israel's kings refused to submit to Nebuchadnezzar's "higher" authority. In actuality, God destroyed Jerusalem with Nebuchadnezzar's sword, and He put the Jews in captivity for seventy years because Israel refused to submit to His "higher" authority. The Bible carefully justifies God's wrath on Israel. To understand God's wrath, we have to start with a conversation between God and Moses. Carefully review these texts:

1. Sabbath Rest Required for the Land - Leviticus 25

A few weeks after the Exodus, **"The Lord said to Moses on Mount Sinai, 'Speak to the Israelites and say to them: 'When you enter the land I am going to give you, the land itself must observe a Sabbath to the Lord. For six years sow your fields, and for six years prune your vineyards and gather their crops. But in the seventh year the land is to have a Sabbath of rest, a Sabbath to the Lord. Do not sow your fields or prune your vineyards. Do not reap what grows of itself or harvest the grapes of your untended vines. The land is to have a year of rest.'"** (Leviticus 25:1-5) This text is self explanatory. God required the land to rest every seventh year. Why would any nation refuse a year's vacation every seventh year? The Lord continues, **"You may ask, 'What will we eat in the seventh year if we do not plant or harvest our crops?' I will send you such a blessing in the sixth year that the land will yield enough for three years. While you plant during the eighth year, you will eat from the old crop and will continue to eat from it until the harvest of the ninth year comes in."** (Leviticus 25:20-22) There is a profound point in these verses: God promised to send a bumper crop every sixth year so there would be enough food to observe a year of rest! Contrary to what many scholars say, the Sabbath rest for the land was not for agricultural purposes. In fact, God made the land produce its greatest harvest during the sixth year – when the land was in its most exhausted condition! The first lesson to be learned from the Sabbath year is simple. God established the Sabbath year rest *to test* His people. Would Israel be loyal or rebellious? (See Exodus 16 for a parallel test concerning the seventh day.)

2. "If You Don't Keep My Sabbath Years" - Leviticus 26

God warned Israel: **"If in spite of this you still do not listen to me but continue to be hostile toward me, then in my anger I will be hostile toward you, and I myself will punish you for your sins seven times over. . . . I will turn your cities into ruins and lay waste your sanctuaries, and I will take no delight in the pleasing aroma of your offerings. I will lay waste the land, so that your enemies who live there will be appalled. I will scatter you among the nations and will draw** out my sword and pursue you. Your land will be laid waste, and your cities will lie in ruins. Then the land will enjoy its sabbath years all the time that it lies desolate and you are in the country of your enemies; then the land will rest and enjoy its sabbaths. All the time that it lies desolate, the land will have the rest it did not have during the sabbaths you lived in it." (Leviticus 26:27,28,31-35, insertion mine) A person does not have to be a rocket scientist to understand these words. God said His land was going to rest, with or without Israel. God wanted His people to understand a profound truth: ". . . [The Lord said] **the land is mine and you are but aliens and my tenants.**" (Leviticus 25:23, insertion mine) God wanted Israel to know that their occupation of His land was conditional on their steadfast loyalty to Him. (Leviticus 18; Deuteronomy 28)

3. Because You Have Rebelled - Jeremiah 25

The Old Testament indicates over and over again that Israel did not remain loyal to God. Their cup of grace overflowed with rebellion and around 615 B.C., God gave a message to Jeremiah. He said, **"I will summon all the peoples of the north and my servant Nebuchadnezzar king of Babylon,' declares the Lord, 'and I will bring them against this land and its inhabitants and against all the surrounding nations. I will completely destroy them and make them an object of horror and scorn, and an everlasting ruin. I will banish from them the sounds of joy and gladness, the voices of bride and bridegroom, the sound of millstones and the light of the lamp. This whole country will become a desolate wasteland, and these nations will serve the king of Babylon seventy years. But when the seventy years are fulfilled, I will punish the king of Babylon and his nation, the land of the Babylonians, for their guilt,' declares the Lord, 'and will make it desolate forever.' "** (Jeremiah 25:9-12) Notice three things: First, God called King Nebuchadnezzar "my servant." This is an important concept. God chose a pagan king to be His agent of wrath against Jerusalem. (Parallel: The Antichrist, the modern king of Babylon, will be God's agent of wrath during the Great Tribulation.) Second, God said that Jerusalem would be destroyed and Israel would be captives in Babylon for seventy years. Third, God said that Babylon would eventually be destroyed for the same sins as Jerusalem.

4. 430 Years of Rebellion

During the seventy years of captivity in Babylon, God raised up two prophets. Ezekiel was a prisoner of war like Daniel, but Ezekiel lived among the captives while Daniel lived in the ivory halls of power. Ezekiel was timid and afraid of public speaking, so the Lord prompted him to "act out" various signs for the elders of Israel to watch. Notice this sign: "**. . . This will be a sign to the house of Israel. . . [Ezekiel] lie on your left side and put the sin of the house of Israel upon yourself. You are to bear their sin for the number of days you lie on your side. I have assigned you the same number of days as the years of their sin. So for 390 days you will bear the sin of the house of Israel. 'After you have finished this, lie down again, this time on your right side, and bear the sin of the house of Judah. I have assigned you 40 days, a day for each year.'** " (Ezekiel 4:3,6, insertion mine) This text is important because we find the length of rebellion to be a total of 430 years. (390 + 40 = 430)   This number should catch the attention of the reader, because it is the same number of years mentioned in Exodus 12:41. These two separate and distinct instances of 430 years have three things in common: apostasy, timing and vigil. First, the apostasy of the Israelites in Egypt is no different than the apostasy of the Israelites in the promised land of Canaan! Apostasy is the direction of fallen man. Second, God's timing was perfect in both instances. The Bible says that God delivered the Israelites from Egyptian slavery exactly 430 years later, *to the very day.* (Exodus 12:41) If God delivered Israel from Egypt on time, then it should come as no surprise that He sent them into captivity on time as well. It should be noted that when Israel had filled up their cup of iniquity by violating seventy Sabbath years, God sent them into captivity! How do we know this? Ezekiel performed the "430 day" sign for the elders of Israel, because they knew there are seventy Sabbatical years in 430 years. In other words, the Babylonian captivity was seventy years in length because that is the exact number of Sabbath years Israel violated.
Remember God's threat in Leviticus 26:34,35? **"Then the land will enjoy its Sabbath years all the time that it lies desolate and you are in the country of your enemies; then the land will rest and enjoy its Sabbaths. All the time that it lies desolate, the land will have the rest it did not have during the**

Sabbaths you lived in it." This text points to a significant parallel between these 430 year periods. Third, God keeps vigil. He does not sleep. He is very much aware of everything that takes place on Earth and He steps into the affairs of men when the timing is perfect. He delivered Israel from slavery in Egypt on time, and He sent Israel into captivity in Babylon on time! Even more, the next text demonstrates that God delivered Israel from captivity right on time!

5. Prophecy Fulfilled

The Bible says, **"God handed all of them** [the Jews] **over to Nebuchadnezzar. He carried to Babylon all the articles from the temple of God, both large and small, and the treasures of the Lord's temple and the treasures of the king and his officials. They set fire to God's temple and broke down the wall of Jerusalem; they burned all the palaces and destroyed everything of value there. He carried into exile to Babylon the remnant, who escaped from the sword, and they became servants to him and his sons until the kingdom of Persia came to power. The land enjoyed its sabbath rests; all the time of its desolation it rested, until the seventy years were completed in fulfillment of the word of the Lord spoken by Jeremiah."** (2 Chronicles 36:17-21, insertion mine) Again, the reason for the Babylonian captivity is simple and obvious. God handed Israel over to Nebuchadnezzar because of disloyalty. Israel refused to keep His Sabbath days and His Sabbath years, so He evicted them and the land rested for seventy years.

Zooming Forward

Now that we understand *why* the Jews were sent to Babylon, we can zoom forward to the fall of Babylon. Historians say Babylon fell on Tishri 16 (around October 13), 539 B.C. Darius began to rule over the province of Babylon during that year (his ascension year), so Darius' first calendar year (according to the religious calendar of the Jews) was 538/7 B.C. The first year of Darius' reign was Daniel's sixty-eighth year in captivity. Daniel knew the end of captivity in Babylon was near. Daniel and his contemporaries knew that Jerusalem had been besieged during the Sabbath year of 605 B.C. (Jeremiah 34:12-21), and Daniel knew the seventy years of desolation decreed upon Jerusalem (Daniel 9:2) would have to end during a Friday year. (Counting inclusively, 605 B.C. minus 536 B.C. equals seventy years, which is ten weeks of seven years.)

Note: When God established the weekly cycle of seven years at the time of the Exodus, God required Israel to set their slaves free at the beginning of the seventh year. The seventh or Sabbath year was observed as a year of freedom from the bondage of slavery. (See Exodus 21:2 and Jeremiah 34:14-16.) Daniel knew of God's requirements, and he understood the operation and synchrony of the Jubilee Calendar. In fact, God used the synchrony and operation of the Jubilee Calendar in Daniel 9 to pinpoint the year of Messiah's death (in the middle year of the week of seven years – Daniel 9:27).

The Political Situation in Daniel's Sixty-eighth Year

It was most unusual in ancient times for a conquering king to give a prisoner of war a position of high authority in his government. The possibility of treason or rebellion was just too great. Incredible as it was, this happened to Daniel three times. Nebuchadnezzar promoted Daniel to one of his highest governing positions after Daniel interpreted his dream. Belteshazzar promoted Daniel to one of his highest governing positions after Daniel read the handwriting on the wall. Finally, Darius promoted Daniel to one of the highest positions in the kingdom when Darius became king. Do you think Daniel's promotions had anything to do with his loyalty to God?

Daniel must have believed that God placed him in a very powerful political position within the government of Darius so that *he, Daniel,* might facilitate Israel's release from captivity. However, Daniel was nearing ninety years of age, and he knew that if he acted on his own, he might interfere with God's marvelous ways as Moses did when he wrongfully killed the Egyptian. (Exodus 2:11-14) Daniel also knew that if any of his actions backfired, many Jews would suffer, as in the days when Moses and Aaron ordered the Hebrew slaves to rest from their weekly labors before the Exodus. (Exodus 5:5) Daniel was aware that he would dishonor God if his actions to free his people aroused suspicion, jealousy or any hint of rebellion against the Medes and Persians. Many of the Chaldeans intensely hated the Jews, and any move on Daniel's part to free his people would probably be construed as treason. If Daniel was convicted in a court of public opinion, he knew the punishment was sudden death.

Note: Hatred for the Jews erupted throughout the Persian kingdom about seventy years after Daniel died. The noble, Haman, obtained a universal death decree from King Artaxerxes for all Jews in the Persian kingdom, but God used a strategically-placed Queen Esther to save His people.

Daniel's dilemma also had other ramifications. During the seventy years of captivity in Babylon, the Jews multiplied and integrated into the province of Babylon. In some cities, the Jews prospered, while others remained servants or slaves of the Chaldeans. When Darius began his reign over Babylon, most of the original captives from Jerusalem had died. Therefore, the next generation had little attachment to Jerusalem, a place they had not seen. In fact, when King Cyrus set the Jews free in 536 B.C., Ezra 2 indicates that a small minority of captives, 29,818 Jewish males, returned to Jerusalem.

Political and Economic Problems

Daniel knew the emancipation of his people after seventy years in Babylon could cause many problems for King Darius. If large numbers of Chaldeans lost their slaves, financial losses could destabilize the economy and produce social unrest. Daniel was also aware that during the seventy years of desolation, tribal nations had moved into Jerusalem and a *returning* Israel would be embroiled in wars and land disputes unless there was a royal land grant decreed by the king who ruled over the territory of Canaan. So, any decree that freed the Jews from the province of Babylon would also require a land grant by King Cyrus, who ruled over Canaan. Daniel's desire, of course, was that his people would recover the land they had lost, but the political and economic problems of setting Israel free greatly perplexed Daniel. What could *he* do to facilitate the freedom of his people? Even if they were set free, how would he motivate a majority of the Jews to return to Jerusalem? Daniel's mind must have churned over these issues for months. As a high government official, he saw how a significant exodus from Babylon could be a political nightmare.

Jealousy Knows No Bounds

From Daniel's point of view, the upcoming seventieth year, 536/5 B.C., would not be a very good year to attempt the release of the

Jews. Even though Daniel held one of the highest positions in the empire, Darius was a new king over the province of Babylon. This meant a new administration was in place adhering to a new set of laws and a new corporate attitude, which included a large group of powerful nobles who hated the Jews. As Daniel pondered his helpless position, it became apparent to him that Israel's deliverance from slavery would have to be an "Act of God," a miracle as great as the Exodus from Egypt. To his credit, Daniel faithfully carried out his responsibilities within Darius' administration, and Darius came to explicitly trust his elder statesman. The Bible says of this time period, **"Now Daniel so distinguished himself among the administrators and the satraps by his exceptional qualities that the king planned to set him over the whole kingdom."** (Daniel 6:3)

Sometime during Darius' first calendar year (538/7 B.C.), Daniel decided the best thing he could do was seek God's wisdom through fasting, praying and wearing sackcloth and ashes. Time was running out! The seventieth year was approaching fast. So, Daniel sought the Lord in utter humility to see what God wanted of him. To be seen in sackcloth and ashes was a sign of mourning or extreme humiliation. To the Medes and Persians, Daniel's appearance must have been very odd since he usually wore clothing appropriate for his exalted office. Regardless, Daniel embarrassed (humbled) himself before God as a man in sackcloth and ashes, demonstrating that God could use him in whatever meaningful or menial way God desired.

Unbeknown to Daniel, King Darius had planned to promote Daniel above the other two governors of his empire. Evidently, Darius decided to do this because he had contracted a degenerating health problem. Darius favored Daniel because Daniel was "pure in heart," a very unusual quality among people in political office. Darius also wanted to make Daniel, "the Jew," his number two man in the kingdom because this would strategically protect his throne when he became too weak to meet the day-to-day needs of his office. Unlike the other two administrators, Darius knew Daniel would be loyal to him instead of an inner or hidden ambition to acquire his throne. Darius knew that even an intelligent Jew could not aspire to be king over an empire of Medes. By putting Daniel in the number two seat, Darius knew his throne would be safe from the schemes of ambitious politicians and administrators.

Somehow, Darius' plans were leaked to the two administrators, and they were filled with jealousy and rage. No self respecting Mede or Persian would be subject to a Jew! Jealousy and hatred for Daniel, "the Jew," led them to search for anything they could use to mar Daniel's reputation and disqualify him from such a position of honor. They closely studied Daniel's personal history, conducted interviews and audited his finances trying to find a flaw in his character. They were unable to find anything. The Bible says, **"At this, the administrators and the satraps tried to find grounds for charges against Daniel in his conduct of government affairs, but they were unable to do so. They could find no corruption in him, because he was trustworthy and neither corrupt nor negligent. Finally these men said, 'We will never find any basis for charges against this man Daniel unless it has something to do with the law of his God.' "** (Daniel 6:4,5) Given the hatred and determination of his enemies, and the notorious behavior of politicians down through the ages, these are amazing words coming from their lips!

Putting the Squeeze on Daniel

Finally, the administrators and satraps concluded that the only way to stop Darius from promoting Daniel was to *prove* to Darius that Daniel's loyalty to his "Jewish" God was higher than his loyalty to Darius. They figured the question of loyalty would prove their point. When it comes to politics, kings have to be gods. Their ego and government rests upon nothing less than total submission and devotion to their will. If no one respects the king, how can he be king? Therefore, "loyalty tests" were sometimes used by ancient kings to ferret out people with bad attitudes. This may explain why Darius did not quibble or hesitate to issue a loyalty decree. Loyalty tests were simple: During the specified month, suspects were arraigned and questioned before a court of political leaders. If the suspect freely confessed allegiance to the king as his highest authority on Earth, the suspect would then affirm his loyalty to the king by swearing an oath. However, if the suspect was hostile toward the king or plotting rebellion, a "loyalty test" became a life and death issue, even though the suspect may not have been caught doing anything wrong. This is why loyalty tests were so effective. If the suspect refused to take an oath affirming his allegiance and submission to the king, he was declared a rebel and killed immediately. On the other hand, if he lied about his allegiance to the king and gave an oath of loyalty, his sympathizers would see that the suspect was a common coward and a liar. Who could respect such a disgusting person? This technique for testing loyalty was simple and effective. Incidently, the Caesars also used loyalty tests. Thousands of Christians perished because they would not bow down before the "man-god," Caesar. (John 19:15; Romans 10:9) During the Great Tribulation, God will use a simple loyalty test. A test of worship will put the "squeeze" on every person and our deepest loyalties will be "squeezed out" for everyone to see. (See Revelation 13:8-18.)

The Perfect Plot

The crafty administrators asked Darius for permission to conduct a "loyalty check" for three reasons: First, a loyalty test was a well-known tactic. Since the province of Babylon was a new territory for Darius, a loyalty test appeared to be a "good idea" to eliminate those who might be rebellious. Second, if Daniel should slip through the thirty-day decree trap, Darius would never know the real motives behind the administrators' request for the loyalty test. Third, if Daniel was caught in their trap, he would be "legally" killed because the law demanded the sudden death of anyone caught in rebellion against the king. If Daniel was destroyed, the administrators would not be implicated in Daniel's death. The "loyalty test" seemed like the perfect way to eliminate Daniel, or so they thought.

When the administrators asked the king for a loyalty decree, they must have known that Darius did not know about Daniel's current state of humiliation. If Darius had been aware of Daniel's behavior, praying to his God three times a day in sackcloth and ashes, this knowledge would have foiled their plot. **"So the administrators and the satraps went as a group to the king and said: 'O King Darius, live forever! The royal administrators, prefects, satraps, advisers and governors have all agreed that the king should issue an edict and enforce the decree that anyone who prays to any god or man during the next thirty days, except to you, O king, shall be thrown into the lions' den. Now, O king, issue the decree and put it in writing so that it cannot be altered–in accordance with the laws of the Medes and Persians, which cannot be repealed.' So King Darius put the decree in writing."** (Daniel 6:6-9)

Daniel Springs the Trap

"Now when Daniel learned that the decree had been published, he went home to his upstairs room where the windows opened toward Jerusalem. Three times a day he got down on his knees and prayed, giving thanks to his God, just as he had done before. Then these men went as a group and found Daniel praying and asking God for help. So they went to the king and spoke to him about his royal decree: 'Did you not publish a decree that during the next thirty days anyone who prays to any god or man except to you, O king, would be thrown into the lions' den?' The king answered, 'The decree stands–in accordance with the laws of the Medes and Persians, which cannot be repealed.' Then they said to the king, 'Daniel, who is one of the exiles from Judah, pays no attention to you, O king, or to the decree you put in writing. He still prays three times a day.' When the king heard this, he was greatly distressed; he was determined to rescue Daniel and made every effort until sundown to save him." (Daniel 6:10-14)

Did you notice how fast Daniel *willfully* disobeyed the king's decree? Why did one of the kingdom's highest officials publicly defy the law of the king? The answer lies in the fact that Daniel understood the motives and reasons behind the *loyalty test*. Daniel remembered his three friends and their fiery furnace test, and he knew he was being tested just like them. Evidently, notification of the decree came suddenly and without warning to Daniel. I find it interesting that Daniel did not go to his immediate superior, King Darius and plead his case! When Daniel learned of the loyalty test, he ran to (not from) his prayer room. This action says volumes about Daniel's loyalty to the God of Heaven!

When Daniel humbled himself by wearing sackcloth and ashes, Daniel's heart was ready and willing to submit, even to death, if that was God's will. Daniel was willing to do *anything* God required of him to facilitate the release of his people. Daniel's loyalty to God was extraordinary and God's approval of Daniel was amazing. In fact, Daniel's loyalty became the very tool that God used to glorify His name before the Medes and Persians so that He could deliver the Jews from captivity! If the plot to kill Daniel was clever, God's use of the situation was even more so. God used the administrators' hatred of Daniel, Darius' affection for Daniel, Daniel's loyalty, and ultimately, the lion's den to set Israel free from slavery. Watch how these elements combined to accomplish God's plan.

King Darius Humiliated

The next morning, "**. . . the king gave the order, and they brought Daniel and threw him into the lions' den. The king said to Daniel, 'May your God, whom you serve continually, rescue you!' A stone was brought and placed over the mouth of the den, and the king sealed it with his own signet ring and with the rings of his nobles, so that Daniel's situation might not be changed. Then the king returned to his palace and spent the night without eating and without any entertainment being brought to him. And he could not sleep."** (Daniel 6:16-18)

Daniel was quickly arraigned before King Darius. When the king saw his elder statesman in sackcloth and ashes, he became furious with his administrators. He saw through their plot immediately. Daniel, "the Jew," was no rebel and Darius knew it. In fact, Daniel was the only administrator the king could trust! According to law, however, Daniel was subjected to the usual "loyalty" interrogation, and without hesitation, Daniel confessed to praying to his God three times a day. Daniel did not offer excuses, plead his case or beg for his life. Even more importantly, he did not swear an oath of loyalty to King Darius as his highest authority. King Darius churned with grief and anger. He condemned himself all night for failing to consider the intense hatred his administrators had for Daniel, "the Jew." How ironic the twist of events. Darius was planning to promote Daniel, but now he would have to kill him instead. Darius knew Daniel was unjustly condemned, but not even the king himself could change the law of the Medes and Persians. With these words, **"May your God, whom you serve continually, rescue you!"** Darius bade farewell to Daniel. The king gave the order and with his own ring and the rings of those who hated the Jew, Darius issued the judgment requiring Daniel to be thrown into the lions' den. Daniel was at peace. Darius was in torment and the administrators were on their way to a secret celebration party.

King Darius Exhilarated

"At the first light of dawn, the king got up and hurried to the lions' den. When he came near the den, he called to Daniel in an anguished voice, 'Daniel, servant of the living God, has your God, whom you serve continually, been able to rescue you from the lions?' Daniel answered, 'O king, live forever! My God sent his angel, and he shut the mouths of the lions. They have not hurt me, because I was found innocent in his sight. Nor have I ever done any wrong before you, O king.' The king was overjoyed and gave orders to lift Daniel out of the den. And when Daniel was lifted from the den, no wound was found on him, because he had trusted in his God. At the king's command, the men who had falsely accused Daniel were brought in and thrown into the lions' den, along with their wives and children. And before they reached the floor of the den, the lions overpowered them and crushed all their bones. Then King Darius wrote to all the peoples, nations and men of every language throughout the land: 'May you prosper greatly! I issue a decree that in every part of my kingdom people must fear and reverence the God of Daniel. For he is the living God and he endures forever; his kingdom will not be destroyed, his dominion will never end. He rescues and he saves; he performs signs and wonders in the heavens and on the Earth. He has rescued Daniel from the power of the lions.' So Daniel prospered during the reign of Darius [the Mede] and the reign of Cyrus the Persian." (Daniel 6:19-28, insertion mine) Thoughtfully consider the profound experience of Darius that morning. Upon hearing Daniel's voice, a pagan king was given every reason to put his faith in the God of Daniel. The tomb was opened and "a dead man" walked out! The king immediately issued another decree requiring every person in his kingdom to fear and reverence the God of Daniel, "the Jew." The news about Daniel's miraculous deliverance was told everywhere! When the intense hatred of the Chaldeans for the Jews is considered, the significance of Darius' actions really stands out. Because of Daniel's loyalty, the God of Heaven was exalted to the highest position by a heathen king! This demonstrates an interesting point that all religious people would do well to remember. *The objective of serving the God of Heaven is to bring honor and glory to God, not to the superiority of one's religion.*

Israel Set Free

The story of Daniel's miraculous deliverance, and the immediate destruction of his enemies by the *same* lions that refused to eat him has been closely examined in this book for some important reasons. First, remember that God's timing is *always* perfect! Evidently, the lions' den episode happened during Darius' first year, 538/7 B.C. This allowed time for Darius to become acquainted with Daniel and to develop such confidence in him that he wanted to make him the number two man in his kingdom. As we are about to see, the timing of the lions' den event is too perfect to be a coincidence!

God used the hatred of the administrators and the loyalty of Daniel in a way that no one could have anticipated. I believe the events unfolded as follows: When Daniel sought the Lord in sackcloth and ashes for instructions on what he should do to facilitate the deliverance of Israel, God heard Daniel's prayer and gave him something that he did not know he was about to need. God gave Daniel *peace* in the face of death. This peace is reflected in Daniel's courageous action after he learned about the law. God did not give Daniel wisdom to outfox the evil administrators, and God did not rain down plagues on Babylon like He did in Egypt. God had a better plan in mind.

After Daniel violated the king's law, God rewarded Daniel's loyalty with protection and enormous notoriety. (Who else has spent a night in a den of wild and ravenous lions and lived to tell about it?) Simultaneously, God eliminated an enormous obstacle that stood in the way of delivering His people. God granted Darius a *legal* opportunity to purge his government of men who were disloyal to the higher interests of their king. Politically speaking, the death of these administrators made releasing the Jews a manageable problem for the king, even though Darius did not know the Jews were about to be set free. After Darius destroyed the administrators who hated Daniel, the king promoted Daniel to the number two position in his kingdom and no one dared to complain!

Evidently, King Darius died soon after this event (the following year) and King Cyrus (the Persian) absorbed the territory of Darius into his expanding kingdom. Therefore, the ascension year of Cyrus over the province of Babylon was 537/6 B.C., and his first calendar year was 536/5 B.C. Because of Daniel's notoriety from the lions' den event and because he was the highest official in Darius' kingdom, Daniel became well acquainted with King Cyrus during his ascension year. During 536/5 B.C., which was the final year or seventieth year of captivity, King Cyrus met with Daniel, and Daniel informed the Persian king that the God of Heaven had chosen Cyrus to be a great king before he was even born. Daniel showed Cyrus the writings of the prophet Isaiah, where Cyrus is called *by name* in Scripture a hundred years before Cyrus was born. (Isaiah 45:1-4) When Daniel explained to King Cyrus why he was fasting and praying – the behavior that ultimately sent him to the lions' den – the king's heart was moved at the loyalty and devotion of this elderly man to the Supreme God over Heaven and Earth.

Daniel told Cyrus that the God of Heaven had appointed the Persian king to set the Jews free, "without price or reward," (Isaiah 45:13) for the purpose of rebuilding His temple. Cyrus was honored to learn of God's approval and blessings, and he issued the decree in Daniel's presence during the seventieth year, a Friday year, in 536/5 B.C. Free at last! Israel was free to enter Canaan a second time. It is interesting to note that Israel's first full year in Canaan after the Babylonian captivity was a Sabbath year. This beautifully parallels their first full year in Canaan after Joshua led them across the Jordan into the Promised Land. In both instances, the slaves had been set free to enjoy the Sabbath year in the Promised Land. The Bible says, **"In the first year of Cyrus king of Persia, in order to fulfill the word of the Lord spoken by Jeremiah, the Lord moved the heart of Cyrus king of Persia to make a proclamation throughout his realm and to put it in writing: 'This is what Cyrus king of Persia says: "The Lord, the God of heaven, has given me all the kingdoms of the earth and he has appointed me to build a temple for him at Jerusalem in Judah. Anyone of his people among you–may his God be with him, and let him go up to Jerusalem in Judah and build the temple of the Lord, the God of Israel, the God who is in Jerusalem." ' "** (Ezra 1:1-3) The timing could not have been more perfect. The decree of Cyrus ended seventy years of captivity (counting inclusively). It is amazing how God took Daniel through the lions' den so that he could present God's will to a pagan king who controlled the province of Babylon, as well as the territory of Canaan. This decree was only possible because Cyrus ruled over the province of Babylon where the Jews were captives, as well as the territory of Judea where Jerusalem was located. God solved the political and economic problems. God's timing is so perfect. His ways are so magnificent! Remember, God required slaves to be released at the end of the Friday year (the sixth year), and this is exactly what He did for the nation of Israel. The captives were emancipated from slavery in 536 B.C., a Friday year.

Calendar of Events

Julian Years

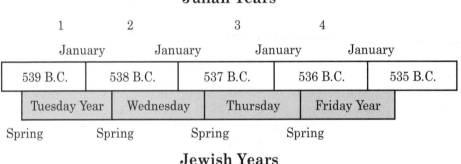

Chart 5.1

1. Babylon falls, ascension year for Darius

2. First year for Darius, lions' den

3. Darius dies, ascension year for Cyrus

4. First year for Cyrus, frees the Jews

Note: There are three good reasons for concluding that the Darius discussed in Daniel 6 died in 537* B.C. First, even though they were contemporary kings, Darius and Cyrus did not rule over the province of Babylon at the same time. History reveals that Babylon fell in 539 B.C. The Bible says that Cyrus, in the *first year* of his reign, which was the seventieth year of Israel's captivity, issued a decree restoring the Jews to their land. **"The land enjoyed its Sabbath rests; all the time of its desolation it rested, until the seventy years were completed in fulfillment of the word of the Lord spoken by Jeremiah. In the first year of Cyrus king of Persia, in order to fulfill the word of the Lord spoken by Jeremiah, the Lord moved the heart of Cyrus king of Persia to make a proclamation throughout his realm and to put it in writing. . . ."** (2 Chronicles 36:21,22) If the seventy years in Jeremiah 25:11 began in the year 605 B.C. as most historians say, the decree of Cyrus had to be issued in the Friday year, 536 B.C. Israel's first full year in their homeland was a Sabbath year. (This timing is consistent with God's command that slaves were to be set free for the Sabbath year rest. Jeremiah 34:14) The count of years and actions of the kings easily align in this case. Babylon fell in 539 B.C. and Darius died in 537 B.C. Cyrus' ascension year over the province of Babylon was 537 B.C. and his first year as king was Friday year, 536 B.C., the year he wrote the decree.

Second, history also reveals that Cyrus had been a Persian king for more than twenty years before he began to rule over the province of Babylon. For Cyrus to have "a first year" as king over the province of Babylon in 536 B.C., Darius had to vacate the throne by dying in 537 B.C. The Bible confirms that Daniel served under these two kings saying, **"So Daniel prospered during the reign of Darius and the reign of Cyrus the Persian."** (Daniel 6:28) Of course, this text could also be interpreted to mean that Daniel prospered during the co-regent reign of both kings. The problem with this argument is that Daniel could not prosper under a king who did not rule over Babylon until the death of Darius in 537 B.C.

The third reason for concluding that Darius died shortly after taking office as king of Babylon comes from written history. The Nabonidus Chronicle, a cuneiform document which describes the fall of Babylon, indicates that an elderly man, Ugbaru, the governor of Gutium, entered Babylon without a battle on Tishri 16 (the seventh

month of a year in a Spring-to-Spring year). Daniel 5:31 says Darius
was 62 years old when he took over the kingdom of Babylon. The
Chronicle also indicates that Ugbaru installed satraps to govern the
province of Babylon. The Bible says, **"It pleased Darius to
appoint 120 satraps to rule throughout the kingdom."** (Daniel
6:1) The Chronicle says that Ugbaru died soon after he began to
reign. He died on the 11th of Arahshamnu (the Jewish equivalent to
Adar, the twelfth month of a Spring-to-Spring year). The province of
Babylon mourned his royal death for seven days. According to the
Nabonidus Chronicle, Cyrus appointed Gubaru as governor over
Babylon after Ugbaru died and Gubaru evidently assumed the name
"Darius." The Bible and other historical documents indicate the
second Darius ruled for several years. For example, **"The temple
was completed on the third day of the month Adar, in the
sixth year of the reign of King Darius."** (Ezra 6:15)

When all of the pieces of history are brought together, there is one
explanation that resolves the puzzle. Once the reign of the kings is
determined and once we understand that two men, Ugbaru and
Gubaru, both using the name "Darius," ruled in Babylon during this
time-frame, the actions and dates given in the Bible fall into perfect
harmony.

*For purposes of discussion, the years mentioned in this addendum
are singular instead of defined as 538/7 B.C.

Chapter 6

Daniel 9 –"God's Timing Is So Perfect"

> ". . . Who foretold this long ago, who declared it from the distant past? Was it not I, the Lord? And there is no God apart from me, a righteous God and a Savior; there is none but me."
>
> – Isaiah 45:21

Introduction

Some of the chapters in the book of Daniel are not in chronological order. For example, Daniel 7 occurred chronologically before Daniel 6. This point is mentioned because the prayer recorded in Daniel 9 occurred during the year that Daniel was sent to the lions' den (Daniel 6). Even though the prayer recorded in Daniel 9 was left unfinished because of Gabriel's unexpected visit, it was included in the book of Daniel for at least two reasons: First, the Bible tells us that God sent an answer to Daniel while he was praying. This information assures us that God hears the prayers of His children and He responds according to His infinite wisdom. Second, this special prayer has been preserved in the Bible because of its amazing content. Daniel states many profound truths in his prayer that everyone should thoughtfully consider.

Part I

The story in Daniel 9 occurred during 538 B.C. and Daniel knew the seventy years of captivity were drawing to a close. He was deeply concerned about Israel's release from captivity and was anxious to fulfill whatever role the Lord might want him to play. So, Daniel turned to the Lord with humility, fasting and prayer. **"In the first year of Darius the [grand] son of Ahasuerus, of the seed of the Medes, which was made king over the realm of the Chaldeans; In the first year of his reign I Daniel understood by books the number of the years, whereof the word of the Lord came to Jeremiah the prophet, that he would accomplish seventy years in the desolations of Jerusalem.**

And I set my face unto the Lord God, to seek by prayer and supplications, with fasting, and sackcloth, and ashes:" (Daniel 9:1-3, KJV, insertion mine)

Commentary on Part I

Consider some of the concerns and concepts that must have been in Daniel's mind before he began to pray:

1. Daniel knew that God had set the descendants of Abraham apart from other nations for a glorious purpose. (Exodus 19:4-6; Isaiah 42:6)

2. Daniel knew why his people were captives in Babylon.

3. Daniel knew that Israel's deliverance would have to be "an Act of God."

4. Daniel knew that *God kept vigil,* and He would not forget His promise to free His people from captivity. (Exodus 12:42)

5. Daniel knew that *God had set a date* for the release of His people and "the Friday year" of 536/5 B.C. was the seventieth year of captivity.

6. Daniel believed he had been placed in a high administrative position to somehow facilitate the release of his people, but he did not know what to do.

Now that some of Daniel's concerns have been identified, carefully examine Daniel's confession and prayer:

Part II

"And I prayed unto the Lord my God, and made my confession, and said, O Lord, the great and dreadful God, keeping the covenant and mercy to them that love him, and to them that keep his commandments; We have sinned, and have committed iniquity, and have done wickedly, and have rebelled, even by departing from thy precepts and from thy judgments: Neither have we hearkened unto thy servants the prophets, which spake in thy name to our kings, our princes, and our fathers, and to all the people of the land.

"O Lord, righteousness belongeth unto thee, but unto us confusion of faces [shame and embarrassment], as at this day; to the men of Judah, and to the inhabitants of Jerusalem, and unto all Israel, that are near, and that are far off, through all the countries whither thou hast driven them, because of their trespass that they have trespassed against thee. O Lord, to us belongeth confusion of face, to our kings, to our princes, and to our fathers, because we have sinned against thee. To the Lord our God belong mercies and forgivenesses, though we have rebelled against him; Neither have we obeyed the voice of the Lord our God, to walk in his laws, which he set before us by his servants the prophets.

"Yea, all Israel have transgressed thy law, even by departing, that they might not obey thy voice; therefore the curse is poured upon us, and the oath that is written in the law of Moses the servant of God, because we have sinned against him. And he hath confirmed his words, which he spake against us, and against our judges that judged us, by bringing upon us a great evil: for under the whole heaven hath not been done as hath been done upon Jerusalem. As it is written in the law of Moses, all this evil is come upon us: yet made we not our prayer before the Lord our God, that we might turn from our iniquities, and understand thy truth." (Daniel 9:4-13, KJV, insertion mine)

Commentary on Part II

Daniel's fasting and prayer must have been motivated by three factors. First, fasting is something we can do when we want God to consider the intensity of our heart's desire. Second, Daniel humiliated (embarrassed) himself with sackcloth and ashes to show God that he was willing to do *anything* God wanted him to do to facilitate the release of his people. Third, Daniel knew about Solomon's prayer, which the Lord confirmed by sending fire from Heaven when Solomon dedicated the temple in Jerusalem. Solomon prayed: "When they [Israel] sin against you – for there is no one who does not sin – and you become angry with them and give them over to the enemy, who takes them captive to a land far away or near; and if they have a change of heart in the land where they are held captive, and repent and plead

with you in the land of their captivity and say, 'We have sinned, we have done wrong and acted wickedly'; and if they turn back to you with all their heart and soul in the land of their captivity where they were taken, and pray toward the land you gave their fathers, toward the city you have chosen and toward the temple I have built for your Name; then from heaven, your dwelling place, hear their prayer and their pleas, and uphold their cause. And forgive your people, who have sinned against you." (2 Chronicles 6:36-39, insertion mine)

Given the content and eloquent language in Daniel's prayer, it is possible that Daniel prepared this prayer for a specific worship service. It is also possible that he prepared this prayer to meet one of the conditions required for deliverance! Notice what the Lord had said when He gave the covenant to Israel at Sinai: "[If you rebel against me] **You will perish among the nations; the land of your enemies will devour you. Those of you who are left will waste away in the lands of their enemies because of their sins; also because of their fathers' sins they will waste away.** *But, if they will confess their sins and the sins of their fathers* **– their treachery against me and their hostility toward me, which made me hostile toward them so that I sent them into the land of their enemies – then when their uncircumcised hearts are humbled and they pay for their sin, I will remember my covenant with Jacob and my covenant with Isaac and my covenant with Abraham, and I will remember the land."** (Leviticus 26:38-42, italics and insertion mine)

Daniel's prayer indicates that he well understood the terms and conditions of the covenant between Israel and God. Daniel acknowledged that God had afflicted Israel with a curse as the covenant stipulated. Daniel knew that Israel deserved captivity because of rebellion. Daniel justified God's righteous actions and he openly confessed that Israel had insulted God. He prayed, ". . . **therefore the curse is poured upon us, and the oath that is written in the law of Moses the servant of God, because we have sinned against him** [the Lord our God]." (Daniel 9:11)

Bilateral Covenant

The curse which God placed on Israel is difficult for some people to understand, so some background information may prove helpful.

God made a unilateral covenant (a one-sided unconditional covenant) with Abraham. God promised Abraham that a) all nations would be blessed through him, b) his descendants would be as numerous as the stars, and c) they would inherit a specific parcel of land. At the Exodus, God made a bilateral (a two-sided or mutually agreed upon) conditional covenant with Israel, and it may be summarized with these words: *"If* you will be my people, I will be your God."* (Leviticus 26:12) However, *"if* you choose to love other gods and rebel against my laws, I will destroy you."* (Leviticus 26:14-39) Bible history indicates that God destroyed Israel several times. The Bible indicates that God began destroying Israel with the first generation that came out of Egypt. The first generation was put to death in the wilderness because of rebellion!

The nation of Israel could uphold their end of the bilateral covenant only if a majority in Israel loved and obeyed the Lord. Moses knew this was a crucial point. In his farewell address to the second generation of Israel – the generation that entered the Promised Land – he said, **"Love the Lord your God with all your heart and with all your soul and with all your strength."** (Deuteronomy 6:5) He also wrote, **"Do not seek revenge or bear a grudge against one of your people, but love your neighbor as yourself. I am the Lord."** (Leviticus 19:18) According to Jesus, these two commandments were the greatest commandments spoken by Moses. (Matthew 22:36-40)

It has been said in this book that God's treatment of Israel is a mirror reflecting how He deals with all nations. The inverse of this statement is also true. Israel's treatment of God is a mirror reflecting how the human race treats God. The carnal nature of individual Jews made Israel's corporate behavior rebellious and ungrateful. A grateful company of slaves was willing and eager to enter into a covenant with God at the base of Mt. Sinai. However, forty days later, they were dancing around a golden calf. After two years, this same group of people became so rebellious that God refused to allow them to enter the Promised Land. (Numbers 14) God confined that generation to the wilderness for forty years so that all of the adults (except Caleb and Joshua) would die without receiving what had been promised to them. (Hebrews 3:10,11) This is a crucial point. Many people have wondered, "Why did God deal so harshly with Israel? Would it have been easier for Him to

abandon Israel and start over with another nation? This almost
happened. God almost destroyed Israel when they bowed down and
worshiped the golden calf in the shadow of Mt. Sinai, but Moses
interceded. (Exodus 32:10) Consider God's love. From the
beginning, God foreknew the offspring of Abraham would fail, so
why did He enter into a covenant with them? This is a profound
point: *God does not treat us on the basis of what He knows the
outcome will be. Instead, God deals with His subjects on the basis of
love.* God loved Abraham and He did everything a heart of love
could do to accomplish His plans through Abraham's children. God
wisely put "a destruction clause" into His bilateral (two-sided)
conditional covenant with the offspring of Abraham because God
had made a unilateral covenant (one-sided non-conditional) with
Abraham. In other words, God unconditionally promised the
patriarch Abraham that *his* descendants would inherit a specific
parcel of land. God foreknew that Abraham's offspring would rebel
against Him time after time, and the only way He could fulfill
everything He promised to Abraham was through a provision in the
covenant that would provide for rebels to be destroyed! Every time
God destroyed Israel, He started over with a remnant. When Israel
rejected Messiah, God did not abandon Israel and turn to the
Gentiles. God redefined Israel by making Gentile believers in
Christ the heirs of Abraham! (Galatians 3:28,29; Ephesians 2) By
doing this, God will be able to fulfill the unconditional covenant He
gave to Abraham!

Blessings and Curses

God's bilateral covenant with Israel was conditional. The covenant
began with "*If* you will be my people, I will be your God." To
motivate Israel to be faithful to the covenant between them, God put
an important balance between blessings and curses in the covenant.
This balance mirrors the two options from which mankind can
choose. Our first option is to love God, submit to His laws and enjoy
His presence, favor and blessings. Our second option is to rebel
against God and experience the pleasures of sin for a short season
and suffer the consequences of sin and destruction. (Leviticus 25;
Deuteronomy 28; Ezekiel 18; Romans 8) These are the only options
available to mankind, because everything in the universe belongs to
God. People who wish to live forever in God's kingdom cannot live
in rebellion against God because God will not tolerate rebellion in

His house. God cast Lucifer and a third of the angels out of Heaven because of rebellion, and God cast Israel out of His favor for the same reason. (Ezekiel 28:17; Revelation 12:7-9; Matthew 23:38) Consider God's words to Israel: **"Follow my decrees and be careful to obey my laws, and you will live safely in the land."** (Leviticus 25:18) **"If in spite of this** [a series of punitive judgments] **you still do not listen to me but continue to be hostile toward me, then in my anger I will be hostile toward you, and I myself will punish you for your sins seven times over."** (Leviticus 26:27,28, insertion mine)

God has demonstrated through Israel's long history that perfect laws cannot change a rebellious heart. (Romans 8:7) God blessed Israel with His magnificent laws and promised them every material benefit if they would follow Him, but unfortunately, God's generosity did not cure their rebellion. Instead of becoming a conduit through which God's blessings could flow to all the nations around them, Israel selfishly appropriated God's blessings to themselves. However, we should not condemn Israel too harshly because every nation has followed the same path! Remember, Israel's treatment of God is a mirror reflecting how mankind treats God. A carnal heart can change. The carnal heart can even do "a good deed" every now and then, but good deeds do not transform the carnal heart into the type of heart that God wants. *The root problem with the carnal heart is that it cannot love God and others as much as it loves itself.* Believe it or not, selfishness and rebellion against God are genetic! Human beings are born with a carnal nature. This is why everyone who wants to be a part of God's kingdom must be *born again*. All sinners can receive a new heart if they surrender to God's will. The carnal heart is self-seeking; therefore, we cannot joyfully submit to God's will until we surrender to His will. If we surrender daily to go, to be and to do all as God directs, He will do something within us that we cannot do for ourselves. God will transform our selfish hearts into selfless hearts through the power of His Spirit. A loving heart does not think less of itself, it thinks more of others than itself. The born-again experience does not occur in groups of people; it occurs within the heart of one individual at a time. *Because most people in Israel did not experience the new birth, the nation of Israel corporately failed to reach the glorious potential which God offered.* Israel's history indicates that most people in Israel were constantly rebellious toward God at any given time. Israel destroyed the prophets God sent, and ultimately, God destroyed His temple and His city along with two-thirds of His people. Then He put the survivors in Babylonian exile for seventy years. (Ezekiel 5:11,12)

This Land Is *My* Land

Few Christians today understand this point: ". . . [The Lord said to Israel] **the land is mine and you are but aliens and my tenants."** (Leviticus 25:23, insertion mine) Many people believe that God's promise to Abraham is still binding, and they believe that modern Israel is entitled to the land that was inhabited by the Palestinians for the past few centuries. This is not true! God did not grant Canaan to Israel without conditions. (Leviticus 18; Deuteronomy 28) In fact, the same requirements hold true for all nations. God owns all of Earth. He created the continents, and through the blood of Christ, He purchased humanity back to Himself. (Romans 5:18) God allows nations to occupy a parcel of land for as long as that nation upholds principles of righteousness. (Acts 17:26) When rebellion within a nation becomes so great that there is no recovery, God cauterizes the malignancy of sin by sending destruction to that nation. He overthrows offending governments and slows the degenerate process of sin by killing off most, if not all, of its inhabitants. God turns the land over to another nation and the process starts over. King Nebuchadnezzar thought Babylon was an invincible city, but Babylon became decadent and rebellious, so God opened the city gates giving the city and the land to the Medes and Persians *in a single night.* (Daniel 5)

Part III

The prayer of Daniel continues: **"Therefore hath the Lord watched upon the evil, and brought it upon us: for the Lord our God is righteous in all his works which he doeth: for we obeyed not his voice. And now, O Lord our God, that hast brought thy people forth out of the land of Egypt with a mighty hand, and hast gotten thee renown, as at this day; we have sinned, we have done wickedly. O Lord, according to all thy righteousness, I beseech thee, let thine anger and thy fury be turned away from thy city Jerusalem, thy holy mountain: because for our sins, and for the iniquities of our** fathers, Jerusalem and thy people are become a reproach to all that are about us.

"Now therefore, O our God, hear the prayer of thy servant, and his supplications, and cause thy face to shine upon thy sanctuary that is desolate, for the Lord's sake. O my God, incline thine ear, and hear; open thine eyes, and behold our desolations, and the city which is called by thy name: for we do not present our supplications before thee for our righteousnesses, but for thy great mercies. O Lord, hear; O Lord, forgive; O Lord, hearken and do; defer not, for thine own sake, O my God: for thy city and thy people are called by thy name." (Daniel 9:14-19, KJV)

Commentary on Part III

Daniel's prayer and Jesus' prayer recorded in John 17 are the best examples of intercessory prayer in the Bible. Prayer coming from a contrite heart *always* gains an audience with God. (Psalm 51:17; Isaiah 57:15; Isaiah 66:2) **"The Lord detests the sacrifice of the wicked, but the prayer of the upright pleases him."** (Proverbs 15:8)

The Bible indicates that God answers the prayers of a humble petitioner in one of three ways: "Yes, No or Wait." (Psalm 66:18; 1 John 1:9; Hebrews 5:7) If, in His omniscient wisdom, God says "No" or "Wait," He knows the consternation His decision will bring, so God sends peace in the middle of the storm if we are willing to receive it. Jesus said, **"Peace I leave with you; my peace I give you. I do not give to you as the world gives. Do not let your hearts be troubled and do not be afraid."** (John 14:27) At best, this world offers a peace that is temporal and fleeting. The carnal nature is at peace when everything is going according to its will, but a new disturbance can rise out of nowhere and ruin its peace in a heartbeat. Jesus offers a different type of peace than the world can give. His peace transcends the anxieties of life. (Isaiah 26:3) When God's peace rests on us, we have joy and we cease worrying – knowing that He is in control. Of course, this does not mean that God's decisions will necessarily be what we think is best; rather, God's peace comes from knowing that He will make the best of the situation. Daniel went peacefully to the lions' den and his three friends went peacefully to the fiery furnace. They were concerned, but they had peace about their decision. We find and receive God's peace "which passes all understanding" when we submit to the wisdom and plans of a sovereign God. Faith in God is not easy to maintain. Israel's history proves this. Without faith, it is impossible to please Him. (Hebrews 11:6)

Part IV

"While I was speaking and praying, confessing my sin and the sin of my people Israel and making my request to the Lord my God for his holy hill [or mountain] **– while I was still in prayer, Gabriel, the man I had seen** *in the earlier vision,* **came to me in swift flight about the time of the evening sacrifice. He instructed me and said to me, "Daniel, I have now come to give you insight and understanding** [into the earlier vision]. **As soon as you began to pray, an answer was given, which I have come to tell you, for you are highly esteemed. Therefore, consider the message and understand the** [earlier] **vision:"** (Daniel 9:20-23, italics and insertions mine)

Commentary on Part IV

The appearance of the angel Gabriel suddenly interrupted Daniel's prayer. Gabriel and Daniel first met during the vision recorded in Daniel 8. So, "the vision" mentioned in verse 21 refers to the vision of the ram, goat, and horn power which occurred about twelve years earlier, in 550 B.C. When Gabriel appeared, he said, **"As soon as you began to pray, an answer was given, which I have come to tell you, for you are highly esteemed."** Daniel's prayer takes about three minutes to read out loud. Since Gabriel flew to Daniel's location with an *answer* as soon as he began to pray, we have to conclude that we are not far away from our Father's ear. (For comparison, it takes about eight minutes for light to travel from the Sun to Earth.)

Gabriel's remarks to Daniel total less than 250 words and the casual Bible student will find them to be cryptic and obscure. Although Gabriel's words were few, they are packed with meaning. Since many people do not understand the architecture of Daniel (which was sealed up until the time of the end) or how the Jubilee Calendar works, many expositors have distorted and manipulated Gabriel's words so that millions of Christians anticipate a series of prophetic events that will never occur. This is a horrible tragedy in the making. Bible prophecy is about to unfold in a way that is contrary to the views of millions of people, and when many Christians are disappointed, they will feel very bitter towards God and their religious leaders who mislead them.

The Question

Gabriel said "an answer" was given when Daniel began to pray, so what was Daniel's question? A personal question had churned within Daniel's heart for twelve years. *Daniel wanted to understand the previous vision, because he was told during the vision of Daniel 8 that God's people would be destroyed by the horn power from the north.* This information was contrary to everything Daniel believed about Israel's destiny. Remember Daniel's mindset before he began to pray? (See my earlier commentary on Part I.) Daniel knew that God had selected the descendants of Abraham from among the nations of Earth to be trustees of the everlasting gospel. Daniel also understood that God had chosen Israel to be a light for the Gentiles. Israel was to show the world the way to God. Even more, Daniel knew that God had promised Abraham that his children would be as numerous as the stars of the sky when God established His kingdom on Earth. However, Daniel was disturbed that Israel was not included in any of the previous visions! Nothing was included about Israel in the visions of Daniel 2 or Daniel 7, and Daniel 8 indicates that God's people would be destroyed by the horn power: "**He** [the horn power] **will destroy the mighty men and the holy people.**" (Daniel 8:24, insertion mine)

Daniel was a devout Jew and he had absorbed a very strong prophetic paradigm as he grew up. In Daniel's mind there was no question that *his* people would play a prominent role when God set up His kingdom on Earth. Jewish culture instilled this prophetic destiny in every child from birth and Daniel was no exception. Daniel believed the Jewish nation would be exalted among the nations of the world as a kingdom of priests. (Exodus 19:3-7) However, reality produced a stark contrast in Daniel's mind. Israel was not a kingdom of priests. Israel was once again a nation of prisoners in a foreign land, and to make matters worse, there was no reference in his previous visions to a glorious role for the Jews. In fact, it was the other way around. Daniel learned the horn would destroy "the holy people." This information greatly distressed the elder statesman.

God is so wise in everything He does. He solved two problems with one action when He sent Gabriel to Daniel. First, God gave Daniel the information he wanted, although "the answer" was not what Daniel had hoped to hear. Second, God ordained that Gabriel's words would be published so that future generations would know about His plans for Israel. God wanted Israel to know that His plans were much more inclusive than merely allowing the Jews to inhabit Jerusalem again. *God wanted Israel to know that their restoration was deliberate and conditional. Israel would be given one last chance to accomplish the mission and purpose for which He had called them out of Egyptian slavery, and now, Babylonian captivity.*

The Answer

Gabriel said, **"I have now come to give you insight and understanding** [into the earlier vision]. **As soon as you began to pray, an answer was given, which I have come to tell you, for you are highly esteemed. Therefore, consider the message and understand the** [earlier] **vision."** (Daniel 9:22-23, insertions mine) When Gabriel began to speak, the angel said nothing about Daniel's prayer, that is, the imminent fulfillment of Jeremiah's prophecy and the release of Israel from Babylon. This is interesting because deliverance from Babylon was the focus of Daniel's prayer. Instead of presenting details about deliverance from Babylon, Gabriel presented *a sequence of events that integrated the nation of Israel into the earlier vision of Daniel 8.* This sequence of events spans 527 years (457 B.C. - A.D. 70), and this span of time began during the time of the ram which Daniel saw in the previous vision. (Daniel 8)

Plan A – Plan B

In essence, Gabriel revealed "Plan B." God had a back-up plan for Israel because Israel had irreparably ruined "Plan A" which was God's original plan for the nation. A new generation of Jews were about to be freed from captivity *to do God's will.* It is interesting to note how deliverance from Babylon parallels Israel's deliverance from Egypt. The first generation had to die because of rebellion before God could start with a new generation. According to Gabriel,

God had much more planned for Israel than merely returning the Jews to Jerusalem. God wanted to establish His eternal kingdom on Earth within 500 years! This could be accomplished *if* Israel fulfilled certain terms and conditions. Consider the following paraphrase of Gabriel's words (Daniel 9:24-27):

1. Seventy weeks of probationary time are determined upon Israel to: a) finish the years allotted for sin on Earth, b) to bring in atonement for sin and establish everlasting righteousness, c) to seal up this vision and its predictions so that its contents might not be known, and d) to anoint the Messiah.

2. From the issuing of the decree to restore and rebuild Jerusalem until Messiah begins His ministry, there will be one Jubilee cycle of 49 years plus 62 weeks (434 years) for a total of 483 years.

3. In the middle of the seventieth week, Messiah will be rejected by His people and be put to death. The execution of Messiah will confirm the unilateral covenant of salvation which God gave to Adam and Eve, and Messiah will put an end to the sacrifices and offerings required since the fall of Adam and Eve.

4. After Jerusalem and the temple are rebuilt, they will be totally destroyed again because of rebellion.

5. Wars and desolations have been decreed upon the Jews and Jerusalem until the end of time.

6. The destroyer, Lucifer, will continue his deadly work until the end of time.

Gabriel's statements are not difficult to understand if a person has a working knowledge of three subjects: 1) God's use of unilateral and bilateral covenants with Adam and Eve, and Abraham and his descendants; 2) the operation of God's Jubilee Calendar; and 3) what history reveals about the timing of Christ's ministry on Earth. When these three matters are properly understood, the events predicted by Gabriel were fulfilled with a precision that is astonishing! Even more, history confirms the alignment of these events within the prophetic matrix that began unfolding in Daniel 2.

(**Note:** A study on unilateral and bilateral covenants is found in Chapters 7 and 8 of my companion volume, *Jesus, The Alpha and The Omega*. A study on the operation of the Jubilee Calendar is found in my reference paper, *Great Clocks from God*.)

Now that we have some ideas about Gabriel's comments, let us examine Gabriel's six statements in detail:

Statement 1

Gabriel said, **"Seventy weeks are determined upon thy people and upon thy holy city, to finish the transgression, and to make an end of sins, and to make reconciliation for iniquity, and to bring in everlasting righteousness, and to seal up the vision and prophecy, and to anoint the most Holy."** (Daniel 9:24, KJV) Many Christians have heard about Daniel's seventy weeks, but few have heard the truth about the seventy weeks. Many scholars claim that sixty-nine of the seventy weeks occurred long ago, but the seventieth week is still to come. This theory forces a large gap of many centuries between the sixty-ninth week and the seventieth week. It will be demonstrated that this gap is artificial and contrived. Inserting a gap of many centuries between the sixty-ninth week and the seventieth week is like inserting a gap of many days between Wednesday and Thursday. The continuum of time cannot be broken. The seventy weeks are seventy *consecutive* weeks. Before we complete this chapter, we will see that Jesus Himself confirms the seventy weeks are 490 consecutive years.

What Is a Week?

What did Gabriel mean when he said, "seventy weeks?" Why did God choose to measure time in weeks and not in years? God's choice of words, as in "seventy weeks" is highly important but poorly understood because of a property called synchrony.

When God created the world, He established four great "clocks" for measuring time. The first clock was called a "day," and the synchrony of a day is set at sundown. A day begins and ends at sundown. The second clock was called a "month," and the synchrony of a month is set by a new moon. A month begins and ends with a new moon. The third clock was called a "year," and the synchrony of a year is determined by the first new moon on or after the Spring Equinox. The fourth clock was a perpetual cycle of seven days called a "week," and the synchrony of each week begins with the first day and ends with the seventh day. The first day *of the week* is always Sunday and the seventh day of the week is Saturday or God's Sabbath of rest. In biblical terms, a week is not Wednesday through Tuesday. Wednesday through Tuesday is seven days, but not a week. A week is a perpetual cycle of time that remains aligned (or synchronous) with the seven days of Creation. (See Chart 6.1)

About 2,500 years after Creation, God added three more clocks to the four established at Creation. God imposed all seven clocks on Israel at the time of the Exodus so that Israel could accurately track the passage of time and seasons, and observe His feasts at the appointed time. (Exodus 12) The fifth clock was a "week of seven months." The sixth clock was a "week of seven years," and the seventh clock was a "week of seven weeks" or forty-nine years. The operation and synchrony of these seven clocks is marvelous. These clocks enabled the ancient Jews to measure the passage of time, and today they allow us to understand something about God's larger timing and plans for Earth.

Seven Clocks from God

1. Day – sundown to sundown

2. Month – new moon to new moon

3. Year – first new moon on or after the Spring Equinox

4. Week – Sunday through Sabbath

5. Week of seven months – synchronized with the month of Nisan

6. Week of seven years – synchronized with the year of the Exodus

7. Week of seven weeks – synchronized with the year of the Exodus

When properly understood, these seven clocks produce a self-correcting calendar which remains properly coordinated with the Sun, moon and the four seasons. A self-correcting calendar is not a small feat when considering the complexity of measuring time via planetary motion. When Israel used God's clocks, their measurement of time was never off by more than one day in any given month. If they happen to miscalculate the arrival of a new month, the error was easily corrected at the beginning of the following month.

You may have noticed that the three clocks God gave to Israel were based on a template of Creation's weekly cycle. Because the weekly cycle was a template, the weekly cycle can be used to represent different periods of time by changing the scale of time. For example, a week of days and a week of years follow the same template, but the scale of time changes from days to years. Each clock has a special synchrony, that is, a specific alignment. For example, the weekly cycle is reset every Sunday because the Creation of the world began on Sunday. Similarly, "a week of seven years" aligns with "the Sunday year" of the Exodus (when this clock began to operate). "A week of seven weeks," which amounts to forty-nine years, aligns with the Sunday year of the Exodus. (Leviticus 25:8) (See Charts 6.1-4.) We will discover that an understanding of these clocks and their synchrony is critical to understanding why God said, "seventy weeks."

The Importance of Synchrony

Because each week starts and stops in perpetual alignment with Creation's week, the weekly cycle has "synchrony" or alignment. *God has placed great significance on the synchrony of the weekly cycles because the observance of His seventh-day Sabbath is tied to Creation.* For example, God withheld manna on the seventh day of the week for forty years in the wilderness to ensure that everyone in Israel knew which day of the week aligned with His Sabbath rest at Creation. (Exodus 16)

Humanity cannot survive without knowing the synchrony of time. The alignment of the Sun with Earth determines the timing of our seasons. Certain crops are planted in the spring because they require a specific number of days of sunlight without frost, while other crops are planted in fall and winter because these plants need the rain and weather conditions necessary for survival during that time. If the human race did not know about the synchrony of the seasons, we would soon starve! If synchrony did not exist, one person could say that it was 4:35 p.m. on January 5, and at the same time, another person could say it was 2:21 a.m. on September 3 and no one could reasonably dispute either claim. For a person to know the time as well as the seasons, he must know about the rotation of Earth, the orbit of the moon around Earth, and the orbit of Earth around the Sun. For a clock to have practical value, it has to synchronize (and stay synchronized) with planetary motion. Otherwise, the information provided by a mechanical clock would mean nothing. Without synchrony, time cannot be measured. When we say this is year A.D. 2003, what do we mean? We mean it has been 2003 years since the birth of Christ (although this is not actually the case, but that's another story). In other words, the Julian/Gregorian calendar is theoretically synchronized with the birth of Christ. When everyone uses the same synchrony of time, everyone knows that a 1954 Corvette is an antique car! With the importance of synchrony in mind, let us examine the three clocks that God created and gave to Israel at the time of the Exodus.

A Week of Seven Months

When God mandated that Israel observe six festivals during the course of a year, He gave them a religious calendar indicating when these feasts were to take place. This religious calendar consisted of **a week of seven months** (Nisan through Tishri). This religious year should not be confused with a full year of twelve months. (Exodus 23:16) Rather, Israel's religious year is similar to a "school year," which lasts for nine or ten months. During the religious year, God required Israel to observe six festivals. For example, Passover was observed on the fifteenth day of the *first* month and the Day of Atonement on the tenth day of the *seventh* month. (See Chart 6.2.) Understand that a religious year did not consist of *any* seven months. The religious year began on New Year's Day (Nisan 1), and New Year's Day was determined by the first new moon on or after the Spring Equinox. The religious year ended (depending on the position of the moon) six or seven days after the Feast of Tabernacles ended. At the time of the Exodus, the Jews often referred to months by number, although they sometimes used Canaanite names for the months. (Exodus 13:4) Centuries later, the Jews adopted Babylonian names for the months of the year. Therefore, Bible writers sometimes call the first month of the year Nisan which is taken from the Babylonian name *Nisanu*. (Nehemiah 2:1) The synchrony of Nisan 1 with the first new moon on or after the Spring Equinox forces Passover to occur in the spring and the Day of Atonement to occur in the fall of the year.

A Week of Seven Years

The **week of seven years** was based on the weekly template, too. Remember, synchrony does not allow a week to start and stop at random times. Likewise, a week of seven years cannot start with just any given year. The Sabbath year (the seventh year) was just as holy to the Lord (Leviticus 25:4) as was the seventh-day Sabbath. (Exodus 20:8-11; Jeremiah 34:13-17) Sabbath years were determined by counting from the year of the Exodus. Because the Jews were required to observe the feasts, they managed to keep track of time. (1 Kings 6:1) The Old and New Testaments demonstrate a perfect synchrony of Sabbatical years. (Isaiah 37:30; Jeremiah 34:14; Nehemiah 8:2,3; Deuteronomy 31:10,11; Daniel 9:24-27; Luke 3:1) At the beginning of the Sabbath year, God required all slaves to be set free and the land was to lay fallow and rest. (See Chart 6.3.)

A Week of Seven Weeks

A **week of seven weeks** equals forty-nine years. Study Chart 6.4 and notice how a week of weeks represents forty-nine years. (Leviticus 25:8) This calendar is called the Jubilee Calendar because the "year of Jubilee" was a special Sabbatical year that occurred *after* each forty-nine year cycle ended. The year of Jubilee was counted as the fiftieth year of the outgoing Jubilee cycle, but it was also counted as the first year of the incoming Jubilee cycle. (See Chart 6.4) Thus, the year of Jubilee always fell on a "Sunday" year. It may seem strange that the fiftieth year of the old Jubilee cycle and the first year of the new Jubilee cycle were the *same* year. This problem vanishes when one realizes this method of counting time parallels the count of days for the feast of Pentecost. The fiftieth day always fell on the first day of the week. (Leviticus 23:15,16) In other words, the only difference is that the count for Pentecost is in days and the count for the year of Jubilee is in years. The weekly template remains the same.

The Bible mentions one year of Jubilee. It took place during the fifteenth year (702 B.C.) of Hezekiah. (Isaiah 36:1; 37:30, see also 2 Kings 19:29) The year of Jubilee was consecrated on the tenth day of the seventh month, on the Day of Atonement (near the end of the religious year). Consecration was delayed until the Day of Atonement because this gave the Israelites six full months into the year of Jubilee to make sure all property was returned to its rightful owner before the Day of Atonement took place.

The beauty of understanding the synchrony of these clocks begins to appear when one realizes that all Sabbath years and Jubilee years – forward and backward – can be easily calculated once a known year is located. For the sake of comparison, one could say that it is easy to calculate paydays – both past and future – when one knows what day of the week payday occurs and how often payday occurs! Synchrony makes this type of calculation possible.

The Weekly Cycle is Alligned with the First Day of Creation

Day One	Day Two	Day Three	Day Four	Day Five	Day Six	**Day Seven**
Sunday	Monday	Tuesday	Wednesday	Thursday	Friday	Sabbath

Chart 6.1

The Week of Seven Months is Aligned with New Year's Day, Nisan 1

Sunday	Monday	Tuesday	Wednesday	Thursday	Friday	Sabbath
Nisan	Ziv	Sivan	Tammuz	Ab	Elul	Tishri

Chart 6.2

The Week of Years is Aligned with the Exodus, 1437 B.C.

Sunday	Monday	Tuesday	Wednesday	Thursday	Friday	**Sabbath**
Exodus 1437 B.C.	1436 B.C.	1435 B.C.	1434 B.C.	1433 B.C.	1432 B.C.	1431 B.C.

Chart 6.3

Look at Chart 6.4 and count off **ten** years beginning with the Exodus year. You should see a Tuesday year, 1428 B.C. Now count off ten **weeks** of years from the Exodus year. What year falls in the middle of the tenth week? (1371 B.C.) Bear in mind, the ten weeks shown on Chart 6.4 are not part of the seventy weeks that Gabriel spoke about. Rather, these weeks mark the beginning of the "weekly

The Week of Seven Weeks is Aligned with the Exodus, 1437 B.C.

	Sunday Year	Monday Year	Tuesday Year	Wednesday Year	Thursday Year	Friday Year	Sabbath Year	
Sunday Week	Exodus 1437 B.C.	1436	1435	1434	1433	1432	1431 (Year 7)	Week 1
Mon Week	1430	1429	1428	1427	1426	1425	1424 (Year 14)	Week 2
Tue Week	1423	1422	1421	1420	1419	1418	1417 (Year 21)	Week 3
Wed Week	1416	1415	1414	1413	1412	1411	1410 (Year 28)	Week 4
Thu Week	1409	1408	1407	1406	1405	1404	1403 (Year 35)	Week 5
Fri Week	1402	1401	1400	1399	1398	1397	1396 (Year 42)	Week 6
Sabbath Week	1395	1394	1393	1392	1391	1390	1389 (Year 49)	Week 7
Jubilee Cycle #2								
Sunday Week	Jubilee 1388 B.C.	1387	1386	1385	1384	1383	1382 (Year 7)	Week 1
Mon Week	1381	1380	1379	1378	1377	1376	1375 (Year 14)	Week 2
Tue Week	1374	1373	1372	1371	1370	1369	1368 (Year 21)	Week 3

Chart 6.4

clock" which God initiated at the Exodus. As we continue to examine the synchrony of time, it will become apparent that inserting a gap of time between days, weeks or years is impossible! When one year ends, another year begins. When one week of seven years ends, another week of seven years begins! When one Jubilee cycle of forty-nine years ends, a new Jubilee cycle begins! If these cycles are broken, the synchrony of the weekly cycle is destroyed and, without synchrony, time cannot be measured.

Why Seventy Weeks?

Gabriel said, **"Seventy weeks are determined. . . ."** Why did God deliberately choose the number "seventy weeks" as a measure of time in Daniel 9:24? We know that God is deliberate and purposeful in everything He does. He could have said, "Four hundred ninety years are determined upon your people. . . ." Instead, God chose to use the term "weeks" as the measurement of time in Daniel 9 instead of "years," because weeks have a synchrony that years do not have! We know that God initiated weeks of years at the Exodus because He required the land to lay fallow during the Sabbath year! This fact produces a key point: *The seventy weeks of Daniel 9 cannot begin with just any year.* God used the word "weeks" because the seventy weeks began with a Sunday year which aligns with the year of the Exodus. Remember, a week of days always begins with Sunday and a week of seven years *always* begins with a Sunday year and ends with a Sabbatical year. When God determined "seventy weeks" of years on Israel, He gave Israel a tremendous hint to identify the specific decree that would start the seventy weeks! Gabriel's words were not intended to be mysterious or secret! Review Chart 6.4 again and notice that a week of years always begins with a Sunday year and that "weeks of years" are always synchronous with the year of the Exodus.

When God sentenced Israel into captivity in Babylon, He did it for a specific period of time. **"This whole country will become a desolate wasteland, and these nations will serve the king of Babylon seventy years."** (Jeremiah 25:11) It is interesting that God said seventy years in Jeremiah's prophecy instead of saying ten weeks. (Ten weeks of seven years equals seventy years.) God's use of "years" instead of "weeks" in Jeremiah's prophecy reflects the fact that the Babylonian captivity did not start in a Sunday year. The seventy years of Babylonian captivity began in 605 B.C., which is a Sabbath year! Therefore, the seventy years in Babylon cannot be called ten weeks of years. This feature, incidently, unlocks a mystery about the 2,300 days in Daniel 8:14. The 2,300 days (or evenings and mornings) amount to 328 weeks plus five days (counting inclusively). Even though the 2,300 evenings and mornings began at the same time as the seventy weeks of Daniel 9 (the decree of Artaxerxes in the Sunday year of 457 B.C.), the 2,300 days are expressed in units of days instead of units of weeks because it takes 2,303 days to make 329 weeks! Since 2,300 days do not equal 329 weeks, God described this time-period using days.

God's Signature

In Chapter 1, remember that seven appears to be God's signature: there are seven days of the week, seven continents, seven colors in the rainbow, seven churches in Revelation, seven seals, seven trumpets, seven bowls, etc. If seven is God's signature, then seventy (ten times seven) must have prominence, too. I believe the number seventy suggests the fullness of God's patience with rebellion. For example, God waited until Israel had violated seventy Sabbath years before sending them into Babylonian captivity. The violation of seventy Sabbath years explains why the captivity in Babylon lasted seventy years. (Leviticus 26:34,25; 2 Chronicles 36:21) Likewise, the *seventy* weeks granted to Israel in Daniel 9 reflect the limits of God's patience with Israel's rebellion. This makes me wonder if there is also a correlation to man's life being approximately seventy years. (Psalm 90:10)

You may recall the following text: **"Then came Peter to him, and said, Lord, how oft shall my brother sin against me, and I forgive him? till seven times? Jesus saith unto him, I say not unto thee, Until seven times: but, Until seventy times seven."** (Matthew 18:21,22) This verse is not translated as it should be. When Peter asked the Lord how many times he should forgive his brother, Jesus did not respond with a numerical count (70 x 7 = 490), Jesus responded with a much larger concept, the idea of seventy sevens. To the Jewish mind, seventy sevens referred to the seventy weeks of unmerited grace given to Israel in Daniel 9. Jesus told Peter that he was to forgive his brother as God had forgiven Israel! In other words, forgiveness was not a numerical total, it was an attitude.

God's signature of seven and the number ten have an important relationship throughout the Bible. For example, God deliberately put the Day of Atonement on the tenth day of the seventh month. (10/7) This annual event on the tenth day of the seventh month marked the end of mercy in the camp of Israel. All sins had to be transferred to the temple before the Day of Atonement arrived. Because everyone knew when the Day of Atonement occurred, every

Israelite knew the limits of God's mercy, and it ended with the arrival of the tenth day of the seventh month.

The great red dragon in Revelation 12 has ten horns and seven heads. (10/7) The dragon-like beast (or composite beast) in Revelation 13 also has ten horns and seven heads. (10/7) This strange anatomy indicates the fullness of rebellion against God during the Great Tribulation! The seven heads represent seven false religions of the world, and the ten horns represent ten kings who will rule with the Antichrist for a short period of time. (Revelation 17:12)

One more point about the number seventy should be considered: The duration of sin appears to last for seventy centuries or a week of seven millenniums. (7/10) If this is true, the one thousand years of Revelation 20 could be a Sabbatical rest from sin for planet Earth. God will destroy sin with fire at the end of seventy centuries. God foreknew how long He would allow sin to exist – even before sin began. My study has convinced me that the number seventy indicates the limits of God's patience with rebellion, and this is why Gabriel told Daniel, "*Seventy* weeks are determined upon your people. . . ." With this vision, God put the nation of Israel on notice that His patience with them as a nation was limited to seventy more weeks, beginning with a specific decree to restore and rebuild Jerusalem that would occur during a Sunday year.

Seventy Weeks Make a Statement

When He defined the probationary time for the Jews as "seventy weeks," God informed the Jews of three things: First, God acknowledged the presence and operation of the weekly cycle of years that He had established at the time of the Exodus. (Leviticus 25:1-4) Weeks of years did not suddenly begin during or after the Babylonian captivity. Second, when God said, "Seventy weeks are determined. . . ," He forced the decree and the first year of the seventy weeks to align with a Sunday year, because a week of years *always* begins with a Sunday year! Last, when God indicated that Messiah would cause sacrifices and offerings to cease in the middle of the seventieth week, He affirmed that His calendar would continue to operate *after* Jesus died on the cross. This is a key point that many people overlook: God's calendar could not cease to operate when Jesus died because He died in the *middle* of the seventieth week! If the week of years ended at the cross, as many scholars claim, then the seventy-weeks prophecy would have been stated as a 69 ½-weeks prophecy, not as a seventy-week prophecy!

Work with Me!

I call God's objectives for the seventy weeks "Plan B." Israel was in captivity because it had ruined "Plan A." If the new Israel cooperated with God, He would bring an end to sin and establish His kingdom on Earth at the end of the seventy weeks. If Israel failed to cooperate, God promised to destroy Jerusalem and displace Israel with a "new" Israel, starting over again. One might call the next plan, "Plan C." Remember Gabriel's words: **"Seventy weeks are determined upon thy people and upon thy holy city, to finish the transgression, and to make an end of sins, and to make reconciliation for iniquity, and to bring in everlasting righteousness, and to seal up the vision and prophecy, and to anoint the most Holy."** (Daniel 9:24, KJV) The objectives presented in this verse are very similar to the objectives God gave Israel ("Plan A") before entering the Promised Land, but the essential difference is timing. In Daniel 9:24, God declared that He was ready to bring in everlasting righteousness *within* 490 years of a particular decree! Talk about excitement! Of course, God's objectives could only be met if Israel allowed the Holy Spirit to have dominion in the hearts of the majority of its citizens. God said, "Work with me and see what I will do *through* you!" *If* Israel had cooperated with Him, God would have accomplished four amazing things:

1. The nation of Israel and the city of Jerusalem would have risen from its ashes and flourished above all nations as an example of God's redemption. (God gave numerous prophecies about Israel's restoration and prominent role to Daniel's contemporary, Ezekiel. If Israel had cooperated with God, the prophecies of Ezekiel would have been fulfilled. *This is a key point that will be discussed further at the end of this chapter, because this point is connected to the 2,300-days prophecy.*) Israel's redemption and release from captivity were to be a pattern of salvation, giving hope to all nations of the world that God would redeem everyone and free them from the captivity of sin and rebellion if they loved Him.

The exciting news which God gave to Daniel was that all this could occur within seventy weeks of years. Think of it! God had allotted the remaining time for sin and rebellion on Earth to be a mere 490 years, but only *if* Israel cooperated! It is such a tragedy to discover that each generation in Israel cared less and less about this amazing opportunity as the 490 years rolled by.

2. God promised to send His Sacrifice, the Lamb of God, and offer Him up for sin within 490 years. The Savior of the world would appear, and He would die in the middle year of the seventieth week. Afterwards, Jesus would usher in everlasting righteousness, but only *if* Israel cooperated.

3. If Israel cooperated with God, they would have the privilege of anointing "The Most Holy." The term, "anointing the most holy," is a Hebraic concept that refers to anointing the most holy officer in Israel, the high priest. (Exodus 29:21; Leviticus 4:3; Leviticus 8:30) Even though Israel had long anticipated the birth of Messiah (the word Messiah means the Anointed One), God told Israel they would have the privilege of anointing the Messiah! Tragically, He came unto His own and His own did not receive Him. (John 1:11) So, the Holy Spirit anointed Jesus at His baptism. (Mark 1:10; Luke 4:18)

4. The fourth objective was an amazing promise. If Israel cooperated, God promised to seal up this vision and all the other prophecies in the book of Daniel, because these prophecies would not come to pass. In other words, if the new Israel cooperated with God so that "Plan B" could be fulfilled, the course of human history would unfold as promised under the original plan. This is a very important point to understand. Once implemented, Daniel's prophecies become unconditional. This means they are not subject to man's cooperation to be fulfilled. The Rock in Daniel 2 will hit the ten kings and destroy them. The little horn power of Daniel 7 would appear and persecute the saints. The goat would overrun the ram in Daniel 8, etc. The point is that *if* the new Israel cooperated with God, He would seal up these visions and

prophecies given to Daniel, and their contents would never be known or implemented. Notice what God is doing. God spoke to Ezekiel at the same time He spoke to Daniel, and God promised a grand and glorious future for Israel *if* they would cooperate with Him. The prophecies of Ezekiel were conditional. Israel would be marvelously blessed if they chose to cooperate with God. However, if Israel did not cooperate, then Daniel's visions and prophecies would be fulfilled. You must see this larger picture of what God is doing to appreciate the contrasting messages that God sent to Daniel and Ezekiel.

Always Starting Over

These four objectives have profound significance, because they show God's intentions *if* Israel would cooperate with Him. The prophecies of Jeremiah, Isaiah, and other prophets pointed to a grand fulfillment of "Plan A." Unfortunately, Israel did not cooperate. Therefore, God destroyed His temple, people and city. After seventy years in Babylon, God offered a new Israel "Plan B," promising to fulfill it within 490 years! It is hard to believe, but the new Israel failed, too. They rejected God and they rejected God's Son. (Luke 20:9-19; John 1; Romans 9-11) Therefore, God destroyed His temple, people and city a final time in A.D. 70. (There's another seventy – A.D. 70!) Mercifully, God started again with "Plan C." Under this plan, God redefined Israel. Israel includes anyone who will believe in His Son, Jesus Christ. (Ephesians 2, Galatians 3) Under "Plan C" there is a new covenant that is even better than the former covenant.

If I were to identify the primary reason for so much prophetic confusion among Christians today, it would have to be this: Scholars are still trying to figure out ways for God to fulfill the many Old Testament prophecies that belong to "Plan A" and "Plan B." However, these scholars are wasting their efforts because God has implemented "Plan C." Instead of looking forward to a rebuilt temple in old Jerusalem, we should be looking forward to the *New* Jerusalem that comes from God out of Heaven. The exciting news is that there will be no temple in the New Jerusalem because the Father and the Lamb will be among their people. (Revelation 21:2,22) Think about this: If Israel had cooperated with God during the 490 years, there would have been no need for a Second Coming. Nowhere in the Old Testament, other than in the book of Daniel, is there a mention of a Second Coming. Instead, God would have established His kingdom on Earth at the end of the 490 years! Sin would have ended and everlasting righteousness would have begun.

Back to Gabriel's Statements, Numbers 2 and 3

"Know and understand this: From the issuing of the decree to restore and rebuild Jerusalem until the Anointed One, the ruler, comes, there will be seven 'sevens,' and sixty-two 'sevens.' It will be rebuilt with streets and a trench, but in times of trouble." (Daniel 9:25)

Four decrees were issued for the restoration of Jerusalem. Cyrus gave the first decree in the Friday year of 536 B.C. (Ezra 1) Darius gave the second decree in the Monday year of 519 B.C. (Ezra 6) Artexerxes gave the third and fourth decrees in the Sunday year of 457 and the Sabbath year of 444 B.C. (Ezra 7 and Nehemiah 2, respectively) Remember that God used the word "weeks" instead of years to indicate the synchrony for this all important decree with His weekly cycle of years established at the Exodus. In verse 25, Gabriel adds another specification that identifies which of the four decrees God will use to count off the seventy weeks: **"From the issuing of the decree to restore and rebuild Jerusalem until the Anointed One, the ruler, comes, there will be seven 'weeks' and sixty-two 'weeks. . . .'"** With these words, Gabriel points to the public ministry of Messiah. Gabriel used seven weeks and sixty-two weeks to highlight the all important synchrony of a decree that would occur in a Sunday year and at the *beginning* of a Jubilee cycle of seven weeks. (See Chart 6.5) By separating the 69 weeks into two smaller pieces – the first of which was a Jubilee cycle, God was doing everything He could to help Israel identify the right decree. Notice how this works: In verse 24, God points to a decree that occurs on a Sunday year by using the words "seventy weeks." (Weeks always begin with a Sunday year.) In verse 25, God indicates the decree will occur at the beginning of "seven weeks" or 49 years. A seven-week cycle is a Jubilee cycle of forty-nine years and it always begins with a Sunday year. Only one of the four decrees meets this specification. The decree in 457 B.C. occurred in a Sunday year, which also happens to start a new cycle of seven weeks (Jubilee cycle). Incidently, if 457 B.C. is a Jubilee year, so is 702 B.C., the only Jubilee year mentioned in the Bible. (Isaiah 37:30) God used language so plain that wise men from Ur figured it out! However, the religious leaders in Jerusalem never did figure it out. Religion can be so blinding.

My reference paper, *Great Clocks from God,* discusses the year of the Exodus (1437 B.C.) and many other issues that accompany this topic. For this study, just consider the possibility that 457 B.C. is a Sunday year and 457 B.C. is the first year of a Jubilee cycle. From the Bible we learn that on or about the very first day of the very first month of the year of Jubilee (Nisan 1), King Artaxerxes issued a decree providing for the refurbishing of Jerusalem and its temple. (Ezra 7) We also know that Ezra left Babylon with the decree in his hand on Nisan 12, the twelfth day of the first month! (Ezra 8:31)

The Decree of Artaxerxes, Nisan 1, 457 B.C. – Jubilee Cycle #21 Since the Exodus

Sunday	Monday	Tuesday	Wednesday	Thursday	Friday	Sabbath	
457 B.C. Decree	456 B.C.	455 B.C.	454 B.C.	453 B.C.	452 B.C.	451 B.C.	Week 1
450 B.C.	449 B.C.	448 B.C.	447 B.C.	446 B.C.	445 B.C.	444 B.C.	Week 2
443 B.C.	442 B.C.	441 B.C.	440 B.C.	439 B.C.	438 B.C.	437 B.C.	Week 3
436 B.C.	435 B.C.	434 B.C.	433 B.C.	432 B.C.	431 B.C.	430 B.C.	Week 4
429 B.C.	428 B.C.	427 B.C.	426 B.C.	425 B.C.	424 B.C.	423 B.C.	Week 5
422 B.C.	421 B.C.	420 B.C.	419 B.C.	418 B.C.	417 B.C.	416 B.C.	Week 6
415 B.C.	414 B.C.	413 B.C.	412 B.C.	411 B.C.	410 B.C.	409 B.C.	Week 7
Jubilee Cycle #22 Since the Exodus							
408 B.C. Jubilee	407 B.C.	406 B.C.	405 B.C.	404 B.C.	403 B.C.	402 B.C.	Week 8
401 B.C.	400 B.C.	399 B.C.	398 B.C.	397 B.C.	396 B.C.	395 B.C.	Week 9
394 B.C.	393 B.C.	392 B.C.	391 B.C.	390 B.C.	389 B.C.	388 B.C.	Week 10

Chart 6.5

Look at Chart 6.5 and count off the "seven weeks" which Gabriel mentioned (457 - 409 B.C.). Notice that first week of the "sixty-two weeks" Gabriel mentioned began with 408 B.C., and if this chart extended long enough, the 69th week would end with the Sabbath year of A.D. 26. Notice that 457 B.C. is both a Sunday year and a Year of Jubilee. (Remember, the Year of Jubilee is the fiftieth year of the old Jubilee cycle, and it is also the first year of the new Jubilee cycle.) *None of the other decrees to restore and rebuild Jerusalem can satisfy the synchrony that God indicates in Daniel 9.* Therefore, none of the other decrees can meet the "seven weeks and sixty-two weeks" requirement that Gabriel specified. If this information does not convince the reader, history proves these three decrees cannot meet the Daniel 9 specifications either. Here's how:

If 457 B.C. is the correct decree and it marks the beginning of the seventy weeks, then we should expect the appearing of Messiah "seven and sixty-two weeks later" (69 x 7 = 483 years), in the Sunday year of A.D. 27. History precisely confirms this to be the case! Jesus waited until His thirtieth birthday, which occurred in the Fall of A.D. 27., to begin His ministry. Notice how Luke documents the year of Jesus' baptism: **"In the fifteenth year of the reign of Tiberius Caesar—when Pontius Pilate was governor of Judea, Herod tetrarch of Galilee, his brother Philip tetrarch of Iturea and Traconitis, and Lysanias tetrarch of Abilene. . . . The people were waiting expectantly and were all wondering in their hearts if John might possibly be the Christ."** (Luke 3:1,15) Have you wondered why people thought John the Baptist might be the Christ? I believe some people were expecting Christ because they knew that 483 years had lapsed since the decree of Artaxerxes. The year had come for the Messiah to appear and John the Baptist, a forerunner of Messiah, was attracting a lot of attention because the power of the Holy Spirit rested on him. (Luke 1:17) Within this context Luke wrote, **"When all the people were being baptized, Jesus was baptized too. And as he was praying, heaven was opened and the Holy Spirit descended on him in bodily form like a dove. And a voice came from heaven: 'You are my Son, whom I love; with you I am well pleased.' Now Jesus himself was about thirty years old when he began his ministry. . . ."** (Luke 3:21-23)

Tiberius and A.D. 27

Some scholars claim that the fifteenth year of Tiberius cannot be A.D. 27., but it was the fifteenth year for the Jews! The Romans did not date Caesar's rule with regnal years. Rather, the official count of years in Roman service was determined by the years Tiberius held tribunician power. Therefore, A.D. 27 would have been the 33rd or 34th year of Tiberius' tribunician power (Tiberius was granted power as a member of the tribune in 6 B.C.). I raise this point because Luke dates the fifteenth year of Tiberius according to Jewish tradition, not Roman tradition. The fifteenth year of Tiberius, according to Jewish tradition, began in the fall of A.D. 27. Here's how:

History says that on August 19, A.D. 14, Augustus died. Tiberius maneuvered the Senate for a few weeks and did not allow it to name him emperor for almost a month. On September 17, A.D. 14, Tiberius became the emperor of Rome at age 56. Because this is what history says, we find that Luke follows the Jewish tradition of inclusive dating. This means Luke counted the ascension year of Tiberius as "year 1," even though the ascension year was just a few days in length before a new civil year began on Tishri 1. Josephus also followed this practice when he dated the reigns of the Herods. (Antiquities xv. 5.2; xvii. 8.1) The Mishnah further confirms this method of Jewish regnal reckoning. (Mishnah Rosh Hashanah 1.1)

During the time of Christ, the Jews observed a fall-to-fall civil calendar. The first month of this calendar was the seventh month of their religious year. It was called Tishri. Therefore, Tiberius ascended to the throne on September 17, A.D. 14, during a Jewish civil year that ended about two months later (November 11, A.D. 14.) So, Luke counted September 17 to November 11 as "year 1" because Tiberius, counting inclusively, ascended to the throne that year. Therefore, the Jews regarded the following civil year Tishri 1 to Tishri 1 (November 12, A.D. 14 to October 31, A.D. 15), as the second year of Tiberius' reign. (See Chart 6.6.)

Luke's Account: The Reign of Tiberius Caesar

Year 1 = A.D. 14/14 (September 17 - November 11)
Year 2 = A.D. 14/15 (Tishri 1 to Tishri 1)
Year 3 = A.D. 15/16 (Tishri 1 to Tishri 1)
Year 4 = A.D. 16/17 Etc.
Year 5 = A.D. 17/18
Year 6 = A.D. 18/19

Year 7 = A.D. 19/20
Year 8 = A.D. 20/21
Year 9 = A.D. 21/22
Year 10 = A.D. 22/23
Year 11 = A.D. 23/24
Year 12 = A.D. 24/25
Year 13 = A.D. 25/26
Year 14 = A.D. 26/27
Year 15 = A.D. 27/28

Chart 6.6

Chart 6.6 shows Tishri 1 to Tishri 1 (October 19, A.D. 27 through November 6, A.D. 28) as the 15th year of Tiberius. According to Roman dating, Jewish reckoning and Luke's report, Jesus was baptized in the fall of A.D. 27, sometime after Tishri 1. (The length of Christ's public ministry on Earth was almost 32 months.) Just as Gabriel predicted, Jesus arrived at the banks of the Jordan River where John baptized Him. Jesus began His public ministry in the Sunday year of A.D. 27, which is the first year of the seventieth week! This is not the end of the story. Two additional facts from history confirm this synchrony of the Jubilee Calendar. In short, God's timing is astonishing.

The Wise Men

The story of Jesus' birth includes a surprising visit by the Magi from the East. Many people do not realize the Magi were careful students of prophecy. Scholars believe they were clergymen from Ur, in the province of Babylon. Evidently, they had discovered and deeply studied Daniel's writings, as well as other books of the Old Testament. The Magi understood that priests and kings in Israel were typically thirty years of age when they ascended to authority. (Numbers 4; Genesis 41:46; 1 Samuel 13:1; 2 Samuel 5:4; 1 Chronicles 23:3) Using this information, they determined when the sixty-nine weeks would end. Then, they subtracted thirty years from that calculation to determine the year of Messiah's birth. When they saw the star appear in the heavens, they knew *it* was a sign from God.

Think about it. Their round-trip journey to see baby Jesus required them to travel more than a thousand miles over a period of a year. The intensity of their desire to see the Messiah was obvious. Their lavish gifts for baby Jesus reveals a love for God that few Jews could understand. (The gifts from the Magi financially sustained Mary, Joseph and Jesus during their exile in Egypt when they escaped Herod's decree to kill all baby boys less than two years of age.) Wise men do not go to these extremes on a whim. Like Simeon and Anna (the elderly prophets of Israel who longed to see Messiah before they died), the wise men longed to see the Savior of the world with their own eyes. Their visit was a powerful affirmation that the decree of Artaxerxes in 457 B.C. is the correct decree for starting the 483-year countdown. Consider their question to King Herod: **"Where is the one who has been born king of the Jews? We saw his star in the east and have come to worship him."** (Matthew 2:2) They were not questioning *whether the king of the Jews had been born.* They were wanting to know *where* He had been born. Perhaps they did not have access to Micah's writings. If they did, they could have gone directly to Bethlehem. (Micah 5:2) Their presence in Jerusalem at just the right time suggests they understood Daniel 9, since *no other prophecy* in the Bible pinpoints the time of Messiah's birth.

How could mere "Gentiles" from a distant land be better informed on the timing of Messiah's appearing than Jewish scholars? How did the Samaritan woman at the well know Messiah's coming was near. She anticipated the appearing of the Messiah because she said: **". . . I know that Messiah (called Christ) is coming . . . when he comes, he will explain everything to us."** (John 4:25) The answer is simple. Centuries earlier, the Lord had said, **"You will seek me and find me when you seek me with all your heart."** (Jeremiah 29:13) Unfortunately, Jewish scholars were not looking for Jesus. They were caught up in their tiny world of pseudo-scholarship. They had nit-picked the Word of God into so many senseless pieces, they could no longer see the big picture. Even though the religious leaders discussed and debated the prophecies of Daniel between themselves, they could not understand Gabriel's words. Ironically, the same situation appears to be true today. Scholars still twist and distort Gabriel's words. Unfortunately, they have led millions of people to anticipate a non-existent pre-tribulation rapture by tampering with the seventy weeks.

Jesus Died in the Middle of the Seventieth Week!

God's timing is incredibly perfect. Let us review the facts. First, 457 B.C. aligns with the weekly cycle of years that began operating at the Exodus in 1437 B.C. Second, 457 B.C. aligns with the forty-nine year Jubilee cycles that began operating at the Exodus. Third, Messiah appeared sixty-nine weeks after 457 B.C., in A.D. 27, to be baptized by John the Baptist. Fourth, 457 B.C. was affirmed by the wise men shortly after Jesus was born. The fifth and best proof that the 457 B.C. decree is the one indicated in Daniel 9, is the timing of Jesus' death. Basically, Jesus began His ministry on time and He died on time. The death of Jesus not only confirms the synchrony of the Jubilee Calendar, it also confirms the decree of Artaxerxes in 457 B.C. to be the right decree. Paul was aware of this phenomenon: **"But when the time had fully come, God sent his Son, born of a woman, born under law . . . You see, *at just the right time*, when we were still powerless, Christ died for the ungodly."** (Galatians 4:4; Romans 5:6, italics mine)

Gabriel's Statement Number 3

Gabriel said, **"After the sixty-two 'sevens,' the Anointed One will be cut off and will have nothing. . . . He will confirm a covenant with many for one 'seven.' In the middle of the** [last] **'seven' he will put an end to sacrifice and offering."** (Daniel 9:26,27, insertion mine) Look ahead to Chart 6.7. Notice how A.D. 30 is located in the *middle* of the seventieth week of years. Of course, Christians have no question that Jesus *confirmed* the covenant that God first gave to Adam and Eve, as well as Abraham and his descendants. There should be no doubt in any mind that He put an end to animal sacrifices and ceremonial offerings when He died on the cross. (Colossians 2) Yet, very few Christians realize that Daniel predicted Jesus' death and Jesus fulfilled Daniel's prophecy when he died in the middle of the seventieth week!

Look again at Chart 6.7. Counting from the decree of Artaxerxes, notice that A.D. 30 is in the middle of the seventieth week. Notice also that A.D. 30 occurs in the middle of the 210th week counting from the Exodus in 1437 B.C. Notice that the seventy weeks of Daniel 9 began at the beginning of the 141st week (or 987 years) since the Exodus, and also notice that the seventieth week terminates 210 weeks of years, which is exactly thirty Jubilee cycles since the Exodus.

Counting Weeks from the Exodus (1437 B.C.) and the Decree of Artaxerxes (457 B.C.)

Sun	Mon	Tue	Wed	Thur	Fri	Sab	Weeks Since Decree	Weeks Since Exodus
1437 B.C. Exodus	1436	1435	1434	1433	1432	1431	--	1
---	---	---	---	---	---	---	---	---
457 B.C.	456	455	454	453	452	451	1st	141
450	449	448	447	446	---	---	2nd	142

Weeks 3 Through 68

Sun	Mon	Tue	Wed	Thur	Fri	Sab	Weeks Since Decree	Weeks Since Exodus
A.D. 20	21	22	23	24	25	26	69th	209
A.D. 27	28	29	A.D. 30	31	32	33	70th	210
34	35	36	37	---	---		71st	211

Chart 6.7

Proving A.D. 30 is the Year of Christ's Death

Daniel 9:27 says, "**. . . In the middle of the 'seven'** [or week] **he will put an end to sacrifice and offering.**" Gabriel said that Jesus would die in the middle year of the seventieth week. (See Chart 6.7.) Since we know that Jesus died at the time of Passover (John 12), and since there is widely accepted astronomical data for A.D. 30 that is accurate to within two hours, there is sufficient evidence to prove beyond reasonable debate that Jesus was crucified on Friday, April 7, A.D. 30. (There is another signature seven in April 7!) If we allow Bible history and the synchrony of God's Great Clocks to resolve the question of the time of His death, all of the data presented in the Gospels concerning Christ's passion week harmoniously fits together. In fact, A.D. 30 *exclusively satisfies* the synchrony required by all seven clocks which the Creator devised! A.D. 30 is the *only* year during which all of the events described in Scripture could have occurred.

How Israel Measured Time

The Jews normally measured time *inclusively*. Any part of a year, month or day counted as a whole unit. Remember how Tiberius came to power about two months before Tishri 1 (the beginning of a new Jewish civil year), but Luke counted those two months as a *whole year.* (Luke 3:1) Similarly, if someone came to your home on Tuesday and left on Wednesday, the ancients would measure the time your guest visited in your home to be two days and two nights – Tuesday and Wednesday – even though the actual time was less than twenty-four hours. Because a day consists of a dark portion and a light portion, any part of two days was called "two days and two nights." This inclusive method for measuring time explains how Jesus could be dead for three days and three nights (Matthew 12:40), even though the Bible says the Father resurrected Jesus *on* – not after – the third day (Acts 10:40), which was Sunday, the first day of the week. (John 20:1-5) Using inclusive reckoning, Jesus was in the tomb for three days and three nights: Friday, Sabbath and Sunday. However, He was slain on Friday afternoon, rested in the Tomb on Sabbath and resurrected on Sunday. The number of hours that Jesus was dead was less than forty hours (two hours on Friday afternoon, twenty-four hours on Sabbath and ten to twelve hours on Sunday). The timing of this matter can be demonstrated beyond the point of reasonable controversy!

One more point about inclusive measurement of time. *Eighteen prophetic time periods are in Daniel and Revelation's seventeen prophecies, and from God's perspective, all of them use inclusive reckoning.* The decree by Artaxerxes in 457 B.C. occurs *during* the first year of the seventy weeks; therefore, the year of the decree is *included* in the count of 490 years. (See Chart 6.7.) The time period of forty years the Israelites spent in the wilderness was measured with inclusive reckoning. (Deuteronomy 2:14; Numbers 14:34) The three days allotted to Pharaoh's cupbearer was measured with inclusive reckoning. (Genesis 40:12,13)

One Moon – Two Months

History says the Jews abandoned God's "new moon" synchrony for
determining the beginning of a new month. In its place, they
adopted the Babylonian method of sighting the first crescent of a
new moon to determine the beginning of a month. Even today, Jews
and Moslems continue the practice of sighting a new moon to
determine the beginning of a religious month. God's synchrony for
starting a new month is based on calculation, not observation. A
new moon occurs when the moon crosses an imaginary line between
Earth and the Sun. Since a new moon cannot be seen (the moon is
between Earth and the Sun), the time of conjunction has to be
calculated. Calculation of a new moon is not difficult. (See
Numbers 28:14; 1 Samuel 20:24-27; Isaiah 66:23.) Of course, when
two different methods for starting a given month are used, there are
two different results. The difference between these two methods is
usually two days. The sighting of the new crescent of a moon occurs
in Jerusalem anywhere between sixteen to forty hours after
conjunction. Because there are two methods for starting a new
month (thus, two calendars) in the New Testament, there is
confusion about the timing of Christ's death.

The Bible indicates that Jesus and His disciples (and other Jews)
observed Passover according to the "new moon" calendar, even
though the nation of Israel observed its corporate Passover
according to the Babylonian method for starting a new month.
(Mark 14; John 13) Since the moon determines the first day of the
month for both groups of people, the position of the moon plays an
important role in determining the date for Passover. God
commanded the Passover lamb to be slain on Nisan 14 as the day
was ending, and after roasting the lamb for a few hours, it was to be
eaten at midnight on the fifteenth day of the first month. The Lord
passed over Egypt at midnight on the fifteenth of Nisan. (Exodus 12;
Leviticus 23:5,6; Numbers 28:16,17; Luke 22:1-8) *Therefore, any
attempt to determine a date and time for the death of Jesus has to
address the astronomical position of a new moon for Nisan 1, as well
as the first sighting of the crescent of a new moon.*

After the Babylonian captivity, the Jews often observed two Feasts
of Passover in the same month. This conflict (and many other
contradictory issues) gave the Romans another reason to mock the

Jews. Even as late as the fourth century A.D., the emperor Constantine used the competing observance of two Passovers to prove that Christians should not depend upon the Jews to determine the correct time for Passover (the observance of Easter was determined by the time for Passover in those days). Notice his denigrating comments: "We ought not, therefore, to have anything in common with the Jews, for the Savior has shown us another way; our worship follows a more legitimate and more convenient course; and consequently, in unanimously adopting this mode, we desire, dearest brethren, to separate ourselves from the detestable company of the Jews, for it is truly shameful for us to hear them boast that without their direction we could not keep this feast [of Easter at the proper time]. How can they be in the right, they who, after the death of the Savior, have no longer been led by reason but by wild violence, as their delusions may urge them? They do not possess the truth in this Easter question; for in their blindness and repugnance to all improvement, they frequently celebrate two Passovers in the same year." (Eusebius, Vita Const., Lib iii., 18-20, insertions mine)

Two Passovers in One Week!

When Jesus came to Earth, He came to declare the truth on many issues which the Jews had distorted. The presence of two calendars (and two Passovers) in Israel solves an interesting mystery, namely, how Jesus could observe Passover at its appointed time with His disciples in the upper room (on Nisan 15 – Mark 14:14-16), and within the same year, also die at the time of the national Passover which took place on Nisan 15 (John 19:14-31)! The solution to this mystery is quite simple. Jesus and His disciples observed Passover in the upper room according to God's synchrony for the month (new moon to new moon), but Jesus died on the cross according to the Babylonian method of starting a new month (the sighting of the first crescent of a new moon)! Since the observance of two calendars was a common part of Jewish life, Gospel writers do not specifically mention that two conflicting calendars existed. For two thousand years, this silence has caused a lot of controversy over the day and date of Christ's death. I hope the following explanation eliminates the confusion surrounding the time of Christ's death.

Jesus was crucified on Friday afternoon, April 7, A.D. 30, which is the precise year required by Daniel 9! Even though most Christians accept A.D. 30 as the year of Christ's death, few understand that it is in the middle of the seventieth week and even fewer understand how this date is determined.

Step 1

Solar and lunar tables posted at the United States Naval Observatory (USNO) website offer astronomical data covering the years Jesus was on Earth. This data has been carefully verified by several astronomers through the years and is accurate to within one or two hours. The dates and times from the USNO are given in Universal Time. Notice the date of the equinox and the time of conjunction for years A.D. 29-31, especially notice the days of the week:

A.D. 29 Vernal Equinox: Tuesday, March 22, 4 p.m.

First New Moon on or after Equinox: Saturday, April 2, 5 p.m.

A.D. 30 Vernal Equinox: Wednesday, March 22, 10 p.m.

First New Moon on or after Equinox: Wednesday, March 22, 6 p.m.

A.D. 31 Vernal Equinox: Friday, March 23, 3 a.m.

First New Moon on or after Equinox: Tuesday, April 10, 12 noon

Source: http://aa.usno.navy.mil/AA/faq/docs/springphenom.html

Step 2

According to the dates and times published by the USNO, a new moon occurred on the same night as the Equinox in A.D. 30. (Jerusalem local time for the new moon was 8 p.m. and for the Equinox, midnight.) Since a new moon and the Equinox occurred on the same day, a new month and a new year began on Wednesday night, March 22, Universal Time. Converting Universal Time to Bible Time: Wednesday night, March 22 becomes Thursday, March 23 and Nisan 1. This translation is necessary because a day in God's calendar begins at sundown. (Genesis 1; Leviticus 23:32) Notice in the New Moon calendar (Chart 6.8) that New Year's day (Nisan 1) occurred on Thursday and Passover (Nisan 15) occurred on a Thursday in A.D. 30.

New Moon Calendar

Jesus Ate Passover Thursday Night (April 6), Nisan 15, A.D. 30

Sunday	Monday	Tuesday	Wednesday	Thursday	Friday	Sabbath
---	---	---	---	Nisan 1 March 23	Nisan 2 March 24	Nisan 3 March 25
Nisan 4 March 26	Nisan 5 March 27	Nisan 6 March 28	Nisan 7 March 29	Nisan 8 March 30	Nisan 9 March 31	Nisan 10 April 1
Nisan 11 April 2	Nisan 12 April 3	Nisan 13 April 4	Nisan 14 April 5	**Nisan 15** **April 6**	Nisan 16 April 7	Nisan 17 April 8

Chart 6.8

If Jesus and His disciples observed Passover according to the new moon calendar, Chart 6.8 indicates that Jesus and His disciples ate the Passover together on Thursday night at midnight. (Remember, in God's calendar the night precedes the light.) We know that God required the Jews to slay the Passover lamb near sundown on Nisan 14. (Exodus 12:6) In this case, the disciples killed the paschal lamb about sundown on Wednesday afternoon and they roasted it until about midnight on Thursday, Nisan 15. Jesus and His disciples then celebrated the Passover, for it was at midnight that the Lord passed over Egypt. (Exodus 11:4) Take a few moments and study the Passion Week Outline. Notice how each of the gospel writers describe the course of events in their order:

The Passion Week Calendar

C=Creation Calendar	B = Babylonian Calendar
(Observed by Jesus)	(Observed by the Jews)

<u>C B</u>

Nisan 11, 9   Sunday night

                  Sunday light

                    –   Jesus arrived in Bethany (John 12:1)

<u>C   B</u>

Nisan 12, 10 Monday night

– Mary washed Jesus' feet at Simon's
house (Mark 14:1)

Monday light

– Jesus went to the temple, publically rebukes the
leaders of Israel (Matt 23)

– Jesus went to Mount of Olives – predicted end of
Jerusalem and world (Matt 24,25)

– Judas went to the chief priests offering to condemn
Jesus (Mark 14:10, Luke 22:1)

– Chief priests held meeting to accept the offer of
Judas to condemn Jesus (Matt 26:3-5)

Nisan 13, 11 Tuesday night

Tuesday light

– Jesus rode into Jerusalem on a donkey
(John 12:12-16)

Nisan 14,12 Wednesday night

Wednesday light

– Disciples made preparations for Passover meal
(Mark 14:12, Matt 26:17)

Nisan 15, 13 Thursday night

– Jesus ate Passover at midnight with disciples
(Mark 14:17,18)

– Jesus predicted His betrayal (Matt 26:20,21)

– Jesus eager to eat this Passover *before* He suffered
(Luke 22:15)

April 6, A.D. 30

– Judas left room after midnight meal to betray
Jesus (John 13:30)

<u>C B</u>

Thursday light

- At daybreak, they sang a hymn and went out to the Mount of Olives (Matt 26:30)

- Jesus spent all day talking to the disciples. (John 13:36-16:33)

- Jesus predicted the scattering of the disciples (Matt 26:31,32)

- Jesus prayed for His disciples. (John 17)

Nisan 16,14 Friday night

- Jesus took Peter, James and John into Gethsemane. (Matt 26:36)

- Jesus betrayed and arrested . (Luke 22:44-47)

- Peter denied knowing Jesus. (Luke 22:60,61)

Friday light

- Jesus taken before the chief priests and elders. (Luke 22:66, Matt 27:1)

- Jesus taken to Caiaphas then to Pilate. (John 18:28)

- Jesus taken to Herod and sent back to Pilate. (Luke 23:7,12)

- Pilate offered to release a prisoner to Jews for goodwill. (John 18:39)

Jesus Crucified:

- Jesus crucified about the third hour. (9 am) (Mark 15:25)

April 7, A.D. 30

- Darkness covered the land from noon to 3 pm. (Mark 15:33, 34)

- Jesus died about the ninth hour. (3 pm) (Matt 27:46)

<u>C B</u>

- Jesus' body was not prepared because Sabbath was so close. (Luke 23:55)

- Jews asked Pilate to have the bodies removed for Passover (John 19:31)

Nisan 17,15 Sabbath night

- National Passover feast eaten at midnight.

- Disciples mourned, chief priests worried that Jesus' body might be stolen.

Sabbath light

- Chief priests asked Pilate to seal the tomb to prevent theft. (Matt 27:62)

Nisan 18,16 Sunday night

- Disciples hid for fear of Jewish leaders.

Sunday light

Jesus resurrected

- Mary and Mary go to the tomb near sunrise. Empty! (Mark 16:1)

- Afternoon: Jesus walked with Cleopas and a friend to Emmaus. (Luke 24:13)

Mark 14:16 clearly indicates that Jesus ate the Passover with His disciples before going to His death. The sequence of events went like this: Jesus ate the Passover on Thursday night. On Thursday (the light part of Thursday follows the night part of Thursday) Jesus spent the day with His disciples on the Mount of Olives. (Mark 14:26) As Friday night settled upon them, Jesus and three disciples went into the Garden of Gethsemane. (Mark 14:32) Jesus was arrested that night while in the garden. His trial began that night and lasted until morning on Friday. He was crucified about 9 a.m. and died around 3 p.m. (Mark 15:25, 34) About the time Jesus expired, the Jews celebrated the slaying of the national Passover lamb at the temple, and to their astonishment, the veil was torn from top to bottom by unseen hands. The Jews hurried home from the temple to kill their own Passover lambs so that they could observe the feast at midnight (Nisan 15). Remember, Sabbath night comes before Sabbath light, so the Jews ate Passover on Sabbath night (or Friday night).

The Bible does not indicate anything unusual about Jesus eating Passover or beginning the Feast of Unleavened Bread at a time that was not in harmony with the national Passover. (Compare Matthew 26:17 with Mark 14:12.) The Bible also does not offer any justification for killing the Passover lamb on late Wednesday afternoon and eating the Passover on Thursday night, even though the national Passover lamb was killed two days later on Friday. This silence is for two reasons. First, the dating of the Passover was a common conflict, one of many conflicts among religious sects in Israel; therefore, a discussion about the presence of two calendars is not included in the gospels. Second, the gospel writers did not attempt to include *for our understanding* everything that was common knowledge in their day. However, with a little background investigation, we find that John dated the Passion week of Jesus with the Babylonian Calendar (John 12) and Mark used the new moon calendar. (Mark 14) This explains why there is an apparent conflict between some of the things Mark and John wrote. Once we understand which calendar they are using, the writings of Mark and John are in perfect harmony.

The Bible clearly indicates two Passovers were celebrated during the year that Jesus was crucified. It would be blasphemous to assert the Creator did not know *the true time* for Passover. Actually, Jesus' actions affirm what is Truth, for He is the Truth. (John 14:6) *Jesus correctly observed Passover* with His disciples in the upper room on Thursday night, the 15th day of Nisan – using God's synchrony for determining monthly cycles (conjunction). The Creator's actions perfectly synchronize with the instructions that Moses recorded in Exodus 12. The timing of the new moon (the USNO tables) and the testimony of the gospel writers confirm it!

Step 3

History reveals the Jewish nation synchronized Nisan 1, with the sighting of the first crescent of a new moon at the time of Christ . (Incidently, this practice has not changed since the time of Christ.) Depending on the visibility afforded by weather and the position of the Sun and the orbit of the moon, the first sighting of the crescent of a new moon in Jerusalem occurs between sixteen and forty hours *after* conjunction. Since it is impossible to precisely determine when the crescent of a new moon was sighted in A.D. 30, we have to let Bible facts help put the pieces together. The following facts help to determine the correct date: 1) since the sighting of the new moon crescent usually occurs two days after a new moon; 2) since Jesus was arrested on the night *after* He ate the Passover with His disciples; and 3) since the Jews observed Nisan 15 on a seventh-day Sabbath the year of Christ's death (John 19:14-31), these facts indicate Nisan 1 (using the Babylonian calendar) had to occur on Sabbath (March 25), and the death of Jesus occurred on Nisan 14, which was Friday, April 7.

Babylonian Calendar

Jesus Was Crucified Friday (April 7), Nisan 14, A.D. 30

Sunday	Monday	Tuesday	Wednesday	Thursday	Friday	Sabbath
---	---	---	---			**Nisan 1** **March 25**
Nisan 2 March 26	Nisan 3 March 27	Nisan 4 March 28	Nisan 5 March 29	Nisan 6 March 30	Nisan 7 March 31	Nisan 8 April 1
Nisan 9 April 2	Nisan 10 April 3	Nisan 11 April 4	Nisan 12 April 5	Nisan 13 April 6	Nisan 14 April 7	**Nisan 15** **April 8**

Chart 6.9

The Lamb of God died on the cross about 3 p.m. Friday afternoon (April 7) and was buried before sundown because a *special* Sabbath was about to begin. Special or *high Sabbaths* occurred when two Sabbath rests coincided. When required feasts like the Passover occurred on a seventh-day Sabbath, a "high Sabbath" occurred. (John 19:31) In summary, we know the following facts: 1) We know the astronomical positions of the Sun and moon for A.D. 30; 2) We know that Jesus properly observed the Passover using God's new moon reckoning for the beginning of a month; 3) We know that Jesus rested in the tomb over Sabbath and rose *on the first day of the week* (John 20:1; Acts 10:40); and 4) We know that A.D. 30 occurred in the middle of the seventieth week. This information leads to a solid conclusion: Jesus was crucified on Friday, April 7, A.D. 30 (Nisan 14). The actions of Jesus (such as eating Passover with His disciples) and the astronomical positions of the Sun and moon are two witnesses that confirm the truth. No wiggle room is left. *A.D. 30 is the only year during the seventieth week that will satisfy all the necessary specifications.*

The Seventy Weeks Nailed Down

If A.D. 30 is the year of Christ's death, the seventy weeks prophecy has no wiggle room left in it. There is amazing harmony from several sides. Consider the following:

1. The seventy weeks have to begin with a Sunday year because a week of years always begins with a Sunday year. The synchrony of the week of years from the year of the Exodus and A.D. 30 proves that 457 B.C. is a Sunday year.

2. The seventy weeks have to begin with a Year of Jubilee because of the specification of "seven weeks and sixty-two weeks." The synchrony of Jubilee cycles from the year of the Exodus confirms that 457 B.C. is a year of Jubilee, and according to Luke 3, Jesus began His ministry 483 years later, in the Sunday year of the seventieth week, A.D. 27.

3. The appearance of the wise men at the birth of Jesus affirms their understanding of the sixty-nine weeks mentioned in Daniel 9. No other prophecy in the Bible points to the time of Christ's birth.

4. According to Luke 1:17, John the Baptist began his ministry before Jesus appeared. The baptism of Messiah occurred during the fifteenth year of Tiberius Caesar, which is A.D. 27 – which is the first year of the seventieth week.

5. The Jublilee calendar and the decree of Artaxerxes in 457 B.C. forces A.D. 30 to be the middle year of the seventieth week – Jesus died at just the right time.

6. The astronomical position of the Sun and moon in
   A.D. 30 confirms that Jesus and His disciples ate
   Passover at the correct time according to God's
   calendar.

7. The actions of the Jews and their use of the moon's
   first crescent method is consistent with the course of
   events described in the four gospels. Jesus was
   crucified on the day when the national Passover
   lamb was slaughtered, Friday, April 7, A.D. 30.

8. Constantine refers to the fact that Jews frequently
   observed two Passovers in the same year and used
   this anomaly to prevent Christians from depending
   on the Jews to set the date of Easter.

9. The writers of the four gospels are in perfect
   harmony on the timing of these events.

When these nine points are woven together, all wiggle room
concerning the timing of the seventieth week is eliminated. **No
other time frame can meet or satisfy the prophetic or
astronomical synchrony required for the seventieth week.**
The overwhelming abundance of harmonious facts supports the
conclusion that the seventieth week occurred from Spring A.D. 27 to
Spring A.D. 34.

The Year of the Lord's Favor

Notice what Luke says about the first days of Christ's public
ministry in A.D. 27: "He [Jesus] **went to Nazareth, where he had
been brought up, and on the Sabbath day he went into the
synagogue, as was his custom. And he stood up to read. The
scroll of the prophet Isaiah was handed to him. Unrolling it,
he found the place where it is written: 'The Spirit of the Lord
is on me, because he has anointed me to preach good news to
the poor. He has sent me to proclaim freedom for the
prisoners and recovery of sight for the blind, to release the
oppressed, to *proclaim the year of the Lord's favor.*' Then he
rolled up the scroll, gave it back to the attendant and sat
down. The eyes of everyone in the synagogue were fastened**

on him, and he began by saying to them, 'Today this
scripture is fulfilled in your hearing.'" (Luke 4:16-21, italics
mine)   Some people twist these words to mean A.D. 27 is a year of
Jubilee. They claim Jesus expressed the idea of freedom from
slavery in this passage because the first year of His ministry was a
year of Jubilee. *The trouble with this argument is that slaves were
not set free in the year of Jubilee.* Slaves were to be set free at the
end of each Friday year. (Exodus 21:2; Jeremiah 34:13-16) Because
God required slaves to be set free at the end of Friday years, there
were no slaves at the beginning of a Jubilee year (the fiftieth year).
Furthermore, if A.D. 27 were a year of Jubilee or even a Sabbatical
year, then several dating changes would be required which history
and prophecy do not support. The astronomical data for A.D. 30,
plus the harmony of the gospels, plus the count of years established
in Old Testament prophecy makes an airtight case. The words of
Jesus in Luke 4 are to be understood within the context that "the
year of the Lord's favor" is the first year of the seventieth week! The
prophecy of Daniel was fulfilled when Jesus spoke these words.
Messiah had appeared!

Time Is Constant

Time on Earth has been constant since Creation. Therefore, the
positions of the Sun and moon can be calculated over long spans of
time. Any deviation from this constant requires massive changes in
planetary physics. Time is a steady and unbroken continuum, and
any tampering with dates will distort everything forward and
backward in time. In Luke 3, we find that Jesus was baptized in
A.D. 27, and in Luke 4, He began His ministry with the declaration
recorded in verses 16-21. The expression "to proclaim the year of
the Lord's favor" that Jesus used indicates that He, God in the flesh,
had come from Heaven to usher in the kingdom of God, *if* Israel was
willing.

Back to Gabriel's Statements, Numbers 4 - 6

Given the amount of information examined so far, I may need to
remind you that we are still studying Daniel 9. Gabriel's comments
to Daniel were brief, but they were full of meaning! Earlier in this
chapter, I paraphrased Gabriel's remarks to Daniel as six
statements. Now that the purpose of the seventy weeks has been
examined (Statement 1), and the timing of Messiah's ministry and

death during the seventieth week has been examined (Statements 2 and 3), Gabriel's final statements about Israel are very sad. Israel could have done so well.   Israel could have sealed up this segment of the vision and prophecy, but it failed to cooperate with God. Gabriel predicted:

4. After they are rebuilt, Jerusalem and the temple will be destroyed again.

5. Wars and desolations have been decreed upon the Jews and Jerusalem.

6. The Destroyer will continue his deadly work until the end of time.

Consider this text: **"After the sixty-two 'sevens,' the Anointed One will be cut off and will have nothing. The people of the ruler who will come will destroy the city and the sanctuary. The end will come like a flood: War will continue until the end, and desolations have been decreed."** (Daniel 9:26) This verse says several things about Jesus and Jerusalem. Verse 26 predicts that Messiah will be rejected and disowned (cut off from Israel, as in having no inheritance). Then, Gabriel told Daniel that Jerusalem and the rebuilt temple will be destroyed *again* by **"the people of the ruler who will come . . . ."** About six hundred years later, Jesus Himself predicted the second temple would be destroyed when He said to His disciples, **" 'Do you see all these things** [pointing toward Jerusalem and the temple]**?' he asked. 'I tell you the truth, not one stone here will be left on another; every one will be thrown down.' "** (Matthew 24:2, insertion mine) The Romans fulfilled this prophecy in A.D. 70. When they broke through the walls of Jerusalem, a soldier threw a firebrand into the temple complex. Thousands of Jews had sealed themselves in the temple thinking that God would not allow His holy temple to be destroyed. They were wrong. Fire quickly ignited the cedar that generously adorned the edifice. To escape the fire the Jews threw open the huge temple doors. As they ran to escape the fire, the Romans slaughtered them. So many Jews were killed that day that history says blood flowed down the temple steps like a river. Because of the intense heat from the fire, millions of dollars in gold ornamentation, utensils and goldware melted and the liquid metal flowed into the cracks of the stones used to construct the temple. To recover the gold, Roman soldiers literally pulled the temple apart – stone by stone.

Another interesting point is found in Gabriel's choice of words. He said, **"The people of the ruler who will come will destroy the city and the sanctuary . . . ."** Why did Gabriel say, **"The people of the ruler. . . ."?** These words have a context and meaning that need to be understood. In the previous verse, Gabriel said, ". . . **From the issuing of the decree to restore and rebuild Jerusalem until the Anointed One, the ruler, comes. . . ."** Did you notice that the Anointed One (Messiah) is called a "ruler." Gabriel elevated the destruction of Jerusalem in A.D. 70 to that of a divine decree issued by "the ruler," Jesus Christ Himself. The Romans were sent to destroy Jerusalem by One who overrules. The Romans were unwitting servants of God, just like the Babylonians had been unwitting servants of God (Jeremiah 25:9) when they destroyed Jerusalem the first time. If Israel had cooperated with God, the world would have enjoyed a glorious outcome when Jesus came to Earth! The kingdom of God would have been established. Israel would have been a kingdom of priests, the head of all nations and not the tail. Unfortunately, Israel refused to accept Messiah and submit to His truth. Therefore, "the Ruler" rejected them again (Matthew 23:37,38), and in A.D. 70, *He* destroyed Jerusalem.

The expression, **"The end will come like a flood. . . ."** accurately portrays Rome's destruction of Jerusalem. The Romans literally carried away everything of value as a flood carries away everything in its path. In ancient times, the most destructive force known to the human race was a flood of water. A pent-up wall of snow-melt descending down a mountain ravine in the spring was an even more devastating force than fire! Such a flood could remove huge stone walls and bury cities in mud and debris, making recovery impossible or impractical. (Hosea 5:10; Isaiah 59:19; Isaiah 8:6,7) Gabriel's words were fulfilled in A.D. 70, when the destruction of Jerusalem and its temple came like a devastating flood.

Gabriel said, **"War will continue until the end, and desolations have been decreed** [upon Jerusalem].**"** (Insertion mine) The history of the city of Jerusalem since A.D. 70 has been one of war and bloodshed, and this will continue until the end of time. Contrary to every human effort, Jerusalem has not been at peace and it will never be peaceful. Jerusalem is not the city of God. Two cultures and religions cannot inhabit the same space and be at peace. Men may negotiate a temporary cease-fire, and Lucifer may establish his throne in Jerusalem when he appears on Earth, but there will be no lasting peace and safety in Jerusalem. God has decreed it.

Gabriel said, "**. . . And on the wing of abominations will come one who makes desolate, even until a complete destruction, one that is decreed, is poured out on the one who makes desolate.**" (Daniel 9:27, NASB) The last portion of verse 27 is hard to translate smoothly into English. This explains why we find such diverse wording in different translations of the Bible. After reviewing several respected translations, I have chosen to use the New American Standard Bible for this particular verse, because the ideas expressed in this translation are easier to understand. Gabriel predicts an unseen destroyer [Lucifer] will continue to cause desolations long after Jerusalem is destroyed. His rage against God's people will not end until God's wrath is poured out upon him. You may recall from Daniel 8, that the stern-faced king will eventually become visible. When he appears, he will destroy everything in his wake, even the holy people. Daniel 8 also assures us that this ruler will be brought to his end, but not by human power.

A great tragedy is predicted in Gabriel's last three statements. These statements are compelling and sobering because Israel's disaster could have been diverted. Jesus cried, **"O Jerusalem, Jerusalem, you who kill the prophets and stone those sent to you, how often I have longed to gather your children together, as a hen gathers her chicks under her wings, but you were not willing. Look, your house is left to you desolate."** (Matthew 23:37,38) John summarized Israel's rebellion and their rejection of Messiah in one verse when he wrote, **"He came to that which was his own, but his own did not receive him."** (John 1:11)

The 2,300 Evenings and Mornings

One final issue has to be addressed before closing this study on Daniel 9. In fact, the timing of the 2,300 days of Daniel 8:14 cannot be established without first understanding the seventy weeks of

Daniel 9. Let us revisit our examination of the 2,300 evenings and mornings by asking two questions: Does God interpret the 2,300 days as 2,300 days or 2,300 years, and when do they start? These are valid questions and they deserve careful answers.

The 2,300 days in Daniel 8:14 share some similarity with the time, times and half a time (1,260 years) mentioned in Daniel 7:25, because neither of these time-periods is given a starting date. This is not a big problem because both time-periods have a definite length and end with an event that can be identified. So, we can calculate backwards from the event at the end to a starting date. Evidently, God did not give a starting event in either of these prophecies because the information in Daniel was sealed up until the time of the end. To be blunt about it, the generation that really needs to understand Daniel and Revelation is the generation that will experience the closing events of Earth's history. Given this emphasis on the final generation, the following steps have led me to conclude that the 2,300 days of Daniel 8:14 represent 2,300 years. Furthermore, I conclude they began at the same time as the seventy weeks of Daniel 9 (457 B.C.).

Step 1

Daniel wrote, **"While I was speaking and praying, confessing my sin and the sin of my people Israel and making my request to the Lord my God for his holy hill – while I was still in prayer, Gabriel, the man I had seen in the earlier vision** [Daniel 8], **came to me in swift flight about the time of the evening sacrifice. He instructed me and said to me, 'Daniel, I have now come to give you insight and understanding. As soon as you began to pray, an answer was given, which I have come to tell you, for you are highly esteemed. Therefore, consider the message and understand the** [earlier] **vision.'"** (Daniel 9:20-23, insertion mine) Daniel identifies Gabriel as the "man" he had seen in his earlier vision. (See Daniel 8:16-19.) Gabriel told Daniel that he had come to give Daniel insight and understanding into the [earlier] vision. Which vision? The *previous* vision given to Daniel is recorded in Daniel 8. This is the vision where Daniel met Gabriel. It does not make sense for Gabriel to say, "I have just been sent to you to give you insight and understanding about a vision that does yet not exist." Gabriel's remarks indicate that Daniel 9 is intimately connected to Daniel 8, which suggests there is a relationship between the 2,300 days in Daniel 8 and the seventy weeks in Daniel 9.

Step 2

Notice the words of Gabriel: **"Seventy 'sevens' are *decreed* for your people. . . ."** (Daniel 9:24, italics mine) The Hebrew word translated *decreed* (NIV) or *determined* (KJV) comes from the Hebrew word *chathak* which means "to cut off" or "to determine by separation." This Hebrew word is used once in the Bible so by itself, it cannot resolve many questions. However, it does make an important contribution to our understanding of the seventy weeks. The word indicates that a smaller period of time (seventy weeks) is "cut off" or "separated" from a larger unit of time (2,300 years). This may sound too simple, but the following process is very important. The Jubilee calender forces seventy weeks to represent 490 years, and the Jubilee Calendar forces the 2,300 days to represent 2,300 years. Therefore, the short time-period of seventy weeks are cut off from the larger time-period of the 2,300 days. In other words, the seventy weeks of Daniel 9 are "separated" from the 2,300 years given in the "earlier vision" of Daniel 8.

Gabriel was sent to Daniel in the first vision to explain the ram, goat and horn power (Daniel 8) and Gabriel was sent to Daniel in the second vision with "an answer" for Daniel's question. Daniel wanted to know how Israel fit into God's larger picture. The details presented in Daniel 9 concern the nation of Israel and they belong within the larger prophecy of Daniel 8. Since the decree to restore Jerusalem and rebuild the temple in Daniel 9 (457 B.C.) was issued during the time of the kingdom of the ram in Daniel 8 (538-331 B.C.), there is a solid link between the timing of Daniel 8 and Daniel 9.

Here is an illustration showing how the word *chathak* functions in this context: Suppose your son asks if he can go play with the kids next door. You notice the trash can in the kitchen is full, so you say, "You can go play for one hour, but your hour includes taking out the trash." In this illustration, the time required to take out the trash is "cut off" or separated out of the hour allotted with the kids next door – and we know that in such a situation, the trash will probably disappear in the twinkling of an eye.

Of course, the word *chathak* does not tell us if the seventy weeks are separated from the beginning or the end of the 2,300 years, but the word indicates the seventy weeks are "cut off" from the 2,300 years because there is no other time-period in Daniel 8. More will be said about starting both time periods with the decree of Artaxerxes (457 B.C.) in a moment.

Step 3

The 2,300 *days* have to be interpreted as 2,300 years for two reasons: First, Rule Four (mentioned at the end of Chapter 1) requires days to be translated as years during the operation of the Jubilee Calendar. Second, if seventy weeks amount to 490 years – using the scale of a day for a year, then the 2,300 days have to use the same scale and represent years as well, because a person cannot separate 490 years from 2,300 literal days (about six years and four months). However, it is possible to "cut off" 490 years from 2,300 *years*. If the seventy weeks are "cut off" from the 2,300 years, this forces the 2,300 years into the operation of the Jubilee Calendar! Interpreting the 2,300 days as 2,300 years is consistent with Rule Four, which states, *"God reckons apocalyptic time in two ways: (a) a day for a year, and (b) as literal time. The presence or absence of the Jubilee Calendar determines how God measures time."*

The Seventy Weeks of Daniel 9 "Cut Off"
from the 2,300 Days of Daniel 8:14

457 B.C. -- A.D. 33   A.D. 34   --------------------------------   1844

Seventy Weeks (490 Years)	1810 Years

<------------------------------2300 Years ----------------------------------->

Chart 6.10

Step 4

Sometimes, an answer to a prophetic question can be given with few words. However, there are segments of Bible prophecy that require a lot of background information before an answer will make much sense. The timing of the 2,300 years is such an issue. We have examined a lot of details in this study, and it is possible to miss seeing the forest when studying a tree. In this light, the following observation is offered for your consideration. Remember, that the book of Daniel contains a set of non-conditional prophecies. In other words, everything given to Daniel is an outline of God's pre-determined plans for Earth. For example, God determined that Babylon would fall to the Medes and Persians and Medo-Persia would fall to the Greeks, and it was predicted the saints would be handed over to the little horn power for 1,260 years, etc. All of the predicted events in Daniel are non-conditional.

While Daniel was receiving visions of non-conditional events, Ezekiel was receiving a series of conditional visions from God. The visions given to Ezekiel are very different than the visions given to Daniel. The visions given to Ezekiel were conditional. Ezekiel is in Babylon just like Daniel, but God told this prophet that 1) He destroyed Jerusalem and the temple because Israel violated Plan A. However, God also told Ezekiel that He has a redemptive plan for Israel (Plan B). The fulfillment of Plan B requires Israel's full cooperation. God will give Israel one more chance to accomplish all that He wanted! Looking at the visions given to both prophets, we find that God places two conditions on Plan B. First, the time allotted is seventy weeks – counting from the decree of Artaxerxes in 457 B.C. Second, Plan B can be accomplished only if a majority of people in Israel experience the miracle of being born again. (Ezekiel 36:25-27)

Consider the contrast between Daniel's prophecies and Ezekiel's prophecies. God told Daniel what would be if Israel failed to cooperate. God told Ezekiel what would be if Israel cooperated. The point is that God cuts off seventy weeks from the 2,300 years to give Israel a chance to terminate (seal up) Daniel's visions and prophecy! If Israel had cooperated with God, the prophecies of Daniel would not have come to pass. The prophecies of Daniel would have remained a secret forever. We have seen God do this before. If Israel had cooperated with God at the time of the Exodus, the first generation would not have had to die in the wilderness. God was willing to put the children of Israel in the Promised Land within two years of leaving Egypt!

When the 2,300 years are seen in this light, it makes sense that a benevolent God would cut off seventy weeks from the beginning of a longer prophecy to allow time for Israel to cooperate. Even though God told Daniel that Israel would fail and that the city and the temple would be destroyed again, God was willing to give Israel one more chance. What a patient God! What a wonderful Savior! It is so amazing to realize that God does not treat us according to His perfect foreknowledge. He compassionately treats us according to His marvelous love. When we begin to see these elements of God's character unfold from prophecy, we know we are on the right track.

Step 5

Because God is the architect of Bible prophecy, perfect harmony is found in the sum of all the parts. Remember, none of the seventeen prophecies in Daniel and Revelation stand alone. Each prophecy contributes something very important to a much larger picture that spans many centuries. The seventy weeks in Daniel 9 are not isolated from the prophecies in Daniel 2, 7, 8 and elsewhere! Each of the seventeen prophecies reveals a piece of the big picture. God is the designer of this great matrix, which means the outcome will be harmonious. Each prophecy requires the others to be present, and in turn, supports those around it. I have often remarked, "A person has to understand the whole thing before he can appreciate anything!"

At the end of Chapter 1, I wrote that a person needs to have a working knowledge of four rules before all of the pieces in both Daniel and Revelation will come together and align harmoniously. Misplacing 2.3 millennia (2,300 years), or even 2,300 days, can create problems that cannot be solved later on. This point was demonstrated in our study on Antiochus IV. If we follow valid rules, the sum of all the prophetic parts will produce *one* harmonious truth. The most compelling reason for interpreting the 2,300 days as 2,300 years and beginning this time-period with the seventy weeks of Daniel 9 is the harmony that it produces. Of course, it takes awhile to discover and understand this harmony because there is no substitute for knowledge and understanding. Carefully read the following statements and refer to Chart 6.11 to see if you can identify the timing of each statement:

> **A.** (Find 457 B.C. in the Daniel 9 row.) The decree of Artaxerxes in 457 B.C. marks the beginning of the

Relationships between Daniel 7, Daniel 8, Daniel 9 and Revelation 6

Rev 6				Seven Seals 123		4		5 6
Daniel 9	457 B.C. A.D. 33 |---Seventy Weeks---|			1798 |				
Daniel 8	|---457 B.C.------------ 2300 Day/Years -----------1844---|							The Time of the End
Daniel 8 (cont.)	Ram with Two Horns	Goat with One Great Horn -- Then Four Horns				Judgment of the Dead	Judgment of the Living	Horn Power From the North: Stern Faced King
Daniel 7	Bear with Three Ribs	Leopard with Four Heads	Monster with 10 Horns	|-------1,260 Years----| A.D. 538 to 1798 Little Horn Persecutes Jesus Found Worthy to Receive the Kingdom in 1798		Books Opened	Little Horn Heard Boasting	Beasts are Burned Up in the Fire at the End
	Medo Persia	Grecia	Rome	Many Kings				10 Kings

Chart 6.11

seventy weeks. Notice that this event begins during the time of the ram, which was discussed in Daniel 8.

B. (Find 457 B.C. in the Daniel 8 row.) If the 2,300 days of Daniel 8:14 are interpreted as 2,300 years, the seventy weeks can be "cut off" from this larger time period. Even though the Bible does not explicitly say the seventy weeks are cut off from the beginning of the 2,300 years, the matrix resolves this question. Daniel viewed the cleansing of Heaven's temple. (Daniel 7:9,10) We know this event has to occur *after* 1798, when the Ancient of Days took His seat. Even though we have not examined the seven seals of Revelation, the opening of the third seal harmoniously aligns with 1844. The 2,300 years began in the Spring of 457 B.C. and they terminated in the Spring of 1844. Jesus began cleansing Heaven's temple in the Spring of 1844.

C. (Find the end of the seventy weeks in the Daniel 9 row.) The public ministry of Jesus (A.D. 27-30) affirms the location of the seventieth week and the accuracy of the 457 B.C. decree. According to Daniel 9, Jesus died in the middle of the seventieth week. The synchrony of the Sun and moon, and the presence of two different calendars in Israel harmoniously align, and altogether they confirm the date of His death, April 7, A.D. 30. The certainty of 457 B.C. as a starting date for the seventy weeks also insures the certainty of the termination of the 2,300 years in 1844.

D. (Locate 1798 in the Daniel 7 row.) The little horn of Daniel 7 persecuted the saints for 1,260 years. As predicted, the persecution of the saints ended in 1798 because the Ancient of Days issued a judgment (a restraining order) on behalf of the saints from His throne in Heaven. (Daniel 7:21,22) This event in Heaven is directly linked with the fall of the papacy on Earth. Generals Waller and Berthier captured the pope and placed him in exile in February 1798. At that time, the Roman Catholic Church's control over Europe was almost fatally wounded. (Daniel 7:26) Since the signing of the Lateran treaty on February 11, 1929, this fatal wound has been healing. (Revelation 13:1-3)

E. (Find 1798 in the Daniel 7 row.) Jesus was found worthy to receive Earth as His kingdom in 1798. (Daniel 7:13,14)

F. (Find 1798 in the Revelation 6 row.) Even though the seven seals of Revelation have not been examined, the following statement is presented to help you see an ever-widening matrix. In Revelation 4-6, Jesus was found worthy to receive the book sealed with seven seals in 1798. Jesus began opening the seals. He opened the third seal in 1844. As a result, people on Earth came to understand the cleansing of Heaven's temple. Christ's judgment bar has been underway since 1844. (2 Corinthians 5:10)

G. (Find 1844 in the Daniel 8 row.) At the end of the 2,300 years, in the spring of 1844, Jesus began going through the books of record and passing judgment on those who have died. Jesus is judging the dead to see who will live in His kingdom. If a person is found to be rebellious, Jesus assigns the guilt of the sinner upon his own head. If a person is found to be submissive to the Holy Spirit, the sinner's guilt is assigned to Lucifer, the scapegoat. Ultimately, Heaven's temple will be cleansed of sin when the seventh trumpet of Revelation 11 sounds. (Revelation 15:7,8)

H. (Find 1844 in the Revelation 6 row.) The world's inhabitants began to hear about the cleansing of Heaven's temple because the third seal was opened in 1844. The fourth seal will open soon. It will happen suddenly and unexpectedly.   When it does, the Great Tribulation and the judgment of the living begins.

Summary

This chapter has covered many issues. Although this has been an involved study, hopefully you can see how the seventy weeks of Daniel 9 and the 2,300 years of Daniel 8 have been fulfilled. God's timing is perfect. Because of God's generous grace to Israel (the offer of Plan B), the seventy weeks were "cut off" from the 2,300 years. God was willing to abort all of the visions given to Daniel if Israel would cooperate with Him. Unfortunately, Israel did not cooperate with God and the "rebuilt" Jerusalem and temple were totally destroyed in A.D. 70. We could say that "Plan C" is now underway, and in the Spring of 1844, the cleansing process of Heaven's temple began. This means that Jesus is currently going through the Books of Record to determine who will live in His coming kingdom. Very soon, Jesus will turn His attention to judging the living in a sequence of events known as the Great Tribulation.

Chapter 7

Daniel 10:1 - 11:35 – Israel's Prophetic Destiny

"So when you see standing in the holy place 'the abomination that causes desolation,' spoken of through the prophet Daniel – let the [Gentile] reader [also] understand – then let those who are in Judea flee to the mountains. Let no one on the roof of his house go down to take anything out of the house. Let no one in the field go back to get his cloak. How dreadful it will be in those days for pregnant women and nursing mothers! Pray that your flight will not take place in winter or on the Sabbath."
— Matthew 24:15-20, insertions mine

Introduction

About 534 B.C., God gave Daniel a compelling vision that came in two installments. The first installment contained scenes from a protracted series of wars and the second consisted of another visit with the angel, Gabriel. Gabriel was sent to Daniel, who was nearing eighty years of age, to explain certain things about the wars which he saw in the first installment. Daniel received these installments about three weeks apart. When Daniel put the vision in written form, he, like all other Bible writers, did not divide his report into the chapters and verses that are found in our Bibles today. This point is made because Daniel 10 through 12 should be understood as one vision, even though it covers three chapters. A similar situation occurred in Daniel 8 and 9. Daniel 8 contains a ram, goat and horn power. Later, Gabriel was sent to Daniel with more information about Daniel 8. (Daniel 9:21)

Today, few religious leaders speak about the last chapters of Daniel. This is unfortunate because this particular vision contains valuable information for the final generation. God does not give visions to His prophets without revealing important information. As we examine this vision, keep four issues in mind:

1. Two Groups of Beneficiaries

God gave this vision to Daniel to benefit two groups of people who would live in the future. The first group lived about 600 years after this vision was given. This group consisted of Christians who lived in Jerusalem at the time of its destruction in A.D. 70. The second group of people for which this vision was given are those Christians who will live on Earth during the Great Tribulation. This vision benefits both groups because they will share a common experience. Early Christians experienced the destruction of Jerusalem, and Great Tribulation Christians will experience the destruction of Earth. Because there are distinct parallels in these two events, God gave one vision for the benefit of two groups of people. This is not unusual, because Jesus, in Matthew 24 and elsewhere in the Bible, compared the destruction of Jerusalem with the end of the world. For example, Jesus told His disciples, **"Then you will be handed over to be persecuted and put to death, and you will be hated by all nations because of me. At that time many will turn away from the faith and will betray and hate each other, and many false prophets will appear and deceive many people. . . . They will put you out of the synagogue; in fact, a time is coming when anyone who kills you will think he is offering a service to God. They will do such things because they have not known the Father or me."** (Matthew 24:9-11, John 16:2,3) History reveals that many of the early Christians, like Stephen, were martyrs for their faith. (Acts 6 and 7) The Jews, including Saul of Tarsus, thought they were doing God a service by killing Christians! (See Deuteronomy 13 and 1 Timothy 1:13.) People living during the Great Tribulation will see similar parallels. Soon, God's people will be persecuted, even martyred for their faith, and amazingly, people who persecute and martyr God's people will think they are doing God a service! (Revelation 6:9-11; 13:1-10; 14:12,13; 16:4-7)

Other parallels in Matthew 24 merit our attention. For example, Jesus said, **"As it was in the days of Noah, so it will be at the coming of the Son of Man. For in the days before the flood, people were eating and drinking, marrying and giving in marriage, up to the day Noah entered the ark; and they knew nothing about what would happen until the flood came and took them all away. That is how it will be at the coming of** the Son of Man." (Matthew 24:37-39) Jesus compared the disbelief and ignorance of the people who lived before the flood with the people who will be living at the end of time. Of course, ignorance is not limited to people living in Noah's day nor at the end of the world. This is why Jesus warned His listeners to anticipate Jerusalem's destruction, " 'Do you see all these things [the temple complex]?' he asked. 'I tell you the truth, not one stone here will be left on another; every one will be thrown down... So when you see standing in the holy place 'the abomination that causes desolation,' spoken of through the prophet Daniel – let the [Gentile] reader [also] understand – then let those who are in Judea flee to the mountains.' " (Matthew 24:2,15,16; Luke 21:22, insertions mine.) Jesus quoted Daniel 11:31, because the vision in Daniel 10-12 lays out a historical sequence of events that includes the destruction of Jerusalem! Not only did early Christians benefit from Jesus' remarks, but the final generation will also benefit from this amazing vision. Remember, God gave this vision to Daniel about 540 B.C., and it was meant to benefit *two* groups of people who would be separated by almost 2,000 years!

2. God's Foreknowledge

The vision of Daniel 10-12, like that of Daniel 8-9, predicted Israel's failure long *before* the seventy weeks began. One of God's most amazing qualities is His ability to treat His children according to the principle of love, even though He knows our choices before we make them. Think this through. If you knew your child would flunk out of college, would you spend $50,000 on his or her college education anyway? If you knew your upcoming marriage was going to end in a bitter divorce, would you still get married? God is all-knowing (omniscient). He knows everything in the past, present and future. Even more, He is also omnipotent, which means He has the power to manipulate everyone and everything in the universe to His satisfaction. However, God does not use His foreknowledge or His omnipotence to manipulate His creatures for His benefit. If He manipulated us according to His desires, He would not be a God of love; instead, He would be a self-serving God. The only way God's creatures can live at peace with God is through trust. We have to believe that He will not violate the principle of love even though we cannot understand His ways at times. God does not ask us to trust

Him with these incredible powers without giving us good reason to trust Him. Calvary proves the Father and the Son are worthy of complete trust.

Here is a profound point. *God uses His mighty powers (omnipotence, omniscience and omnipresence) to insure the principle of love will be exalted throughout the universe.* God does not use His incredible powers to keep Himself on the throne! The principle of love is essential for eternal happiness (there is no alternative). The humiliation and death of Jesus assures every created being that the principle of love will forever be the basis of God's government. In other words, if God could have resolved the sin problem without Jesus' death, He would have done so. But, **"God so loved the world that He gave His only begotten Son. . . . "** This is why John wrote, "God is love." (1 John 4:8) What a marvelous God!

God deals with us according to His great love, even though He knows our choices may not be good. In other words, God is not like us. A selfish heart will use manipulation, deceit and any other means at its disposal to satisfy its selfish desires! God does not work this way. He is motivated by pure love. God is selfless. The vision recorded in Daniel 11 reveals Israel's failure long before the seventy weeks began. If God foreknew their failure, why did God give Israel 490 years of probationary time? (For that matter, God foreknew the failure of Lucifer and Adam and Eve, yet He gave them life and probationary time.) These examples highlight what is so amazing about God. Even though He foreknew Israel's failure, God granted seventy weeks of grace because He wanted Israel *to have the opportunity* to succeed or fail. The potential was awesome. If Israel *chose* a life of faith and submission to God, God was ready and willing to establish His kingdom on Earth at the end of the 490 years decreed in Daniel 9. If Jesus had been able to establish His kingdom on Earth, Israel would have become a kingdom of priests who served the Lord on behalf of all the nations of Earth. (Exodus 19:5,6) However, we now know that Israel *chose* the way of rebellion, and God abandoned the nation of Israel and destroyed Jerusalem. If the Jews had experienced God's love and properly understood Daniel 10-12 before Jesus came to Earth, world history would have been so different.

3. Caught in the Middle

The Daniel 10-12 vision tells the story of a series of protracted wars fought over several centuries. In a geographical, religious and political sense, Israel was trapped in the middle of endless wars between nations from the north and the south. Israel's unique position mirrors the general experience of God's people in a fallen world. Many times God's people are "caught in the middle" between opposing forces. Moreover, God forbade Israel from taking sides or making alliances for protection (Isaiah 30), because He wanted Israel to understand that they were only safe if they remained allied with Him.

Keep three entities in mind as you study this vision: the kingdom of the north, the kingdom of the south and the kingdom of God. God placed the ancient nation of Israel geographically "in the middle of the nations." (Ezekiel 5:5) He deliberately placed Israel in this strategic location to be representatives of His love and truth. God wanted the nations of the world to become acquainted with a special group of people. However, a prominent position can have adverse consequences, too. When Israel failed to honor God, He humiliated them by making them a reproach to all of the surrounding nations. (Ezekiel 5:14) God displayed His wrath against Jerusalem two times; first in 605 B.C., and again in A.D. 70.

Israel's prominent location was to be an asset or a liability, depending on their relationship with God. The vision given in Daniel 10-12 proves that God deliberately restored tiny Israel to their homeland at the end of seventy years in Babylon, but their return home put them *between* two huge warring forces If Israel had cooperated with God, they would have had a powerful impact on the nations to the north and to the south. Israel could have used this prophecy to demonstrate the superiority of their God above the gods of the pagans, *because this vision discloses the outcome of numerous wars before they happened!* God wanted His people to be informed about *His* larger plans, and He wanted Israel to tell the nations that other than Jehovah, there are no other gods. (Isaiah 44) God did not want Israel to be afraid of the larger nations, but God's plans were not realized because of Israel's rebellion. As a result, the only group that has benefitted from this vision thus far was early Christians.

Caught Between Two Groups of People

Since we are considering Israel being caught in the middle of a series of wars, a few comments about this concept is necessary. Several parallels can be made of ancient Israel's position between the kings of the north and the kings of the south. For example, after Jesus went to Heaven, early Christians found themselves caught between Rome's hatred for the Jews and the Jew's hatred for the Romans. The Romans viewed Christians as an offshoot sect of the Jews, and the Jews viewed Christians as traitors worthy of death. Both groups hated the Christians! What a terrible place to be. God's people will have a similar experience during the Great Tribulation. As the Great Tribulation unfolds, three groups of people will appear:

1. **Religious wicked.** These will be people like the Pharisees of old. They will devise and endorse the false doctrines of Babylon. This group of people will embrace the Antichrist when he appears because they will believe that he is God. These people are identified in Daniel 11 as followers of the king of the north (Lucifer).

2. **Non-religious wicked.** These people will be like the Moabites of old. The Moabites did not worship Jehovah; they had their own gods. These people will rebel against the laws imposed by Babylon. They will refuse to submit to the laws and authority of Lucifer, the Antichrist. This group of people is described in Daniel 11 as the followers of the king of the south. Wicked people of Earth will be divided in their loyalties – the north versus the south.

3. **Saints.** The saints will make up a third group of people during the Great Tribulation. They are identified as "the holy people" mentioned in Daniel 12:7 and Revelation 11:2. The saints will oppose the false doctrines of Babylon and they will refuse to submit to the laws of Babylon because of their faith in Jesus and obedience to His commandments. Because the saints will not join either group, the groups in the north and in the south will both hate the saints. (See also Revelation 12:17; 13:7; 14:12.)

Lucifer and his angels will eliminate the kingdom of the south by killing its people. (Revelation 9:15) Many saints will also be martyred during this time. (Revelation 6:9) The net effect is that when Jesus appears at the Second Coming, two groups of people will remain: one-third of the world's population worshiping the Lamb of God, and two-thirds of the world worshiping the Antichrist, Lucifer. (Zechariah 13:8,9)

Remember, God gave this vision to benefit two groups of people. The first section of this vision (Daniel 10:1-11:35) lays out a chronological sequence of historical events for the benefit of early Christians. By following the sequence of events in this vision, they could determine and anticipate the outcome of Jerusalem's fate. The second section of the vision (Daniel 11:26-12:13) belongs to Great Tribulation Christians. For them, this vision describes the future actions of the stern-faced King from the North (Daniel 8), as well as some information about the persecution of the saints during the Tribulation. If you understand the first section of this vision (pertaining to early Christians), the second section will make a lot more sense because there are parallels between the two sections.

4. The Region of the North

The title, "The king of the north," is used nine times, and the title, "The king of the south," is used ten times in this vision. These titles have geographic value, as well as figurative value, because the kings of the south and the north stand in opposition. Because the devil will appear as the king of the north during the Great Tribulation, review the following points about him (the Horn Power) in Daniel 8 before we proceed:

Horn Power from the North

1. The Horn Power will come out of one of the four winds.

2. The Horn Power will come out of the north, but will grow toward the south, east and west.

3. Divine destruction in the Old Testament consistently comes out of the north.

4. God's throne is located on the north side of His temple.

You may recall that King Nebuchadnezzar came out of "the north" to implement divine judgment against Jerusalem. (Jeremiah 6:1,22;

25:9) Likewise, divine judgment against Babylon came out of "the
north." (Jeremiah 50:2,3) When the Antichrist appears, he will also
come out of the north. (Daniel 8:9; 11:36-40) Finally, when Jesus
returns, He will come out of the north with divine destruction. (Job
37:22; Daniel 11:44) Of course, from our point of view on Earth,
which rotates in a counter-clockwise direction, Jesus will physically
show up in the East!

Initial Summary

Try to keep the following four issues in mind as you examine this
vision: (1) It was given for the benefit of two groups of Christians;
(2) God has perfect foreknowledge, but He does not use His foreknowledge to manipulate the outcome of events; (3) God's people will
be caught in the middle of opposing forces; and (4) God will empower
the Antichrist, the stern-faced king that comes out of the north, to
cause great destruction because of the world's rebellion. (2 Thessalonians 2:11,12)

What Did Jesus Mean?

Before we examine the details of Daniel 10-12, one more point needs
to be presented. Jesus warned His disciples, **"So when you see
standing in the holy place 'the abomination that causes
desolation,' spoken of through the prophet Daniel – let the
reader understand – then let those who are in Judea flee to
the mountains."** (Matthew 24:15:16) When Jesus spoke these
words, He knew that Daniel 11:31 would be fulfilled forty years
later. According to Webster, an abomination is "a despicable act, an
insult having no equal, a defiant act of insolence and total disdain."
The highest insult or abomination that anyone can commit is to
insult or defy God. Consider the following texts taken from the
Kings James Version and notice how the Bible defines an
abomination:

1. Exodus 8:25, 26 **"And Pharaoh called for Moses and for
Aaron, and said, Go ye, sacrifice to your God in the land. And
Moses said, It is not meet so to do; for we shall sacrifice the
abomination of the Egyptians to the Lord our God: lo, shall
we sacrifice the abomination of the Egyptians before their
eyes, and will they not stone us?"** The ancient Egyptians
believed in the transmigration of the soul. They considered the

slaughter of animals to be a grave insult to their ancestors (who might be living in an animal). They also considered the killing of animals an abomination to their gods. Knowing this, Moses wanted to leave Egypt and offer animal sacrifices to God in the wilderness to avoid agitating the Egyptians with inflammatory behavior.

2. Leviticus 18:20-22 **"Moreover thou shalt not lie carnally with thy neighbor's wife, to defile thyself with her. And thou shalt not let any of thy seed pass through the fire to Molech, neither shalt thou profane the name of thy God: I am the Lord. Thou shalt not lie with mankind, as with womankind: it is abomination."** God considers a homosexual relationship to be an abomination. He created us in His image (Genesis 1:26) and is insulted when we debase His image. God also considers a sexual relationship with an animal to be an abomination. (Leviticus 20:15)

3. Deuteronomy 17:1 **"Thou shalt not sacrifice unto the Lord thy God any bullock, or sheep, wherein is blemish, or any evilfavouredness: for that is an abomination unto the Lord thy God."** When God established the ritual of animal sacrifices, He forbade anyone from presenting an offering that was considered a "second" or that had a known blemish on it. Each sacrificial animal represented the perfect "Lamb of God" who would take away the sins of the world. If any flaw was found in Jesus, He could not be man's perfect substitute! Therefore, presenting a blemished sacrifice was an insult or abomination to God.

4. Proverbs 6:16-19 **"These six things doth the Lord hate: yea, seven are an abomination unto him: A proud look, a lying tongue, and hands that shed innocent blood, An heart that deviseth wicked imaginations, feet that be swift in running to mischief, a false witness that speaketh lies, and he that soweth discord among brethren."** God hates these seven things because they destroy love. God will not tolerate these forms of behavior in His coming kingdom because they ruin life, and this is an insult to the Author of Life.

These few verses (and there are many others in the Bible) define certain actions that God considers an abomination. An abomination is a despicable act directed towards God. As you might expect, God may wink at our ignorance, but He does not tolerate insults very

long. King Sennacherib insulted God and an angel struck 185,000 of
his soldiers dead in a single night! (2 Kings 19:35)

". . . .That Causes Desolation"

Now that we know that an abomination is a great insult toward
God, it should be easier to make sense of the prophetic phrase, "the
abomination that causes desolation." This phrase comes from a
Jewish mindset because the Jews regarded their homeland as the
"holy land," that is, land set apart or separated from other nations
for Abraham's descendants. They also considered their homeland to
be God's "holy land" because God dwelt in their land; at the temple
in Jerusalem. Notice King David's song of praise: **"He struck down
all the firstborn of Egypt, the firstfruits of manhood in the
tents of Ham. But he brought his people out like a flock; he
led them like sheep through the desert. He guided them
safely, so they were unafraid; but the sea engulfed their
enemies. Thus he brought them to the border of *His holy
land*, to the hill country his right hand had taken. He drove
out nations before them and allotted their lands to them as
an inheritance; He settled the tribes of Israel in their
homes."** (Psalm 78:51-55, italics mine)

The word *holy* means "set apart" from the common or usual. The
term "holy land" defines land as that which is set apart from all
other lands. God set Israel apart from Egypt as a holy nation of
people. (Exodus 19:4-6) He placed Israel in the center of the
nations, at a special location, called "His holy land." (Ezekiel 5:5)

The Levites and Their Pastureland

You may recall that God did not give a share of the Promised Land
to the tribe of Levi when Israel entered Canaan. **"The Lord said to
Aaron, 'You will have no inheritance in their land, nor will
you have any share among them; I am your share and your
inheritance among the Israelites. I give to the Levites all the
tithes in Israel as their inheritance in return for the work
they do while serving at the Tent of Meeting.' "** (Numbers
18:20,21) God did this because He wanted to tie the prosperity of the
tribe of the Levites to their effectiveness as teachers and pastors of
His flock. If the priests were faithful and taught the people the
ways of the Lord, the nation would prosper, and the Levites would

prosper from the increase in tithe! If the priests failed to teach the people the ways of the Lord, the nation would suffer, and the Levites would suffer because of Israel's economic failures.

When the time came for Israel to possess the holy land, God gave Moses certain instructions about the Levites. Notice the size, place and role of the pasturelands that were set apart for the priests: **"On the plains of Moab by the Jordan across from Jericho, the Lord said to Moses, 'Command the Israelites to give the Levites towns to live in from the inheritance the Israelites will possess. And give them pasturelands around the towns. Then they will have towns to live in and pasturelands for their cattle, flocks and all their other livestock. The pasturelands around the towns that you give the Levites will extend out fifteen hundred feet from the town wall. Outside the town, measure three thousand feet on the east side, three thousand on the south side, three thousand on the west and three thousand on the north, with the town in the center. They will have this area as pastureland for the towns.** *Six* **of the towns you give the Levites will be cities of refuge, to which a person who has killed someone may flee. In addition, give them forty-two other towns. In all you must give the Levites forty-eight towns, together with their pasturelands. The towns you give the Levites from the land the Israelites possess are to be given in proportion to the inheritance of each tribe: Take many towns from a tribe that has many, but few from one that has few."** (Numbers 35:1-8, italics mine)

When the Israelites finally possessed the land, Joshua sanctified, or "made holy," Bezer, Ramoth, and Golan as cities of refuge on the east side of the Jordan River, and Kedesh, Shechem and Kiriath Arba on the west side of the Jordan River. (Joshua 20:7,8) These six cities became known as "holy cities" because they were *set apart* as cities of refuge. If a murder was committed, the murderer could seek refuge by fleeing to one of these cities for either temporary or permanent safety from the avenger of blood. About four hundred years after Israel occupied the Promised Land, King David overthrew the city of Jebus and established his throne there. David renamed Jebus, "Jerusalem" (city of peace), and it became the seventh (and last) of the holy cities. After Solomon's death, the kingdom of Israel was divided into two states and in 722 B.C., the northern kingdom was destroyed. At that time, Jerusalem became *the* only holy city remaining for the tribes in the south, Benjamin and Judah.

When each "holy city" was established, the nearby pastureland around the walls of the city was "set apart" for the Levites as a place for their gardens and flocks. They called the pastureland around the walls of each city "the holy place" or "holy ground" because it was set apart for the Levites. When Jerusalem became a holy city, the pastureland just outside the city was also set apart for the priests to use exclusively. Even after the Babylonians destroyed Jerusalem, God planned for the rebuilt city to have "holy ground" surrounding its walls. (Ezekiel 45:1-6) Now that you know how the language is used to describe the pastureland around the walls of the holy cities, closely examine these two texts:

1. Jesus said, **"So when you see standing in the holy place 'the abomination that causes desolation,' spoken of through the prophet Daniel – let the [Gentile] reader understand – then let those who are in Judea flee to the mountains. Let no one on the roof of his house go down to take anything out of the house. Let no one in the field go back to get his cloak. How dreadful it will be in those days for pregnant women and nursing mothers! Pray that your flight will not take place in winter or on the Sabbath."** (Matthew 24:15-20, insertion mine)

2. Jesus said, **"When you see Jerusalem being surrounded by armies, you will know that its desolation is near. Then let those who are in Judea flee to the mountains, let those in the city get out, and let those in the country not enter the city. For this is the time of punishment in fulfillment of all that has been written. How dreadful it will be in those days for pregnant women and nursing mothers! There will be great distress in the land and wrath against this people."** (Luke 21:20-23)

There is an interesting difference between these two texts. Both Matthew and Luke heard Jesus give the same discourse. Years later, when the gospels were written, Matthew, the Jew, wrote as a

Jew would have remembered Jesus' prediction. Luke, a Gentile converted to Christianity, wrote according to what he understood Jesus to mean. Both men understood the meaning of Christ's words. In the Jewish mind, the city of Jerusalem was an object of highest adoration and exaltation. Jerusalem was the hub of Judaism. Jehovah's temple was located on Mount Moriah, and the Jews regarded Jerusalem as the invincible City of God. Given this ideology, the Jews considered the presence of an uncircumcised Gentile army standing in the land dedicated to the Levites to be an insult to God. Luke confirms this understanding. He interprets Jesus' words to mean "when you see Jerusalem being surrounded by foreign armies, you will know that its desolation is near." Jesus was trying to warn His followers about a future event that was something unbearable to hear! Why would God allow *His* holy city and *His* temple to be subjected to barbarians bent on destruction? *His* justification for destroying Jerusalem a second time was the same as the first destruction of the city and temple by Nebuchadnezzar. God destroyed Israel because of defiant apostasy.

Jesus quoted Daniel 11:31 saying, **"So when you see standing in the holy place 'the abomination that causes desolation,' spoken of through the prophet Daniel . . ."** because the first section of the prophecy in Daniel 10-12 was about to reach fulfillment in A.D. 70. This portion of Daniel's prophecy was fulfilled when Vespesian set siege to Jerusalem in A.D. 68. He surrounded Jerusalem so that no one could enter or leave the city. However, Nero died shortly after the siege began, and Vespasian ordered his troops to return to Rome to secure his position on the throne. The following year, the siege was renewed under the leadership of Vespesian's son, Titus. In A.D. 70, the city of Jerusalem fell and was totally destroyed. When Vespasian lifted the siege on Jerusalem and returned to Rome because of Nero's death, a short window of time opened up. The retreat gave believers enough time to escape the city of Jerusalem. Early Christians understood Daniel's words, as well as Jesus' warning. When Titus destroyed Jerusalem the following year, few, if any, Christians perished. Thousands of Christians survived because Jesus pointed them to Daniel 11:31! Incidentally, the dispersion of thousands of Christians from Jerusalem in A.D. 69 forced the gospel into many places where it had not gone before.

A Different Commentary Style

Because the vision in Daniel 10-12 has one section applying to early Christians and a second section applying to Great Tribulation Christians, I have divided this vision into two sections. This chapter deals with early Christians and the next chapter deals with Great Tribulation Christians.

Because this vision presents several wars that can be somewhat complicated to follow, a different style of commentary will be used. According to the dictionary, a paraphrase is an attempt to clarify the meaning of an author's words by restating his or her original idea using different words. On the other hand, a translation is a direct conversion of words or their equivalent sense from one language to another. *The commentary style that follows is neither a paraphrase nor a translation.* The following commentary style should be called interlacing. The text from Scripture will be presented first, then my commentary will be interlaced with Scripture so you can follow the vision as it moves back and forth between the armies of the north and the south.

Daniel 10:1-6 (KJV) – Part I

"In the third year of Cyrus king of Persia a thing was revealed unto Daniel, whose name was called Belteshazzar; and the thing was true, but the time appointed was long: and he understood the thing, and had understanding of the vision. In those days I Daniel was mourning three full weeks. I ate no pleasant bread, neither came flesh nor wine in my mouth, neither did I anoint myself at all, till three whole weeks were fulfilled. And in the four and twentieth day of the first month, as I was by the side of the great river, which is Hiddekel; Then I lifted up mine eyes, and looked, and behold a certain man clothed in linen, whose loins were girded with fine gold of Uphaz: His body also was like the beryl, and his face as the appearance of lightning, and his eyes as lamps of fire, and his arms and his feet like in colour to polished brass, and the voice of his words like the voice of a multitude."

Interlaced Commentary on Part I

"During the third year of Cyrus (534 B.C.), king of Persia, I, Daniel – also called Belteshazzar by the Babylonians, received a vision. This vision contained scenes of a great war and I did not understand the vision. When the vision ended, I was sad and distressed for three weeks because of what I had seen. I petitioned the Most High God for understanding. I ate no delicious food; no meat or wine touched my lips; and I used no cologne until the three weeks were over. Then, on Nisan 24, I had another vision to help me understand the vision of the great war. I was standing on the banks of the Tigris. I looked up toward the sky and there I saw a glorious man dressed in linen, wearing around his waist a belt of the finest gold. His body was as bright as sunlight shining on gold, his face was brighter than lightning, his eyes were like flaming torches, his arms and legs had the gleam of polished bronze, and his voice could be heard for miles, like the sound of a great multitude."

Daniel 10:7-14 (KJV) – Part II

"And I Daniel alone saw the vision: for the men that were with me saw not the vision; but a great quaking fell upon them, so that they fled to hide themselves. Therefore I was left alone, and saw this great vision, and there remained no strength in me: for my comeliness was turned in me into corruption, and I retained no strength. Yet heard I the voice of his words: and when I heard the voice of his words, then was I in a deep sleep on my face, and my face toward the ground. And, behold, an hand touched me, which set me upon my knees and upon the palms of my hands. And he said unto me, O Daniel, a man greatly beloved, understand the words that I speak unto thee, and stand upright: for unto thee am I now sent. And when he had spoken this word unto me, I stood trembling. Then said he unto me, Fear not, Daniel: for from the first day that thou didst set thine heart to understand, and to chasten thyself before thy God, thy words were heard, and I am come for thy words. But the prince of the kingdom of Persia withstood me one and twenty days: but, lo, Michael, one of the chief princes, came to help me; and I remained there with the kings of Persia. Now I am come to make thee understand what shall befall thy people in the latter days: for yet the vision is for many days."

Interlaced Commentary on Part II

"I, Daniel, was the only one who saw the glorious man. The men with me did not see Him, but when they saw His glory, they were filled with terror and fled for refuge. So, I was left alone, gazing at the glorious man; my body had no strength, my face turned deathly pale and I was utterly helpless. Then I heard him speak, and as I listened, I fell unconscious and I crumbled to the ground. An angel, Gabriel, came to me and helped me up on my hands and knees. He said, 'Daniel, you are highly esteemed; carefully consider the words I am about to speak to you. So, stand up, for God has sent me to you.' After he said this to me, I stood up even though I was trembling. Then Gabriel said, 'Do not be afraid, Daniel. Since the day you received the vision and began humbling yourself with fasting and prayer – requesting understanding, the Lord heard your words, and has sent me to you. I would have come sooner, but a conflict over the king of Persia thwarted my efforts for the past twenty-one days. Then Michael Himself, the archangel, came to my aid because I could not overcome the prince of darkness. Now that this crisis has passed, I have come to explain what will happen in the future, for this vision reaches far beyond the expiration of the seventy weeks.' "

Daniel 10:15-21 (KJV) – Part III

"**And when he had spoken such words unto me, I set my face toward the ground, and I became dumb. And, behold, one like the similitude of the sons of men touched my lips: then I opened my mouth, and spake, and said unto him that stood before me, O my lord, by the vision my sorrows are turned upon me, and I have retained no strength. For how can the servant of this my lord talk with this my lord? for as for me, straightway there remained no strength in me, neither is there breath left in me. Then there came again and touched me one like the appearance of a man, and he strengthened me, And said, O man greatly beloved, fear not: peace be unto thee, be strong, yea, be strong. And when he had spoken unto me, I was strengthened, and said, Let my lord speak; for thou hast strengthened me. Then said he, Knowest thou wherefore I come unto thee? and now will I return to fight with the prince of Persia: and when I am gone forth, lo, the prince of Grecia shall come. But I will show thee that which** is noted in the scripture of truth: and there is none that holdeth with me in these things, but Michael your prince."

Interlaced Commentary on Part III

"While Gabriel was saying this to me, I bowed with my face toward the ground and was speechless. Then the angel touched my lips, and I opened my mouth and began to speak. I said to the angel, 'I am overcome with anguish because of the vision, my lord, and have no strength; I am helpless. How can I, your servant, talk with you, my lord? My strength is gone and I can hardly breathe.' So the angel touched me, and instantly I received strength. 'Do not be afraid, O man highly esteemed,' he said. 'Peace! Be strong now; be strong.' When he spoke to me, I was strengthened and said, 'Speak, my lord, since you have given me strength.' Gabriel continued, 'I have come to explain things that will help God's people in days to come. Soon, destruction will overtake Persia, and the kingdom of Greece will rise to power. First, however, I will tell you some secrets that are written in the Book of Truth containing God's master plan for Earth. No one else has access to these secrets except Michael, the Prince of Heaven.' "

Daniel 11:1-4 (KJV) - Part IV

"In the first year of Darius the Mede, even I, stood to confirm and to strengthen him. And now will I show thee the truth. Behold, there shall stand up yet three kings in Persia; and the fourth shall be far richer than they all: and by his strength through his riches he shall stir up all against the realm of Grecia. And a mighty king shall stand up, that shall rule with great dominion, and do according to his will. And when he shall stand up, his kingdom shall be broken, and shall be divided toward the four winds of heaven; and not to his posterity, nor according to his dominion which he ruled: for his kingdom shall be plucked up, even for others beside those.

Interlaced Commentary on Part IV

"Gabriel said, 'According to God's will, I began to support and protect the conquests of Darius the Mede in the first year of his reign, but due to illness, his kingdom did not last long. Three more kings will rule over Persia after the present king, Cyrus, dies.

Cambyses, False Smerdis and Darius I will become kings and rule over Persia. Then a fourth king, far richer than the others, will come to power. When Xerxes has gained much power from his wealth, he will militarily resist the developing kingdom of Grecia. Later, a mighty king, Alexander the Great, from Grecia, will ascend and rapidly gain control of the world. He will rule with astonishing power and do as he pleases. After he reigns about ten years, he will die an untimely death and God will divide his great empire into smaller kingdoms in the north, south, east and west. Alexander's empire will not go to his descendants, nor will his successors have the sweeping power he exercised. In time, God will dissolve Alexander's empire and pass the government of the world to the Romans.' "

Historical Note: After Alexander's death, the Grecian empire was eventually divided into four kingdoms, and four generals from Alexander's empire ruled over them. Ptolemy ruled in the south, Cassander in the west, Lysimachus in the north and Seleucus in the east. After Greece was divided, the empire experienced many changes, including national borders (the four generals fought each other continuously over their borders); however, most of the border wars did not drastically affect the tiny nation of Israel. When Grecia fell in 331 B.C., Israel had completed most of its post-Babylonian restoration of Jerusalem. Naturally, the Jews in Jerusalem were concerned about the tensions that existed between the nations, because Israel occupied a strip of strategic land that served as a "land bridge" between the nations in the north and south. (Ezekiel 5:5) Because the Great Sea to the west and the Great Desert to the east were natural geographical barriers, large armies from the north or the south had no option but to march directly through Judea in their attempts to defeat each other. As a result of Israel's geographic location and the titles of the kings used in this prophecy, we can identify the kings of the north and the south without too much difficulty.

Daniel 11:5,6 (KJV) - Part V

"And the king of the south shall be strong, and one of his princes; and he shall be strong above him, and have dominion; his dominion shall be a great dominion. And in the end of years they shall join themselves together; for the

king's daughter of the south shall come to the king of the north to make an agreement: but she shall not retain the power of the arm; neither shall he stand, nor his arm: but she shall be given up, and they that brought her, and he that begat her, and he that strengthened her in these times."

Interlaced Commentary on Part V

"Gabriel said, 'One of Alexander's generals, Ptolemy I Soter, will become the king of Egypt. As king of the south, he will become strong, but a second general from Alexander's empire, Seleucus I Nicator, will become even greater than Ptolemy. Seleucus I will extend his dominion and eventually rule over the north. After a few years, these two kings will die, but their descendants will seek peace through marriage. Bernice, the daughter of Ptolemy II, the king of the south, will go to Antiochus II, the king of the north, to make an alliance. Antiochus II will divorce his wife, Laodice, to marry Bernice and they will produce an heir. However, the new marriage will not last long. The vacillating Antiochus II will eventually divorce Bernice, and reconcile with his first wife, Laodice. After Antiochus II and Laodice reconcile, Laodice will kill Bernice, her royal escort, and her son by Antiochus II. Laodice will then kill Antiochus II because he divorced her to marry Bernice.' "

Daniel 11:7-10 (KJV) - Part VI

"**But out of a branch of her roots shall one stand up in his estate, which shall come with an army, and shall enter into the fortress of the king of the north, and shall deal against them, and shall prevail: And shall also carry captives into Egypt their gods, with their princes, and with their precious vessels of silver and of gold; and he shall continue more years than the king of the north. So the king of the south shall come into his kingdom, and shall return into his own land. But his sons shall be stirred up, and shall assemble a multitude of great forces: and one shall certainly come, and overflow, and pass through: then shall he return, and be stirred up, even to his fortress.**"

Interlaced Commentary on Part VI

"Gabriel continued, 'After Bernice's death, her brother in Egypt, Ptolemy III, will come to the throne in the south. To avenge

Bernice's death, he will attack the army of Seleucus II, the king that took the place of Antiochus II. Ptolemy III will be victorious. He will seize their gods of metal images and valuable articles of silver and gold and take them to Egypt. For some years, Ptolemy III will leave the king of the north alone. After several years pass, Seleucus II will invade the domain of the king of the south to retrieve the gold and silver that Ptolemy III took from him. However, Seleucus II will be defeated again and will return to his own country empty-handed. To avenge the defeat of their father, Seleucus III and Antiochus III, the two sons of Seleucus II, will prepare for war and assemble a great army. They will sweep through the land of the king of the south and cause damage that is like the devastation caused by an irresistible flood. The two sons will carry the battle as far as the area of Transjordan, which will be the fortress of the next king of the south, Ptolemy IV.' "

Daniel 11:11-13 (KJV) - Part VII

"And the king of the south shall be moved with choler, and shall come forth and fight with him, even with the king of the north: and he shall set forth a great multitude; but the multitude shall be given into his hand. And when he hath taken away the multitude, his heart shall be lifted up; and he shall cast down many ten thousands: but he shall not be strengthened by it. For the king of the north shall return, and shall set forth a multitude greater than the former, and shall certainly come after certain years with a great army and with much riches."

Interlaced Commentary on Part VII

"Gabriel continued, 'Then Ptolemy IV will march out in a rage and fight against Antiochus III, the king of the north, at Raphia, and the large army of Antiochus III will be defeated. The army from the north will be humiliated and Ptolemy IV, the king of the south, will become full of arrogance and continue his mighty conquests. He will slaughter thousands as his army moves as far as the border of India, yet he will not remain triumphant. Both he and his wife will die mysteriously. In their place, Ptolemy V Ephiphanes, their five-year-old son, will ascend to the throne of the south. Meanwhile, Antiochus III, the king of the north, will muster another army, larger than the first. After several years, his forces will plunder

Jerusalem and advance toward Egypt with a huge, well-equipped army.' "

Daniel 11:14,15 (KJV) - Part VIII

"And in those times there shall many stand up against the king of the south: also the robbers of thy people shall exalt themselves to establish the vision; but they shall fall. So the king of the north shall come, and cast up a mount, and take the most fenced cities: and the arms of the south shall not withstand, neither his chosen people, neither shall there be any strength to withstand."

Interlaced Commentary on Part VIII

"Gabriel continued, 'Daniel, understand that during the reign of Ptolemy IV, many people will try to rebel against this arrogant king of the south. Even some of the zealots and violent men among your own people will rebel against him in fulfillment of this vision, but they will not succeed. However Antiochus III, the king of the north, will come and build siege ramps and will capture the fortified city of Sidon. The forces of the king of the south will not be able to resist; even their best troops will not have the strength to resist.' "

Daniel 11:16,17 (KJV) - Part IX

"But he that cometh against him shall do according to his own will, and none shall stand before him: and he shall stand in the glorious land, which by his hand shall be consumed. He shall also set his face to enter with the strength of his whole kingdom, and upright ones with him; thus shall he do: and he shall give him the daughter of women, corrupting her: but she shall not stand on his side, neither be for him."

Interlaced Commentary on Part IX

"Gabriel continued, 'Many years later, a new group of invaders from the north will appear and they will do as they please for a long time; no one will be able to resist them. They will eventually establish themselves as a military force all over the world, including the Beautiful Land, Israel. They will have power to destroy anyone who rebels against them. These invaders from the north will be called Romans. As ruler of the north, Julius Caesar, will come with the might of many legions and make an alliance with Ptolemy XI, the king of the south. The two children of Ptolemy XI, Cleopatra and Ptolemy XII, will be placed under the guardianship of Rome. In the years to come, Cleopatra and Ptolemy XII, who are heirs to the throne in the south, will try to eliminate Roman control over Egypt. Cleopatra will conduct illicit love affairs with Julius Caesar and Mark Antony to gain power. But later, Julius Caesar will be assassinated and Mark Antony will be killed in battle. So her plans will not succeed or help Egypt.' "

Daniel 11:18-20 (KJV) - Part X

"After this shall he turn his face unto the isles, and shall take many: but a prince for his own behalf shall cause the reproach offered by him to cease; without his own reproach he shall cause it to turn upon him. Then he shall turn his face toward the fort of his own land: but he shall stumble and fall, and not be found. Then shall stand up in his estate a raiser of taxes in the glory of the kingdom: but within few days he shall be destroyed, neither in anger, nor in battle."

Interlaced Commentary on Part X

"The angel then told me more about Julius Caesar. 'After an alliance is made with Ptolemy XI, Julius Caesar will make war against the people living on the islands of the coastlands of Africa and will subdue them. Thus, Julius Caesar will end the rebellion of Scipio and turn his rebellion into defeat. Julius Caesar will then return home and receive many honors and titles, but he is mortal. An assassin will kill him and he will be seen no more. Caesar's successor, Octavius – later named Augustus – will send tax collectors all over the kingdom to maintain his royal splendor. After reigning 40 years, he too will die, not in anger or in battle, but of natural causes.' "

Daniel 11:21,22 (KJV) - Part XI

"And in his estate shall stand up a vile person, to whom they shall not give the honour of the kingdom: but he shall come in peaceably, and obtain the kingdom by flatteries. And with the arms of a flood shall they be overflown from before him, and shall be broken; yea, also the prince of the covenant."

Interlaced Commentary on Part XI

"Gabriel continued, 'Tiberius, a contemptible person who will not come through the royal line, will succeed Augustus Caesar. This is possible because Augustus Caesar will adopt Tiberius, making Tiberius the legal heir to the throne. Tiberius will take the throne of the kingdom without open conflict. He will seize it through intrigue and the help of his manipulating mother, Livia. Tiberius Caesar will prove to be a brilliant general. He will be eminently successful against powerful armies that oppose him in Germany, Armenia and Parthia. During his reign, the Holy One, the anticipated Messiah, will be baptized, but Israel will reject Him. He will be cut off from His people as a criminal. The great Prince of God's everlasting covenant, the Messiah, will be murdered.' "

Daniel 11:23,24 (KJV) - Part XII

"And after the league made with him he shall work deceitfully: for he shall come up, and shall become strong with a small people. He shall enter peaceably even upon the fattest places of the province; and he shall do that which his fathers have not done, nor his fathers' fathers; he shall scatter among them the prey, and spoil, and riches: yea, and he shall forecast his devices against the strong holds, even for a time."

Interlaced Commentary on Part XII

"Gabriel continued, 'Daniel, this is a summary of Rome's rise to power and how that kingdom will specifically affect Israel in those days. During its rise to power, Rome will offer treaties and pacts to various kingdoms throughout the world. After these kingdoms have reached a friendly agreement with Rome and spared themselves from deadly conflict, Rome will act deceitfully and betray them. With only a few people controlling its great army, the Romans will become dominant over the world and no one will be able to defend themselves against them. When the richest provinces feel secure, Rome will invade them and either destroy or dominate them. Rome's authority will extend far beyond that of earlier kingdoms. Rome will finance its conquests by distributing the spoils of war to mercenary soldiers. Consequently, its army will become large and powerful. Rome will plot the overthrow of kingdoms everywhere, but only for a time. As with all other nations, Rome's dominion will come to an end.' "

Daniel 11:25-28 (KJV) - Part XIII

"And he shall stir up his power and his courage against the king of the south with a great army; and the king of the south shall be stirred up to battle with a very great and mighty army; but he shall not stand: for they shall forecast devices against him. Yea, they that feed of the portion of his meat shall destroy him, and his army shall overflow: and many shall fall down slain. And both these kings' hearts shall be to do mischief, and they shall speak lies at one table; but it shall not prosper: for yet the end shall be at the time appointed. Then shall he return into his land with great riches; and his heart shall be against the holy covenant; and he shall do exploits, and return to his own land."

Interlaced Commentary on Part XIII

"Gabriel continued, 'The Roman ruler, Augustus Caesar, will raise a large army with strength and courage to attack Antony, the king of the south. At the Battle of Actium (31 B.C.), Antony will wage war with a large and powerful army, but will not be able to endure the plots devised against him. Some people who are very close to Antony, even the ones who eat with him, will attempt to destroy him. Antony's army will be ruined. However, Antony will remain in power for a little longer. Augustus and Antony, with evil in their hearts, will sit at the same table and lie to each other, but to no avail. Both men want to control the world, but neither of them will attain world dominion.

Daniel, the Most High God has a great plan to exalt Jerusalem during the Roman rule. He will fulfill "Plan B" at the end of the seventy weeks *if* Israel honors His covenant. Kingdoms and empires will come and go, but the nation whose God is the Lord will remain forever. Augustus Caesar, the king of the north, will return to his own country after the Battle of Actium with great wealth from Egypt. Years later, the Jews, who are trustees of God's holy covenant, will anger Caesar. Vespasian will be sent to attack many cities and he will specifically target Jerusalem for destruction. However, news about the death of Nero will cause him to lift the siege and return to his own country without subduing Jerusalem. This will be *the sign* to flee Jerusalem.' "

Daniel 11:29-31 (KJV) - Part XIV

"At the time appointed he shall return, and come toward the south; but it shall not be as the former, or as the latter. For the ships of Chittim shall come against him: therefore he shall be grieved, and return, and have indignation against the holy covenant: so shall he do; he shall even return, and have intelligence with them that forsake the holy covenant. And arms shall stand on his part, and they shall pollute the sanctuary of strength, and shall take away the daily sacrifice, and they shall place the abomination that maketh desolate."

Interlaced Commentary on Part XIV

"Gabriel continued, 'At the appointed time, Titus, the son of Vespasian, will invade the south again with a different result. Countries with many ships from the western coastlands of Africa and Egypt will fight Titus, but he will lose his desire to fight them. Instead of retreating, Titus will turn his frustration and fury towards the rebellious city of Jerusalem, because of his hatred for the Jews. When Titus resumes the siege of Jerusalem which his father began, he will spare the lives of the Jews who will forsake their religion and join forces with him against Israel. Eventually, the forces of Titus will level the city and completely destroy the temple complex which the Jews think is impregnable. The Jews will not be able to conduct the daily temple services again after Titus destroys the temple in A.D. 70.

These things are revealed so that God's people can know that wrath is determined upon Israel unless Israel cooperates with God. Rome will execute the wrath of God on Israel. This future desolation will occur and be fulfilled in A.D. 70, because your people will violate the covenant, and consequently, negate the grace which God granted to them.' "

Daniel 11:32-35 (KJV) - Part XV

"And such as do wickedly against the covenant shall he corrupt by flatteries: but the people that do know their God

shall be strong, and do exploits. And they that understand among the people shall instruct many: yet they shall fall by the sword, and by flame, by captivity, and by spoil, many days. Now when they shall fall, they shall be holpen with a little help: but many shall cleave to them with flatteries. And some of them of understanding shall fall, to try them, and to purge, and to make them white, even to the time of the end: because it is yet for a time appointed."

Interlaced Commentary on Part XV

"Gabriel continued, 'The Romans will corrupt the people of God with flattery and false ideas. However, a few people will resist compromise with Rome. People filled with the Holy Spirit will keep the truth about the Most High God alive in their hearts. In time, Christianity will become popular and many insincere people will become part of the church. As a result, Christianity will become corrupt. The true people of God will be persecuted with sword, flame, captivity and forfeiture of their property for a predetermined period of time – 1,260 years. Even though many people will die for the Word of God, God's people will not entirely perish. God will give them strength to keep the torch of truth burning. Some of God's people will stumble because they lack faith, but their failures will be lessons of refinement and purification for those who live at the time of the end. Be patient, Daniel, for the end does not come until Earth's history reaches the appointed year set by the Most High God.' "

Summary

After reading this far, it is easy to see why Daniel described this vision as "a great war." (Daniel 10:1) Several points in this vision warrant our consideration. First, early Christians understood the first portion of this vision well enough to escape Jerusalem when Vespesian lifted his siege in A.D. 68 and returned to Rome. Second, the predicted failure of Israel to meet God's requirements during the seventy weeks comes as no surprise. Even though this vision mentions Israel's failure, it also contains a much larger story that demonstrates how God uses one nation to destroy another whose cup of iniquity has been filled. This vision emphatically demonstrates why the perpetual destruction of degenerate rulers and governments never ends. God is Sovereign. He sets up kings and takes them down when they become decadent and arrogant. (Daniel 2:21; 5:20-24) Historians may report the actions of the kings of the north and south, but God manages the governments of Earth through a phenomenon called war. (Ecclesiastes 3:8) Much could be written about this subject, but in a nutshell, God originates "the spirit of war" from time to time to accomplish His larger purposes. (Leviticus 26; Deuteronomy 32; Ecclesiastes 3; Isaiah 45:7) When a nation fills its cup of iniquity, God arouses and empowers another nation to destroy the decadent one. This process cauterizes the malignancy of sin. Eventually, the destroying nation also becomes decadent and is destroyed for the same reason it destroyed the earlier nation. This cathartic process explains why Jerusalem and pagan nations have been destroyed. This limiting process never ends in a fallen world! This is the core message in Daniel 10-12 for all generations to study.

The third point in this vision is that God's people are frequently caught in the middle of political and military forces that are much greater than themselves. The world always considers God's people to be weak, but He deliberately designed this. *God knows that it is impossible for a Christian government to function in a world of sin!* If a Christian government had been possible, Jesus would have set up His kingdom on Earth when He came the first time. Do not misunderstand the point. It is possible for a government to espouse and defend Christian principles. In fact, as long as a nation does this, God prospers such a nation! However, Bible history confirms that Israel was unable to sustain a Godly government because a majority of Israel's population did not become born-again people! Let's face it – this world is not our home! Christians are represented as pilgrims passing through a foreign land. Yet, we have hope. We look forward to a city whose foundation is righteousness and whose walls of love are built by God. (Psalm 89:14) Therefore, this continual and perpetual conflict between nations should not discourage God's people. Jesus said, **"You will hear of wars and rumors of wars,** *but see to it that you are not alarmed. Such things must happen,* **but the end is still to come. Nation will rise against nation, and kingdom against kingdom. There will be famines and earthquakes in various places. All these are the beginning of birth pains."** (Matthew 24:6-8, italics mine) Unfortunately, wars are a necessity in a sinful world. God causes war when He wants to "purify" various parcels of *His* Earth so that future inhabitants may have a chance to satisfy *His* purposes. (See Jeremiah 25:15-17; 27:6,7; 50:1-3; Ezekiel 38; Matthew 10:34) In this light, it is no mystery that Earth itself ends with the battle of Armageddon.

Chapter 8

Daniel 11:36 - 12:13 – The King of the North

"At that time Michael, the great prince who protects your people, will arise. There will be a time of distress such as has not happened from the beginning of nations until then. But at that time your people— everyone whose name is found written in the book [of life] – will be delivered."

— Daniel 12:1, insertion mine

Introduction

Remember, I have divided the vision of Daniel 10:1-12:13 into two segments for clarity. Even though Daniel 10-12 is one vision, there is a natural divide at Daniel 11:35, because the vision makes a transition from the destruction of Jerusalem in A.D. 70 to the destruction of the world during the Great Tribulation. This transition parallels Daniel 8. You may recall how the ram and the goat were part of ancient history, but the horn power will appear during the time of the end. In the previous chapter, we saw how the first portion of this vision benefited early Christians. In this chapter, you should discover why the last segment of this vision will benefit Christians who live during the Great Tribulation.

Conflicts between the kings of the north and the south continued long after the Romans destroyed Jerusalem in A.D. 70. In fact, as the Christian church increased in popularity, theological battles between the Church of Rome (on the north side of the Mediterranean) and the Church of Alexandria (on the south side of the Mediterranean) began to occur. The Church of Rome strongly opposed the doctrine, "Christ was created by the Father," which the Church of Alexandria supported. In this controversy, one could say "Rome, the religious king of the north" eventually uprooted "Arius, the religious king of the south." You may recall from Daniel 7 that three nations were plucked up by their roots by the little horn power (Roman Catholic Church). These tribal nations have been identified as the Ostrogoths, Heruli and Vandals.

In Daniel 11:36, Gabriel made a transition from ancient times to end times, but continues to use the same language throughout the vision, that is, the king of the north versus the king of the south. The chronological sequence also continues without interruption. Gabriel uses the same language so that the final generation can see parallels from centuries past and better understand the course of coming events.

This is a key point: The forthcoming actions of Lucifer, represented as the "king of the north" in the last segment of this vision, have no historical equal. The behavior of the Antichrist during the Great Tribulation will be off the scale of human expectations. This is why parallel language from the past is so helpful. If you have a basic understanding of Daniel 8 and Revelation 9, 13 and 17, this transition is not hard to follow or understand. Unfortunately, most people do not have this understanding, so Daniel 11:36 and onward is difficult for many people to decipher.

The Antichrist

The king of the north mentioned in verses Daniel 11:36-45 is the same King *from* the North (also known as the stern-faced king or the horn power) that was introduced in Daniel 8. Notice how this point is demonstrated. Verse 35 points to *the appointed time of the end,* and verse 36 describes a king who will be successful until *the time of wrath is completed.* **"Some of the wise will stumble, so that they may be refined, purified and made spotless until the time of the end, for it will still come at the appointed time. The king will do as he pleases. He will exalt and magnify himself above every god and will say unheard-of things against the God of gods. He will be successful until the time of wrath is completed, for what has been determined must take place."** (Daniel 11:35,36)

1. Who is the "king" in verse 36? Part of the answer is found in the timing of this verse. The king to whom this verse applies is the king who **"is successful until the time of wrath is completed . . ."** When does **the time of wrath** occur? We learned from Daniel 8 that the horn power from the north (the stern-faced king) will appear during *the appointed time of the end*, which is a time of wrath. **"He [Gabriel] said: 'I am going to tell you what will happen later *in the time of***

wrath, **because the vision concerns** *the appointed time of the end.'* **"** (Daniel 8:19, italics mine) Revelation indicates the Great Tribulation will be a time of wrath for everyone. People who obey God's Word will suffer persecution from Babylon. (Revelation 13:5) People who obey Babylon's laws and the Antichrist will suffer God's wrath. (Revelation 14:9,10) Therefore, the appointed time of the end is a time of wrath for everyone. The Great Tribulation consists of two segments of time. The seven trumpets will last 1,260 days. The seven-trumpet judgments of Revelation will be a time of invitation and mercy for those who have not heard the gospel of Jesus Christ. The seven bowls will follow the seven trumpets. They will last for seventy-five days and will contain no mercy. During the seven bowls, God's wrath will be poured out upon all who receive the mark of the beast. When the seven last plagues are completed, God's wrath will end. **"I saw in heaven another great and marvelous sign: seven angels with the seven last plagues – last, because with them God's wrath is completed."** (Revelation 15:1) When these facts are aligned, we are left with one conclusion. The king mentioned in Daniel 11:36 must be the horn power of Daniel 8 (the Antichrist), because he will be successful until the time of wrath is completed. The time of wrath occurs during the appointed time of the end, which is also called the Great Tribulation. (Daniel 12:1)

2. The king of the north will be successful even though he demands obedience to religious beliefs that are contrary to every religion on Earth! Remember, God empowers the stern-faced king, allowing him to have a moment of glorious deception. (Daniel 8:24; Revelation 13:14) Daniel 11:36 says, **"The king will do as he pleases. He will exalt and magnify himself above every god and will say unheard-of things against the God of gods. . . ."** Compare Daniel's words with those of the apostle Paul: **"Don't let anyone deceive you in any way, for that day will not come until the rebellion occurs and** *the man of lawlessness* **is revealed, the man doomed to destruction. He will oppose and will exalt himself over everything that is called God or is worshiped, so that he sets himself up**

in God's temple, proclaiming himself to be God."
(2 Thessalonians 2:3,4, italics mine) The Antichrist is called
"the man of lawlessness" or "the man of sin" (KJV) because
the Bible says, **"The king will do as he pleases."** He will be
accountable to no one! He will be capricious, temperamental
and arbitrary. No one can stop him or prevent him from
saying or doing the evil he wants. The devil will stand in
opposition to all religions of the world. Daniel says, **"He will
exalt and magnify himself above every god and will say
unheard-of things against the God of gods."** Paul says,
"He will *oppose* **and will exalt himself over everything
that is called God or is worshiped, so that he sets
himself up in God's temple, proclaiming himself to be
God."** (Italics mine) Remember the comments about the
stern-faced king in Daniel 8:24. **"He will become very
strong, but not by his own power. He will cause
astounding devastation and will succeed in whatever
he does. He will destroy the mighty men and the holy
people."** The coming Antichrist has no equal in past history.
He will appear during the time of wrath, the Great
Tribulation. This modern king of Babylon will successfully
oppose the religions of the world because God will empower
him (just as He empowered the ancient king of Babylon,
Nebuchadnezzar) to establish a one-world government. This
coming king can be none other than the Antichrist, the devil
masquerading as God.

3. If there is any doubt remaining on the identity of this king,
    notice this verse: ***"At the time of the end* the king of the
    south will engage him in battle, and the king of the
    north will storm out against him with chariots and
    cavalry and a great fleet of ships. He will invade many
    countries and sweep through them like a flood."***
    (Daniel 11:40, italics mine) The king of the north will gain
    control over all of his adversaries *at the time of the end*. We
    know the horn power in Daniel 8 will come from the north,
    will appear during the appointed time of the end, will destroy
    many people, will exalt and magnify himself above every god,
    and will blaspheme the God of Heaven. Only one being can
    meet these specifications. That being is Lucifer, the Antichrist.

A New Series of Wars

We know this vision covers a series of great wars. The last segment of this vision focuses on the wars that will occur during the time of wrath (the Great Tribulation). The Bible predicts the king of the north will wage war against the saints and will conquer them. (Revelation 13:7) The devil will be invincible for a period of time. He will destroy those who oppose him (the kingdom of the south). God grants this authority to Lucifer for two reasons. First, God raises up a destroyer to destroy those who pass the point of no return. Second, God empowers Lucifer for a season because He wants a watching universe to see what dominion under a sinful being like Lucifer would be like. *God wants the universe to see how sin affects authority.* Because Lucifer is the embodiment of sin, his actions will demonstrate what any sinner would do if given enough time and power. The contrast will be profound. If God were not a God of love, His reign over the universe would resemble Lucifer's horrible reign on Earth. If we ponder this thought for just a moment, every Christian should rejoice to know that God is nothing like Lucifer. God is love! With these things said, my commentary begins with verse 36:

Daniel 11:36-39 (KJV) - Part I

"And the king [of the North] **shall do according to his will; and he shall exalt himself, and magnify himself above every god, and shall speak marvelous things against the God of gods, and shall prosper till the indignation be accomplished: for that that is determined shall be done. Neither shall he regard the God of his fathers, nor the desire of women, nor regard any god: for he shall magnify himself above all. But in his estate shall he honour the God of forces: and a god whom his fathers knew not shall he honor with gold, and silver, and with precious stones, and pleasant things. Thus shall he do in the most strong holds with a strange god, whom he shall acknowledge and increase with glory: and he shall cause them to rule over many, and shall divide the land for gain."** (Insertion mine)

Interlaced Commentary on Part I

"Gabriel said, 'Daniel, I must tell you more about the stern-faced king from the north; the horn power you saw in the earlier vision of

Daniel 8. When the devil physically appears on Earth personating
Christ, he will claim to be God. Masquerading as God, he will
receive honor from the religions of the world. They will believe that
he is God. [**Note:** Lucifer is called the *king of the north* in this
section of the vision for two reasons. First, as a point on the
compass, north symbolizes God's dwelling place – on the sides of the
north. (Isaiah 14:13, KJV) North also represents the direction from
which divine destruction comes. Like Nebuchadnezzar, the ancient
king of Babylon, Lucifer, the modern king of Babylon, will inflict
destruction on those people who have rejected God's truth. Second,
in the first portion of this prophecy, Israel was caught between two
great rivals – the kings from the north and south. In the last days,
God's people will again be caught between two great rivals; the
people who believe the devil is God (followers of the king of the
north) and people who refuse to submit to the demands of Lucifer
(followers of the king of the south).] The opposition of men will not
slow Lucifer for long. The devil will do as he pleases, for no one can
stop him. He will exalt and magnify himself above every god known
to man and will say unheard-of things against the Most High God.
He will succeed mightily until the seven bowls are completed, for
what has been predetermined by the Most High God will occur.

Daniel, because of apostasy, Israel rebelled against the God of their
forefathers, the God of Abraham, Isaac and Jacob. Similarly, when
Lucifer appears, the religious wicked will do the same thing. They
will abandon the gods of their fathers and worship this new "living"
god. The devil will have no regard for Christ, the Holy One of Israel,
which every virgin in Israel hopes to bear. The devil will exalt
himself above them all. **Be warned**. The king of the north will
appear as a glorious god-man – subject to no law or authority
created by man. He is called the man of lawlessness because he will
not be subject to any law and will demand that people obey his
commandments. Instead of respecting the gods of the religions that
people know and trust, he will demand the establishment of a new,
one-world religion. He will exalt himself as lord of lords and king of
kings. He will use force when and where necessary to consolidate
the world under his authority. He will demand that all people obey
his laws or be killed. A one-world religion has not existed since
Adam and Eve sinned, but it will come. Everyone who refuses to
submit to the demands of the devil will be targets of persecution. **Be**

prepared. At the appointed time (fifth trumpet), the devil will appear on Earth and consolidate the world's seven religious systems into one colossal organization. He will exalt and honor himself by receiving gold and silver, precious stones, and costly gifts.

When Lucifer has gained a great following, he will fiercely attack the brave people who have remained faithful to the Most High. The 144,000 and their disciples will resist the devil's schemes. Great numbers of people will be deceived and join the devil in rebellion against the clearest evidence of God's truth. The world has not seen anything like this since the time of Noah's flood. The devil will bestow great honor on the leaders of Earth who acknowledge him to be God. The devil and his angels will slaughter a third of mankind during the sixth trumpet war. When the devil dissolves the political and religious boundaries of the world, he will set up ten puppet kings over the people of Earth. Lucifer will honor people who participate in his evil ways by distributing the land to the highest bidder.' "

Daniel 11:40-43 (KJV) - Part II

"And at the time of the end shall the king of the south push at him: and the king of the north shall come against him like a whirlwind, with chariots, and with horsemen, and with many ships; and he shall enter into the countries, and shall overflow and pass over. He shall enter also into the glorious land, and many countries shall be overthrown: but these shall escape out of his hand, even Edom, and Moab, and the chief of the children of Ammon. He shall stretch forth his hand also upon the countries: and the land of Egypt shall not escape. But he shall have power over the treasures of gold and of silver, and over all the precious things of Egypt: and the Libyans and the Ethiopians shall be at his steps."

Interlaced Commentary on Part II

"Gabriel said, 'When the sixth trumpet sounds (Revelation 9:13-21), the devil will attack his adversaries by land, air, and with a great fleet of ships. He will invade and destroy many countries, and his forces will sweep through the nations like an irresistible and devastating flood. Lucifer's angels will kill one-third of mankind. The devil will invade the homeland of Israel and many countries around will fall, but throughout the world, a remnant of people will remain faithful. Remember how some of your people escaped Nebuchadnezzar's destruction by fleeing to the remote areas of Edom and Moab? God will sustain His people in the same way during the end time. Like the leaders of Ammon, who protected your people when Nebuchadnezzar destroyed Jerusalem (Jeremiah 40:11,12), God will deliver His people from the devil's hand. As the ruler of Earth, the devil will extend his power over many countries. Egypt, which represents Pharaoh's opposition to God (the king of the south), will not escape Lucifer's dominion. The devil will control all of the treasures of gold and silver. All of the riches of the world will be his. No person will be able to buy or sell unless he obeys the devil's laws and submits to his beastly government.' "

Daniel 11:44-12:1 (KJV) - Part III

"But tidings out of the east and out of the north shall trouble him: therefore he shall go forth with great fury to destroy, and utterly to make away many. And he shall plant the tabernacles of his palace between the seas in the glorious holy mountain; yet he shall come to his end, and none shall help him. And at that time shall Michael stand up, the great prince which standeth for the children of thy people: and there shall be a time of trouble, such as never was since there was a nation even to that same time: and at that time thy people shall be delivered, every one that shall be found written in the book."

Interlaced Commentary on Part III

"Gabriel said, 'Near the end of the Great Tribulation, people throughout the Earth will hear peals of loudest thunder. At that time, Jesus will announce that the king of the north is to be destroyed. The devil will be alarmed when he hears this thunder because he will know that his rule has ended. In a rage, he will attempt to annihilate all of God's people by setting up a universal death decree, but God's people will be delivered.

The devil will establish a palace in Jerusalem. He will sit enthroned as though he were Almighty God. Jerusalem will serve as one of the palaces of Babylon, that great city that rules over the nations of Earth. The devil will consolidate the world into one empire and he will have undisputed rule over the world for a short time. Yet, the devil will come to his end and no human being will be able to prevent these things from happening. When the devil implements the mark of the beast (a tattoo showing allegiance to Lucifer), he will take his seat on his throne to rule over Earth. He will claim to be lord of lords and king of kings. At that very moment Michael/ Jesus, the great Prince of Heaven who protects His people, will arise from His seat at the right hand of God's throne. Jesus will bring His intercessory work on behalf of the human race to a close. At that time, Jesus will send the seven last plagues upon His enemies. The distress and suffering caused by the plagues will be terrible. Never, since the history of humankind, has such suffering covered the face of the Earth. But your people – everyone whose name is found written in the Book of Life – will be delivered from death and these plagues.' "

Daniel 12:2-4 (KJV) - Part IV

"And many of them that sleep in the dust of the earth shall awake, some to everlasting life, and some to shame and everlasting contempt. And they that be wise shall shine as the brightness of the firmament; and they that turn many to righteousness as the stars for ever and ever. But thou, O Daniel, shut up the words, and seal the book, even to the time of the end: many shall run to and fro, and knowledge shall be increased."

Interlaced Commentary on Part IV

"Gabriel said, 'A few days before the Second Coming, Jesus will resurrect multitudes of martyrs who died during the fifth seal in a special resurrection. He will also resurrect those who crucified Jesus, so that they can see the Son of Man coming in clouds of glory. Their shame and contempt will remain on them until Jesus destroys them at the Second Coming. On that glorious day, the 144,000 will be declared victorious. They will shine with the brightness of Heaven because they led many people to righteousness, and the 144,000 will be the "movie stars" in the new Earth. But you, Daniel, close up and seal the words of this vision. This information is reserved for the time of the end. Many generations will try to understand these prophecies; they will go here and there to increase knowledge, but the Most High God has sealed this book until the final generation arrives.' "

Daniel 12:5-9 (KJV) - Part V

"Then I Daniel looked, and, behold, there stood other two, the one on this side of the bank of the river, and the other on that side of the bank of the river. And one said to the man clothed in linen, which was upon the waters of the river, How long shall it be to the end of these wonders? And I heard the man clothed in linen, which was upon the waters of the river, when he held up his right hand and his left hand unto heaven, and sware by him that liveth for ever that it shall be for a time, times, and an half; and when he shall have accomplished to scatter the power of the holy people, all these things shall be finished. And I heard, but I understood not: then said I, O my Lord, what shall be the end of these things? And he said, Go thy way, Daniel: for the words are closed up and sealed till the time of the end."

Interlaced Commentary on Part V

"Then I, Daniel, looked up and saw two glorious angels. One angel stood on this side of the river and the other stood on the opposite bank. One of the angels said to Jesus, the Man who was clothed in linen and was standing above the waters of the Tigris, 'How long will it be before the astonishing events in these visions are fulfilled?' Jesus lifted His right and left hand toward Heaven, and I heard him swear by the Most High God who lives forever, saying, 'The gospel of salvation will be preached throughout the whole world during 1,260 days. When the power given to the 144,000 has come to an end, all these things will be completed.' I heard these words, but I did not understand their meaning. So I asked, 'Lord, what will be the outcome of all these events?' He replied, 'Do not worry about this Daniel, because the words of this prophecy are closed up and sealed until the final generation arrives. The righteous who live during those days will understand this vision.' "

Daniel 12:10-13 (KJV) - Part VI

"Many shall be purified, and made white, and tried; but the wicked shall do wickedly: and none of the wicked shall understand; but the wise shall understand. And from the time that the daily sacrifice shall be taken away, and the abomination that maketh desolate set up, there shall be a thousand two hundred and ninety days. Blessed is he that waiteth, and cometh to the thousand three hundred and five and thirty days. But go thou thy way till the end be: for thou shalt rest, and stand in thy lot at the end of the days."

Interlaced Commentary on Part VI

"Gabriel said, 'God's people must be refined, purified, and made spotless. The wicked will continue to be wicked. None of the wicked will understand these things, but at the appointed time of the end, the people who are wise in spiritual matters, the ones who are listening for my voice through the Spirit, will understand the importance of these things. Daniel, write the following things down because God's people will need to know them when the appointed time arrives. A time is coming when Jesus will end His intercession on behalf of the world. At that time, Jesus will cease from the daily work He has been doing on behalf of humanity ever since sin began. He will no longer stand between God's wrath and a guilty world. When He steps aside, a great earthquake will shake the Earth. This event will mark the end of Christ's corporate ministry in the Heavenly sanctuary. From the day that Christ's daily intercession ceases until the devil establishes a universal death decree for God's people, there will be 1,290 days. Blessed are the saints who patiently endure the Great Tribulation to reach the end of the 1,335 days.' **Then the King will say to those on his right, 'Come, you who are blessed by my Father; take your inheritance, the kingdom prepared for you since the creation of the world."** (Matthew 25:34) 'As for you Daniel, go on with your business until the end of your life. Then, you will rest with your fathers in sleep. At the end of Earth's days, you will be resurrected to receive your allotted inheritance. The Lord will surely reward you for your faithfulness.' "

Summary

Even though the information in Daniel is very important, the book of Daniel does not tell us everything we need to know about the end-time. This is why God gave John the vision recorded in Revelation. When the prophecies in the two books of Daniel and Revelation are properly related, the alignment of details and the harmony of facts are astounding! So, after my commentary on Revelation becomes available, please review this chapter.

The prophecy in Daniel 10-12 contains a warning message for those who will live during the Great Tribulation. Man's great adversary is coming and will crush every religion and government. He will destroy hundreds of millions of people and will establish himself as Almighty God on Earth. He will do everything in his power to destroy the people of God. The Great Tribulation will last a maximum of 1,335 days, and the final abomination that causes desolation (a universal death decree upon God's people) will occur on the 1,290[th] day. For 1,335 days, God's people will be caught in the middle of a series of wars. Many of God's people will perish. Christians need to know these facts *now*. Christians need to understand God's plans; otherwise, the horrors of tomorrow could overpower our faith in God. Most Christians have no idea about the events that are coming. They are like the Jews living inside ancient Jerusalem. Vespesian's departure did not mean an end to Rome's hostilities against Jerusalem, as the Jews mistakenly presumed. It was merely a signal of a reprieve – a window of opportunity to escape. Christian believers who understood Jesus' words knew what was coming next and fled the doomed city. In our day, people who understand Daniel's words can know what is coming next and when the time becomes appropriate, they will flee from Babylon and separate themselves from this horrible system that will form. God wants His people to understand the big picture before it happens. He wants His people to know His plans so they will not be overwhelmed with loss, disappointment and depression. Therefore, God had the book of Daniel written for *our generation so that coming events will confirm our faith instead of destroying our faith.* What a thoughtful and caring God.

Epilogue

Gabriel told Daniel that his visions were sealed up until the time of the end. (Daniel 12:4,9) Has the time of the end arrived? Has the book of Daniel been unsealed with the discovery of the four rules that govern the interpretation of apocalyptic prophecy? Time will soon tell. Now that the four rules of Daniel are known, and the books of Daniel and Revelation interlock into one comprehensive harmonious story, we better understand the plans of God. We have carefully examined the contents of Daniel and we now know several things that previous generations could not have known.

1. We found in Daniel 2 that our current generation is living during the time period of the feet which are composed of iron and clay. When the Antichrist appears, he will gain control of the world and will appoint ten puppet kings to be responsible for administrative details. (Revelation 17:12) The toes of Daniel's metal man represent these ten kings. (Daniel 2:42) During the days of these ten kings, Jesus will return to Earth and destroy all of the wicked. (Daniel 2:34,35) Daniel 2 indicates that the kingdom of God will not coexist with the kingdoms of sinful men.

2. We found in Daniel 7 that Heaven's court convened in 1798 and billions of angels were summoned to attend. Shortly after the court convened, Jesus began to review the books of record and decide the eternal fate of every person who has ever lived. We also found that the little horn power in Daniel 7 represents the Roman Catholic Church, and we know that the deadly wound inflicted on the church in 1798 will be healed on or about the time the Great Tribulation begins.

3. We found in Daniel 8 that Jesus began reviewing the books of record in 1844 – at the end of the 2,300 day/years mentioned in Daniel 8:14. We also found that the horn power coming from the north in Daniel 8 will be the Antichrist. He is the stern-faced king who will bring destruction upon the whole world. He will cause evil to prosper and will inflict astounding devastation on Earth. He will take away the daily from Jesus, man's intercessor. Many of God's people will perish because of his actions. From a human perspective, he will be invincible. The devil's *personation* of Christ (a physical body) will be destroyed when Jesus arrives in clouds of glory. Lucifer is not annihilated until he is destroyed at the end of the 1,000 years.

4. We found in Daniel 9 that Jesus came to Earth and died on time – April 7, A.D. 30. God's original plan ("Plan A") to establish His kingdom on Earth at the end of the seventy weeks was not fulfilled because Israel rejected the Messiah.

Jerusalem and the temple were destroyed in A.D. 70 as predicted.

5. We found in Daniel 10-12 that Israel's unbelief led to Jerusalem's destruction by the Romans. Through Daniel, God warned early Christians to escape this destruction. In a similar manner, people who live during the Great Tribulation will be caught in the middle of a great war. Christians will be on Earth during the world's destruction and God has included clues in the final prophecy of Daniel describing the actions, identity and objectives of the Antichrist. This vision tells us that the Great Tribulation will last a maximum of 1,335 days, and the vision indicates there will be a universal death decree for the saints which occurs on the 1,290th day of the Great Tribulation.

6. We find in Daniel a prophetic architecture that conforms to four rules. This architecture is a framework that enables us to understand God's plans in advance. God has hidden the knowledge of this framework for twenty-six centuries. Now that this architecture has been discovered, the book of Revelation becomes an extension of the book of Daniel. The two books combine to form one comprehensive story. The book of Daniel provides the final generation with advanced information about God's plans for terminating the sin problem. This is not a casual matter. Given what is coming upon Earth, this knowledge is of greater value than anything the world can offer. The present Heaven and Earth will soon pass away, but God's Word will never fail.

7. The book of Daniel declares that **God rules and overrules**. God is eternal and God is sovereign. He manages the nations of Earth and He knows the hairs on each of our heads. This scope of knowledge is hard to comprehend. God deals with macro issues (the rise and fall of empires) and yet, He deals with His children on the micro level. He treats each one of us with the tenderest care. The book of Daniel demonstrates these things. Whether God is destroying one empire or delivering one man from a lion's den, the message of Daniel is clear: God rules and overrules. The book of Daniel makes it clear that God overrules events on Earth from time to time

so that He can produce the best possible outcome. He manages to do this even within the chaos and suffering that sin has caused without violating the will of men.

The book of Daniel has taught me a sublime lesson: If I surrender my will to God, to go, to be and to do according to all that He has commanded (go-be-do), I have a place within His plans. Whether His plans mandate life or death for me in a temporal sense does not matter, for with God, death is nothing. What really matters is that each of us finds our place within His plans. When Daniel went to the lion's den, he did not know ahead of time what the outcome would be. Yet, he willingly went to the lion's den because he knew he was within God's plans. This is total trust in God. May God grant within each of us total trust and complete peace!

At the end of his last vision, Gabriel told Daniel that he was going to die and that at the end of Earth's history, he would live again. Daniel was told that he would **"stand in his lot at the end of the days."** This phrase means that Daniel will serve in his appointed place in God's kingdom when Jesus resurrects the saints at the Second Coming. Think about it. What greater honor is there than to serve in an *appointed* position throughout eternity? This outcome is possible if we live a life of faith in God. Daniel's visions and experiences are evidences of this truth: God rules. The good news is that God uses His incredible powers, omnipotence, omniscience, and omnipresence, not to secure His position on the throne of the universe, but to insure that the law of love is eternally exalted throughout His universe. No wonder He is called the King of Love, whose dwelling is on the sides of the north, and He will forever rule over His children with love. They will have peace and joy and endless happiness because **". . . . The government will be on His shoulders."** (Isaiah 9:6, insertion mine)

Note: Revelation's commentary will be available soon.

Bible Cross Reference

Recorded Seminar Series

Many seminar series have been recorded on CD and DVD. Call for a free catalog from the Wake Up America Seminars office at (800) 475-0876. Many subjects are available including righteousness by faith, the sanctuary, the plan of salvation, the book of Hebrews, God's justice and mercy, and great clocks of God.

A special video series is available using this book as a study guide. Call the office at (800) 475-0876 for more details.

The Book of Revelation

The Book of Revelation video presentation by Larry W. Wilson, is a comprehensive, chapter by chapter study on the last book of the Bible. It contains 34 segments, each 90-minutes in length, recorded in broadcast quality. This presentation represents Mr. Wilson's conclusions on apocalyptic prophecy gathered from over 30 years years of study. The series can be purchased as a complete set or single topics as you can afford.

- **The Seven Churches**
- **The Seven Seals-Book of Life**
- **The 144,000**
- **The Two Witnesses**
- **The Seven Trumpets**
- **The Four Beasts of Revelation (includes Mark of the Beast)**
- **The 3 Angel's Messages**
- **7 Last Plagues**
- **Revelation 17-21**

We would like to receive comments about this book or questions you may have. Please send your comments to us at the address below. Thank you.

Wake Up America Seminars, Inc.
P.O. Box 273
Bellbrook, OH 45305

http://www.wake-up.org

email: *wuas@wake-up.org*

Books

Warning! Revelation is about to be fulfilled

What do the books of Daniel and Revelation have to say about soon coming events? *Warning! Revelation is about to be fulfilled* outlines Revelation's story in an easy to read format. Revelation predicts and describes many incredible events that will soon occur. These events will not happen in random order nor will they be freak manifestations of violent weather. The coming events predicted in Revelation are carefully designed and executed by the Creator of Heaven and Earth.

To learn more about what the prophecies of Daniel and Revelation have to say about coming events, contact the Wake Up America Seminars office at (800) 475-0876 or access the web site at *http://www.wake-up.org*.

A Study on the
Seven Seals and the 144,000

Every Bible prophecy student should consider the introductory chapter of this book. Why do we have so many interpretations of prophecy? Because the importance of valid rules or methods of interpretation are often overlooked. This book demonstrates how valid rules of intrepretation allow the Bible to speak for itself.

A STUDY ON THE SEVEN SEALS AND THE 144,000

LARRY W. WILSON

Jesus
The Alpha and The Omega

Jesus, The Alpha and The Omega provides a basic framework to understand Bible prophecy. This frame-work, based on five essential Bible doc-trines, helps the serious student of Bible prophecy appreciate the prophecies of Daniel and Revelation. This compelling book examines Jesus' character, minis-try, and example. Cross-references to Bible texts provide a basis for in-depth Bible study. This 280 page book can be yours by contacting Wake Up America Seminars at (800) 475-0876.

Coming Soon . . .

If you enjoyed *Daniel – Unlocked for the Final Generation,* you will appreciate the upcoming studies on the book of Revelation. Apply-ing the foundation and rules of apocalytic prophecy developed in the study of the book of Daniel, Larry Wilson will lead you through a study of the amazing prophecies of Revelation. These books will show God's plans for Earth's final generation.

Other Books by Larry Wilson. . .

17 End-Time Bible Prophecies
*A Study on the Seven Trumpets, Two Witnesses, and Four
    Beasts*

Wake Up America Seminars, Inc.
P.O. Box 273
Bellbrook, OH   45305
(800) 475-0876
http://www.wake-up.org

About the Author

Larry Wilson, Director of Wake Up America Seminars, became a born again Christian after returning from a tour of duty in Vietnam. The understanding of the gospel, the plan of salvation, and the atonement of Jesus Christ has thrilled his soul for the past 30 years. Since his conversion, he has spent over 25 years intensely studying the prophecies of Daniel and Revelation.

In 1988, he published the book *Warning! Revelation is about to be fulfilled* and since then, he has written several books (over 800,000 books in circulation throughout the world in more than 60 countries). He gives seminar presentations, produces video programs which have been broadcast from various locations throughout the United States, and is a guest on radio talk shows.

About the Organization

Wake Up America Seminars (WUAS) is both a non-profit and a non-denominational organization. With God's blessings and the generosity of many people, WUAS has distributed millions of pamphlets, books and tapes around the world since it began in 1988. WUAS is not a church, nor is it affiliated or sponsored by any religious organization. WUAS does not offer membership of any kind. Its mission is not to convert the world to a point of view. Although WUAS has well defined views on certain biblical matters, its mission is primarily "seed sowing." It promotes the primacy of salvation through faith in Jesus Christ, His imminent return, and is doing its best to encourage people with the good news of the gospel. People of all faiths are invited to study the materials produced by WUAS.